PRAISE FOR EDWARD HOAGLAND

"No contemporary essayist sifting through his own experience can match the unadorned clarity of Hoagland's voice."
—*The Los Angeles Times*

"The Thoreau of our time, an essayist so intensely personal, so sharp-eyed and deep-sighted, so tender and tough, so lyrical and elegiac as to transmute a simple stroll into a full-blown mystical experience."
—*The Washington Post*

"Hoagland is an involved observer, participant, and commentator, regardless of the time, place, condition, activities, or subject matter, and like a fine novelist, he has the skill to involve readers in whatever he describes or discusses."
—*Publishers Weekly*

"A powerful writer with an invaluable perspective, Hoagland belongs in every American literature collection."
—*Booklist*

"Hoagland distinguishes himself from many other nature writers by being equally interested in people and their natural surroundings. Hoagland's writing is provocative, direct, raw, sometimes painful, and always full of his passion for life and living things."
—*Library Journal*

"Hoagland is surely one of our most truthful writers about nature."
—*The New York Times Book Review*

SEX
and the
RIVER
STYX

SEX
and the
RIVER
STYX

EDWARD HOAGLAND

Foreword by Howard Frank Mosher

CHELSEA GREEN PUBLISHING
WHITE RIVER JUNCTION, VERMONT

Grateful acknowledgment is given to *Harper's Magazine* for originally publishing the essays: "Sex and the River Styx," "Circus Music," "The American Dissident," "Last Call," "Curtain Calls," "Endgame," and "Small Silences." *Worth* published "Visiting Norah," and *Orion* "Barley and Yaks." Appreciation is also expressed to *The American Scholar* for publishing "The Glue Is Gone" and "A Country for Old Men," to *Civilization* for "A Last Look Around," and *Outside* for "East of Everest."

Project Manager: Patricia Stone
Editorial Contact: Joni Praded
Copy Editor: Nancy Ringer
Proofreader: Susan Barnett
Designer: Peter Holm, Sterling Hill Productions

Printed in the United States of America
First printing February, 2011
10 9 8 7 6 5 4 3 2   11 12 13 14 15

Our Commitment to Green Publishing

Chelsea Green sees publishing as a tool for cultural change and ecological stewardship. We strive to align our book manufacturing practices with our editorial mission and to reduce the impact of our business enterprise in the environment. We print our books and catalogs on chlorine-free recycled paper, using vegetable-based inks whenever possible. This book may cost slightly more because we use recycled paper, and we hope you'll agree that it's worth it. Chelsea Green is a member of the Green Press Initiative (www.greenpressinitiative.org), a nonprofit coalition of publishers, manufacturers, and authors working to protect the world's endangered forests and conserve natural resources. *Sex and the River Styx* was printed on Natures Natural, a 30-percent postconsumer recycled paper supplied by Thomson-Shore.

Library of Congress Cataloging-in-Publication Data

Hoagland, Edward.
Sex and the River Styx / Edward Hoagland ; foreword by Howard Frank Mosher.
    p. cm.
ISBN 978-1-60358-337-4 -- ISBN 978-1-60358-336-7
1. Hoagland, Edward. 2. Hoagland, Edward--Travel. 3. Authors, American--20th century--Biography. 4. Authors with disabilities--United States--Biography. 5. People with visual disabilities--United States--Biography. 6. American essays.

PS3558.O334Z467 2011
818'.5409--dc22
[B]

2010048877

Chelsea Green Publishing Company
Post Office Box 428
White River Junction, VT 05001
(802) 295-6300

www.chelseagreen.com

For Oren and Rafie

— *contents* —

EDWARD HOAGLAND
The Thoreau of Our Times

*L*ately, I've been dismayed and astonished by the almost total absence of "nature," not only as a theme but even as a background or setting, from a great deal of our contemporary literature. Of course, there are notable exceptions. *Cold Mountain* springs to mind. So does almost anything written by Wendell Berry, John McPhee, or Barbara Kingsolver. But stop and imagine. Whatever would *Huckleberry Finn* read like without the Mississippi winding through it? *Moby-Dick* without the whale? *Walden* without Walden Pond? I could go on, but there's no need to. Without the natural world, and not just in the background, but up front and center, those classic works of American literature wouldn't exist *at all*.

Fortunately, at least for those of us who can't conceive of a world without literature or nature, the natural world—or its alarming diminution in the early twenty-first century—is the principal subject of Edward Hoagland's latest, and best, collection of essays. *Sex and the River Styx* is a memoir-like evocation of the current embattlement of wild and unspoiled places and the once nearly infinite variety of species that lived there, from northern Vermont to the African veldt. Employing, as its chief narrative prism, the perspective of an aging, but almost preternaturally alert, lifelong writer, *Sex and the River Styx* examines, in thirteen linked essays, what it means to be a human being in an era when "not just honeybees and chimpanzees are disappearing, but incomprehensibly innumerable species that have never been discovered at all."

Hailed by John Updike as "our finest living essayist," and by *The Washington Post* as "the Thoreau of our time," Edward Hoagland wrote his first book, *Cat Man*, an exuberant novel inspired by two stints working with the Ringling Bros. and Barnum & Bailey Circus, when he was still a student at Harvard. Since then, he's gone on to publish twenty. His titles include the acclaimed essay collections *Walking the Dead Diamond River*, *Red Wolves and Black Bears*, and *The Courage of Turtles*; one of the seminal works of fiction inspired by our relentless westering quests, the novel *Seven Rivers West*; and the highly praised literary travel memoirs *Notes from the Century Before* (set in northern British Columbia) and *African Calliope*. In its clear-eyed celebration of subjects as diverse as the New York City harbor, outback Alaska, and the splendid diversity of wildlife on the Vermont mountain where he has lived part of each year for four decades, much of Hoagland's early work is indeed Thoreauvian. A self-described "rhapsodist by temperament," he could fairly be considered our last great transcendentalist. That, at least, is how I often think of him.

As he tells us in "Small Silences," the highly autobiographical opening essay of his new collection, Edward Hoagland moved, at eight, from the city to rural Connecticut, where he enjoyed a Tom Sawyer-ish, out-of-doors boyhood. Thoreau tells us little or nothing about his early youth. Hoagland, for his part, revels in his recollections of the backyard brook he explored down to a secluded pond abounding with mud turtles, sunfish, and ribbon snakes, with even its own resident mink. In between college semesters, he ventured out with the Big Top as a "cage boy," helping tend to the lions, tigers, and other large animals, sometimes sleeping under the stars on one of the circus train's flatbed cars. "We had charge of some of the most glorious and legendary creatures," he writes, but even then he sensed the doom awaiting those "legendary" animals and their untamed brothers and sisters. The elephants, especially, "appeared to recognize the tenor of events. They were not optimistic—at least I thought not—and forty years later, seeing shattered herds in India and Africa, I was surer still that the road for them shambled off downhill."

As a young man, Hoagland thumbed across America "with a $20 bill for emergencies tucked in his shoe," and drove a rattling Model A Ford over Route 66. After a tour of duty for Uncle Sam, he ranged out farther still as a traveler and a writer. Like the drifter in the old Hank Snow roadhouse jukebox favorite, Edward Hoagland really does seem to have "been everywhere"—even, in his case, Antarctica. It's Africa, however, along with his beloved mountain in northern Vermont, that he's kept coming back to, as indeed he does in many of the essays in *Sex and the River Styx.*

Time was when, on early trips to the great plains of East Africa, Hoagland, like Hemingway before him, witnessed "pristine herds . . . browsing among the thorn trees as creatures do when engaged in being themselves." No more. Today those wild herds are "shattered" and much of the continent a "crucible of mayhem, torture, and murder." Yet for all of his passion for elephants and lions and reptiles large and small, it has always been *human* nature that has concerned Edward Hoagland the most. In "A Last Look Around," he reports that roughly two million people have died recently in the southern Sudan alone, where "the very air smelled burnt." "Visiting Norah," a wonderfully poignant, personal essay, chronicles his first visit to a Ugandan family he's been sending money to for years—a $20 bill here, $50 or $100 there, slipped into "a greeting card so that they wouldn't show through the envelope if a larcenous clerk were looking for them." Somehow, Norah has kept part of her family alive and intact through famine, war, and the AIDS epidemic. But then, with the laser-like, startling truthfulness that has characterized his writing from the beginning: "With these new friends, there remained the tacit barrier that they were nearly destitute and I was not."

Turning to those long-ago days and nights riding the rails with the Greatest Show on Earth, in "Circus Music" Hoagland reveals the harsher truths just under the glitter and stardust of circus life: the "Ten in One"—ten different "freaks" to gawk at under one sideshow tent; and the way the circus reflects, in its ruthless code of survivalism, our own lives, "rolling, juggling, and strutting our stuff." He's marvelous on the "bull men"—the cookhouse crew and "seat men" and aerial-act riggers with "a seaman's way with ropes." They're drifters, mainly, ex-cons, alcoholics, misfits who nonetheless dreaded, above all else, that pink slip that said "no rehire." Where is their like today? Gone the way of the fabled railroad circuses themselves: "They'd slammed around with their hats pulled down over their eyes, every mother-in-law's nightmare, and knew how to jump on a moving train without saying goodbye to anybody—knew the Front Range of the Rockies and the Tex-Mex border."

Of our contemporary writers, perhaps only Edward Hoagland could pull off the sentence cited just above. I love its racy diction, reminiscent of Malamud's and Bellow's, the roustabouts "slamming around. . . every mother-in-law's nightmare," and the indelible image of these circus tramps, hats pulled low, hopping a freight without so much as a backward glance, then waking up to the vista of those soaring, snow-capped mountains.

Nowhere does Hoagland use his gift for what H. L. Mencken called the "American language" more effectively than in his essays on his own aging at a time when so much of the natural world, as he once knew it, is vanishing. He's funny and lively on the indignities and advantages, to the species Homo sapiens, of growing older, dropping terms like "coots," "codgers," "old dogs," and "old crocks" the way a canny major-league pitcher, aging himself, drops a sneaky backdoor curveball over the outermost corner of the plate for a surprise called strike three (How'd he ever do *that*!). Then, look out, lest we readers, like an aggressive hitter, begin to dig in and get *too* comfortable. Here's that still-blazing, inside fastball knocking you right back off the dish, as he reminds us that death, when untimely, can "stink like cordite," and wonders, Job-like, why lightning "lathes down one tree but not another." At the end of "Small Silences," Hoagland's legendary fastball hits 100 mph as he bluntly warns us that "nature, when abused, may react eventually like a tiger whose tail has been pulled. We shall see, indeed, if that is the case. We will definitely find out."

Still, Edward Hoagland is no raging Jeremiah, shrieking down imprecations upon his fellow men and women from some pillar in the wilderness. Like Thoreau, he sees more day to dawn, in Hoagland's case in the blessedness of children at play, animals "being themselves," the spark of divinity in an unexpected act of generosity, and the mere existence of a being as wondrous as an elephant. Like all great writers, what's more, he can't quite be classified. The Thoreau of our times? Well, yes, right down to his fierce egalitarianism. But while Wendell Berry celebrates the traditions of agrarian life, and John McPhee, that greatest of all nature *journalists*, tells us all we could ever wish to know about our geological history, it seems to me that Hoagland's rightful literary bedfellows, in addition to Thoreau, are Faulkner, Whitman, and Twain.

What, then, might a twenty-first-century reader take away from Edward Hoagland's magnificent and unforgettable portraits of landscapes beleaguered and our last frontiersmen and frontierswomen, circus aerialists, African matriarchs, and New England cattle dealers, not to mention the displaced Tibetan yak herder he bumped into not long ago in China's Forbidden City who asked "if he couldn't find him a job herding yaks in the United States"? In his title essay, "Sex and the River Styx," Hoagland remarks that the "disjunction between the sexes keeps the world on an even keel." To me, each of the essays in his latest collection serves the same purpose, of helping us, as creatures of the natural world ourselves, maintain our natural equilibrium.

"My allegiance," Edward Hoagland writes in "Last Call," "is to what's alive, or was. Sea wrack, and the crab that eats a hangnail I spit into it; the porcupine on an apple limb folding leaves into its mouth at dawn, while a nightcrawler, as pink as my fingertip, disappears into the soil under the tree before an early bird wakes up and grabs it. Giraffes licked salt off my cheeks when I worked in the circus at eighteen and discovered that sweat often coexists with pleasure but that everything should be seen as temporary . . . except I was going to love elephants at a throbbing level as long as I lived."

Me, too, Mr. Hoagland. *Us*, too. All of us who have read and marveled over your essays for decades and will for decades to come. "Rather than love, than money, than fame, give me truth," Thoreau writes in the conclusion of *Walden*. Edward Hoagland has spent his entire writing life doing just that. Yes, he is most assuredly telling us in *Sex and the River Styx* that it's late in the game. Yet there's always the sense, in this sobering and beautiful book, that this is a world, and we are a species, eminently worth saving. No one, from the author of the "Song of Solomon" to Henry David Thoreau himself, has ever said it better.

HOWARD FRANK MOSHER

SEX
and the
RIVER
STYX

SMALL SILENCES

*W*andering to the edge of Dr. Green's woods, next door to our new house, at the age of eight, I found a little brook running— my first, because we had just moved from the city to the country. The floating twigs and leaves, the ripples, and yet the water's mirroring qualities, and the tug on my fingers or feet when I dipped them in, plus the temperature, so remarkably different from the air's, fascinated me. We, like the other neighbors, had some brush and untrimmed trees in back of our lawn, so the brook picked up interesting flotsam before entering Dr. Green's pines, where except for scattered boulders or stones the ground was less varied, all needly. The sounds the stream made, thocking and ticking, bubbling and trickling, were equally beguiling, however, and, like the wind-nudged boughs twisting over- head, never precisely the same.

This was in Connecticut during World War II, so we kept a dozen brown hens for their eggs, and I watched their pecking order develop, and other habits, endlessly. But the brook was a near second for curi- osity, and because it was undomesticated I recognized in it a wilder power. I felt like part of the flock—feared for them at nightfall, when they would duck inside the coop through an entrance I never forgot to close, and rejoiced with them when a New Hampshire Red rooster was acquired to trumpet their accomplishments. But the woods were an adventure, more mysteriously reverberant. By nine I was probably daring enough to follow the stream (knee-high, so nobody was afraid I might drown in it) through the forest far enough to catch sight of

Dr. Green's pond and approach its spongy inlet. I must have heard about its existence, but no one had taken me there—my father golfed, my mother gardened. The distance is now elastic in my mind's eye, but no roads or houses intervened and my discovery caused no alarm. My parents, retracing the path, notified Dr. Green, a retired and retiring widower whose given name I never learned. They owned two acres; he, I would guess in retrospect, at least fifteen. Then there was Miss Walker's estate, in back of both properties, and lending them a bit more wildlife, such as the foxes that threatened my chickens. She was a fiftyish spinster, with servants, who may have had about three times as much land. My parents had never met her, but she caught me trespassing as a "nature boy" once or twice—climbing the spruces in her overgrown fields—and summoned me inside her manorial stone house (ours and Dr. Green's were white clapboard) and gave me and the friend who was with me a proper glass of apple juice with chocolate-chip cookies. A real-estate agent who wanted to subdivide the place surprised me too and was less friendly, afraid that I might start a wildfire, but I would sooner have harmed myself, and I think Miss Walker surmised as much and knew you couldn't stop a boy from crossing stone walls and wire fences.

The pond was the great revelation, after, first, the stream and before I could climb a sixty-foot Norway spruce and swing with the wind. Amber, black, and silver, with moss on one bank and cattails on another, it had frogs plopping—leopard and green frogs and bullfrogs with large eardrums who said *jugarum*. I saw crayfish and a ribbon snake, yellow-striped, and a muskrat swimming in a moving V. Greenish pollywogs and salamanders. The pines, in retrospect, were red pines, and red squirrels of course were chattering in them from all angles, much more vociferous than the gray squirrels that nested in the maple shade trees in front of our house. Also my dog, Flash, an English setter and constant companion, who barked at them, sniffed out an opossum, longhaired, long nosed, pouched like a miniature kangaroo, who promptly swooned and played dead when I picked it up by the tail, just as it was supposed to do. The pines, with their thousand jewely shards of light as you looked up on a sunny day, didn't like wetting their feet and gave way to white birches whose curling strips of bark you could write on not just with a pencil but with your fingernail if you had to, and dark hemlocks, droopy-branched and unbelievably tall and somber, in the soggy ground, while the pond itself might be as bright as a lens of glass, with tree crowns, mackerel clouds, and blue sky reflected on its surface.

I was a good student and not as friendless or solitary as this may sound. My trouble was a bad stutter that made Flash's companionship and the flock of chickens and communing out-of-doors important to me. But I generally had an intimate friend of my own age whom I could lead to these precious places—Miss Walker's lordly spruces, like the beanstalk that Jack climbed, or Dr. Green's miraculous, jam-packed pond—discovering, however, to my astonishment, that they didn't matter as much to him. He would prefer listening to Mel Allen broadcast the Yankee games with me, gossiping about our class, inventing piratical schemes. Ice-skating, yes, we shared, or throwing rocks into the water to watch the thumping splash, but when we were past the volcanic stage, why go? Dr. Green was a cranky, softhearted soul almost too old to walk to his pond by the time I discovered it, but he made the effort to inspect both me and it when he heard from his gardener that I was there, telling me not to treat the frogs inhumanely or to fall through the ice. Brooks, the silent Irishman whom he had long employed, had no interest in woods or ponds, so I seldom encountered him, and he was easy to avoid, sitting smoking in his chilly greenhouse—just nodded at me as an authorized visitor if we did chance to meet.

I saw a mink trap an eel, and a musk turtle diving out of reach on the bottom, and tree frogs in the bushes, and "pumpkinseeds," or sunfish; learned how to fish with a worm and a pole. A blue heron bigger than me would sometimes flap over from the larger ponds (Dr. Green's, though huge to a ten-year-old, may have been scarcely an acre in size) after amphibians. Or on my repeated expeditions I might see a kingfisher diving for shiners. Nobody could spot me from the road as I circled the water, looking at the strange jointed plants called horsetails, or ferns at the margins. The ordeal of stuttering at school seemed distant indeed, and I was learning how to swim well enough at my parents' country club not to be a danger to myself if I fell in. I was cautious anyway, as stutterers must be if they are to survive—bicycled home after swimming lessons, before I'd have to try to talk to people on the patio. I could talk to Flash with absolute abandon, and loved Mel Allen, and Tommy Henrich, "Old Reliable," the Yankees' right fielder, and watched the New Hampshire Reds' social goings-on like a budding ethnologist, although I tended to downplay my various excitements in the house lest they be restricted or used against me. It was not a silly instinct because my parents did soon tell me I was reading too much, and by prep school were telling my favorite teachers that I was too intrigued by nature and writing; that these were dodges due to my handicap and might derail a more respectable career in law or medicine—angering the teachers who nurtured me.

I was an only child until, at ten, we adopted a three-month-old baby girl named Mary Elizabeth, from Chicago. So this event may have been another force pushing me into the woods. Within a few years she and I became close, though in the beginning I used to proclaim that she wasn't my "real sister" in order to watch my mother's distress. And from the pond, after school, I would often go uphill, not back along the stream, to Dr. Green's house, skirting both Brooks and, in particular, the doctor himself. That is, he was always indoors, but I would take care not to be heard in his bedroom or sitting room upstairs, and knock softly instead at the kitchen door so that Hope alone heard me. She, as cook, like Brooks, had worked for Dr. Green for many years but had not established the same fellow feeling. She was brown-skinned and tacitly more intelligent and ironic than Brooks was, and took good care of her employer without receiving the hearty although formal daily greetings Brooks did. He was white and had a family in town to repair to, which also made him more of an equal, perhaps, than a large-waisted, large-breasted, light-colored Negress in a pink uniform, far from wherever her grownup children were located, or other friends. Being small and mute, I never inquired of Hope where she had originated. I was grateful for her kindness in inviting me in, to sit on a white chair, with the kitchen clock ticking and the scents of baking. Like the pond, it soon became a dependable sanctuary where nobody asked me to speak. We simply sat quietly, she with her hands in her ample lap, while Flash and the doctor's cocker spaniel lay down together on the back porch. Sometimes I forgot my handicap, but if we talked for a minute it was in low tones so that the lonely doctor wouldn't tromp downstairs and interrupt us, asking angrily why I hadn't come to see him. To a little boy he appeared formidably crabby and diagnostic—naturally wanting to hear, analyze, and cure my stutter.

Jimmy Dunn, in the house on the other side of ours, was a good playmate for cards and chess and imaginary games; and Tommy Hunt, at whose house the school bus stopped, was a likable guy—he eventually became a minister—more mature than us, who worked on a jalopy about as much as I went to the pond and had a crush on the girlfriend of our football quarterback, who became an airline pilot after high school and college, when she married him. By eighth grade I had a silent crush on her too; she was our most down-to-earth, approachable blonde. Though nobody picked on me, some of the other boys collected at Tommy's after the bus dropped us off for BB-gun fights or to drive that hoodless jalopy around and around Tommy's parents' vacant field or to squeeze each other's balls in the bedroom in a manhood test or to tie each other up or masturbate their dogs, including mine if they could catch him (to my cowardly shame). I sometimes hunted rats with Flash in our relic barn with my own BB gun, after I had ceased to need to seek out Hope so much. But the wonder isn't why these kids didn't beat me up—even the Kane boys, sons of a drunken "black Irish" gardener, gap-toothed, tricky and sly, who threw stones at cars and went to the public school, not ours, did not, though I was certainly warier when crossing their employer's meadow—as much as why nobody ever has. Not when I honeycombed Boston on foot for years and New York for decades in late-night walks, or in five trips to Africa and nine to Alaska, and so on. I don't need to belabor the point, but neither cowardice nor caution alone explains it. A naturalist's and a stutterer's intuition maybe more so—I've swung around and looked into an approaching mugger's eyes occasionally, which caused him to sheer off—and a berserk streak that I have when sufficiently angered that perhaps sets other people back on their heels long enough for a bad situation to defuse. Stutterers learn to distinguish genuine danger from the ersatz, and also to manipulate their anger for the fluency that a shot of adrenaline will momentarily bestow. And they may develop a well of empathy that, again, deflects the rage of sufferers looking for someone to attack, and learn to distinguish the fulcrum of power in any group. While bullies, for example, will persecute the closest target, real predators look into the middle distance—as I learned in my late teens when taking care of lions and tigers in the Ringling Bros. and Barnum & Bailey Circus. So you avoid a bully, but stand in closer proximity to a predator and join him in gazing out.

Girls were another puzzle. One of my sister's babysitters would coax me to lie on the sofa with my head in her lap, before I was ready to, so that she could practice what she wanted to do when she was with her boyfriend. Or she would ask me to reach for something on a high shelf, then press her breasts against my back, as if to help. At a dancing class another girl taught me to cut in on her when she was burdened with a partner she didn't like, but after I took this to mean she was partial to me she got mad because I cut in on her when she was fox-trotting with a boy whom she *did* like. Dr. Green died while I was away at boarding school, so I can't recall whether Hope retired somewhere down South, being of an age to, or sought other employment. But she was authentically welcoming to me, and suitably erotic to a prepubescent too, sitting catty-corner to me across from the big old-fashioned stove and oven—with invariably a roast in it for the solitary old man upstairs—and her hands loosely clasped, a gentle expression, big hips, lax bosom, and her uniform collar unbuttoned. I was never interrupting anything; she'd have the clock to listen to, the radio on low, a newspaper the doctor had finished with folded on the counter. Live-in maids in our neighborhood, black or not, had no cars to visit one another and would not have been permitted by the police to walk the roads. I took care not to trigger my stammer by telling her I had just seen watercress, water striders, eelgrass, mudpuppies, duckweed, pickerelweed, horned pout, and water with trembling algae, wavy larvae, and waterlogged trees like slumbering alligators three feet down. The clouds had piled up like smoke signals over the pond and the pines, and I had nibbled rock tripe and touch-me-nots. One winter I'd accidentally angered a friend by grabbing at him as I fell through the ice, pulling him into an icy bath. Our families thought, oh, dirty water, but I knew that, no, it was where life lived, and part of my heart. By twenty I would be climbing unobserved into a mountain lion's cage, but already I trusted my faith in nature and was biking to larger ponds, then every week or two basking in my secret refuge at Hope's kitchen. I didn't eat there or stay as long as an hour, just dropped in to decompress, resting.

———

Hope was not the first colored person I'd known. (The term "black" then was an epithet of insult, equivalent to "nigra.") When my mother brought my baby sister home on the train from the Chicago adoption agency, she had hired a woman from the South named Arizona, much younger than Hope, vigorous, boisterous, taller, darker, and less acclimated to the behavior expected of servants in an upscale Wasp suburb up North. She was a blithe spirit, as I remember her, assertive, gleeful, expansive, loud and goofy with me when, to tease her, I'd pull on the bow of her apron strings—which, though I was about ten or eleven, quickly alarmed my Missouri-born father as, I suppose, proto-miscegenation. In a few years he would begin boycotting the Metropolitan Opera for permitting the great black contralto Marian Anderson to sing on its stage. Arizona had big buttocks under the thin fabric of her uniform that made the butterfly of the bow doubly tempting, and he perceived a sexual element in our giggles. My mother, not being from a former slave state, was more startled by Arizona's guileless tales of growing up barefoot in a hovel, and chewing her own babies' meals for them when she couldn't afford to buy prepared food. It sounded unsanitary, barbarian, "African," like her strangely untrammeled name (evocative to me now of wanting to "light out for the Territories") and her maid's-day-off visits every Thursday to Harlem by taxi and train. Goodness knows what diseases she might bring back to her attic room and our dishes and pantry. My mother rang a tinkly bell at the dining-room table, rather than possibly interrupt a polite conversation with guests, to call Arizona to clear each course off the table, but Arizona didn't seem to fathom the gentility of the ritual; was likely to holler out helpfully to ask what was wanted. So they got rid of her, my father believing afterward that it reduced a property's value, at least in Connecticut, if a colored person had ever lived in it, even in a servant's capacity.

I learned from the episode not to betray to a third party affection for anybody who might get fired because of it, or to divulge any passion that might thereafter be denied me. "I'm going to the pond," I'd say casually to my mother; then dodge carefully past the stolid, deracinated Brooks (like a tug-on-the-forelock-when-the-gentry-go-past footman), toward the trillium and columbine, the toadstools and fairy-ring mushrooms, the nematodes and myriapods, the blueberries or blackberries, near the opaque yet shiny stretch of hidden water, deep here, shallow there, with the wind ruffling the surface to conceal such factual matters, and cold at its inlet but warm where it fed into a creek that ran to the Silvermine River and finally the ocean. Getting hold of a live trap, I caught a couple of weasels that screamed at me through the mesh until I released them, and a burglar-masked coon, and the inevitable beautifully whitecaped skunk, who didn't let me have it when I let him go.

The plopping raindrops, wobbly riffles, crosscurrent zephyrs, the penny-sized and penny-colored springs that replenished the margins of the pond from underground, pluming hazel colored, endlessly rising-and-falling individual grains of sand, irislike around the black pupil of the actual hole, lent variance to the velvet water, near dusk, or bright mornings, when it shone in the mini-forest like a circlet of steel. During a thunderstorm it seethed, fingered madly. Then when the clouds cleared off, in the batty moonlight, the shadows seemed crafted differently than might be cast by any sun. I was delighted watching bats flutter after hatching mosquitoes in the wetland that bulwarked the pond, and thrilled when the pair of barn owls that nested in an abandoned water tower on the hill would shriek as they skimmed across Miss Walker's second growth. It was more frightening to be alone upstairs in my own house at night than to tiptoe about the woods. Nor was it as scary peering at a copperhead on a ledge one noontime that a schoolmate whose mother was a birdwatcher took me to see. And I loved the whirligig beetles and water boatmen, the damselflies and fireflies, the sticklebacks and freshwater snails. My favorite turtles were the wood turtles, *Clemmys insculpta,* seven or eight inches long, that have almost disappeared from New England now, with their sculptured carapaces, like Cellini's metalwork, and salmon-red legs, which I would watch breed in the stream in the spring, but that roamed the fields until hibernation time, when they'd return again to the streambed's leaves and mud.

Snappers lurked in the muck of the pond year-round, platter-sized, but didn't bite if you left them there, even if you happened to step quite close or purposely touched their serrated tails: only if you picked up a female on her big day in June when she left the water to lay her eggs. The bottom, when you waded, was painted with fallen leaves and so varied you'd stand with one foot sucked ankle-deep and the other supported on hard feldspar sand—little fish angrily nipping at you because you had begun to infringe on their nesting terrain—and one warm but one chilled, and a branch knifing out of the water alongside you much like a fin. Wood frogs and peepers were to be found in the bushes, and a water snake tasseled in lovely russets and tans somewhere down the bank. A green frog or bullfrog couldn't survive the snake's visits simply by holding its breath underwater; it had to swim in zigzags or leap fast. But speed was not a defense when the great blue heron, gangly legged, slow flapping, maneuvered down from the sky. It had a spear beak and watched as sternly as a sentinel, once it had landed, for the first frog buried in mud that needed some air. Similarly, a mamma duck might be clever at concealing her ducklings in the reeds from me—but not from the mamma snapping turtle, who grabbed them one by one through the late spring before laying her own eggs. Even a seagull dropped by from Long Island Sound to forage on crappies or what not, and Mrs. Morris, my sixth-grade biology teacher, told me that my eels, too, had migrated in from the sea. The Canada geese barked like beagles, going north or south.

On sunny days a certain woodchuck liked to clamber up onto the leaning bough of an apple tree next to the stream and straddle it as comfortably as if she thought she were not just a matriarch but an arboreal creature. I'd face the ethical dilemma of whether to notify Flash and provide him some fun at the expense of panicking her miserably. An old apple tree's outreach, like that one's, carries an idiosyncratic eloquence because season by season the weight of its fruit has twisted each individual limb. This generosity speaks, whereas a white spruce's symmetry is more visually generous, and climbing high to rock with the wind was to plumb a power no truck tire roped like a pendulum to a maple or an oak tree could approach. I'd lie on my back on a patch of moss watching a swaying poplar's branches interlace with another's, and the tremulous leaves vibrate, and the clouds forgather to parade zoologically overhead, and felt linked to the whole matrix, as you either do or you don't through the rest of your life. And childhood—nine or ten, I think—is when this best happens. It's when you develop a capacity for quiet, a confidence in your solitude, your rapport with a Nature both animate and not so much so: what winged things possibly feel, the blessing of water, the rhythm of weather, and what might bite you and what will not. In the circus a tapir, a tiger, a mandrill, a rhino, but building really upon the calm that Dr. Green's modest woods and pond, forty-five miles out of New York City, had bestowed on me.

Nature indoors—that plump bobby-soxer stroking my hair while holding my head in her lap to practice up for her boyfriend—made me more jittery, but I was not really somebody who "liked animals more than people," as the cliché goes. Animals didn't sometimes smile sardonically or in wonderment when I stuttered and avert their eyes, turn their backs, but I had close friends and was enjoying my sister's presence now too. I loved her, and even found she was deflecting about the right amount of attention away from me in family politics (but not too much). I didn't go swimming in crashing surf or lightning flashes or climb cliffs with ropes and pitons or kayak in whitewater rapids or spelunk claustrophobically, I wasn't trying to conquer nature or prove my testosterone. But nature as simply night or a height or a lonely menagerie animal or a small limestone cave to crawl down in or the lip of the crest of an unpretentious mountain to hunker on for an hour felt just right, and often as if my throttled mouth and bottled-up emotions had engendered a sort of telepathy in me. Not of course to warn of inanimate events, like a flash flood or a rock slide, but the bear around the bend or the desired milk snake in the woodshed. My sixth sense was unstoppered.

I never totaled a car (machines may not have interested me enough) or broke my bones, and had an upbeat view of life, experiencing the kindness of many strangers when I hitchhiked, for instance. I speculated as to what the anthropological purpose could be of the brimming, broad-gauge affection people like me felt when watching a wriggling tadpole or clouds wreathing a massif—sights that have no reproductive or nutritional aspect. Call it "biophilia" or *agape;* it wasn't in response to a hunter's blunt hunger, or kinship-protective, or sexual in some way. Was it a religious wellspring, then? Silence and solitude are fertile if the aptitude is there, and love in its wider applications is also, I think, an aptitude, like the capacity for romantic love, indeed—stilling for a few minutes the chatterbox in us. That massif wreathed in clouds, or the modest pond that has been left in peace to breed its toads, is not a godhead. Like sparks flung out, each perhaps is evidence instead (as are our empathy and exuberance), but not a locus. And yet a link seems to need to take hold somewhere around nine, ten, or eleven—about Mowgli's age, in Kipling—between the onset of one's ability to marinate in the spices of solitude, in other words, and puberty, when the emphasis will shift to contact sports, or dress and other sexual ploys and fantasies or calculations.

But nine was fine; and when you came to feel at home in Connecticut's woods, New Hampshire's were not a large step up the ladder, or Wyoming's expansive mountains after that, then California's by twenty, building toward British Columbia's and Alaska's, Africa's and India's, in the course of the future. The sea was different, however. I admired it from the beach or a steamship but never acquired the nonchalance required for solo sailing; was afraid of drowning. On the other hand, having been born in New York City and then returned to live there as an adult, I loved metropolises and saw no conflict between exulting in their magnetism and in wild places. Human nature is interstitial with nature and not to be shunned by a naturalist. This accidental ambidexterity enriched my traveling because I enjoyed landing and staying awhile in London on the way to Africa, or exploring Bombay and Calcutta en route to Coimbatore or Dibrugarh. Didn't just want to hurry on to a tribal or wildlife wilderness area without first poking around in these great cities, which I rejoiced in as much. Although there are now far too many people for nature to digest, we are all going to go down together, I believe. We are part and parcel of it, and as it sickens so will we.

In the meantime, joy is joy: the blue and yellow stripes of a perfect day, with green effusive trees and the dramatic shapes of the streaming clouds. Our moods can be altered simply by sunlight, and I found that having cared for primates, giraffes, and big cats in the circus made it easier to meander almost anywhere. Few people were scarier than a tiger, or lovelier than a striding giraffe, or more poignant than our brethren, the chimps and orangutans, and you can often disarm an adversary if you recognize the poignancy in him. Nevertheless, I preferred to step off the road, when I was walking in the woods at night and saw headlights approaching. Better to take one's chances with any creature that might conceivably be lurking there than with the potential aberrations of the drive-by human being behind the wheel. It may seem contradictory that for reverence and revelation one needs a balance. You can be staggered by the feast of sensations out-of-doors, but not staggering. Your pins ought to be under you and your eyes focused. As in music, where beauty lodges not in one note but in combining many, your pleasure surges from the counterpoint of saplings and windthrow, or the moon and snow. Both are pale and cold, yet mysteriously scrimshawed—the moon by craters, mountains, and lava flows, the snow by swaying withes or maybe a buck's feet and antler tines. Although like snow, the moon will disappear predictably and reappear when it's supposed to, moonlight is an elixir with mystical reverberations that we can pine and yet grin over, even when "empty-armed." It's off-the-loop, a private swatch of time, unaccountable to anybody else if we have paused to gaze upward, and not burdened with the responsibility of naming birdcalls, identifying flowers, or the other complications of the hobby of nature study. One just admires a sickle moon, half-moon, full moon that, weightless and yet punctual, rises, hovering. Sometimes it may seem almost as if underwater, the way its dimensions and yellow-ruddy coloring appear to change to butter, or russet, or polar. The Hungry Moon, Harvest Moon, Hunter Moon, are each emotional, and expertise about their candlepower or mileage from the earth is a bit extraneous. Although our own cycles are no longer tied to whether they are waning or gibbous, we feel a vestigial tropism. This is our moon. *It's full*, we'll murmur; or *It's a crescent*, or like a cradle lying partly tipped. And a new moon is no moon.

Twilight, the stalking hour, itself can energize us to go out and employ that natural itch to put our best foot forward and "socialize." The collared neck, the twitching calf, and tumid penis will respond to daylight's variations or the moonrise, as we gulp raw oysters and crunch soft-shelled crabs that still possess that *caught* quality, not like precooked pig or processed cow. If we've lost the sense of astrological spell and navigational exigency that the stars' constellations used to hold, we at least present fragrant bouquets and suck the legs of briny lobsters like savages on important occasions. The stunning galaxies have been diminished to blackboard equations that physicists compute, and our dulled eyes, when we glance up, instead of seeing cryptic patterns and metaphors, settle rather cursorily for the moon.

Water does retain a good deal more of its ancient power to please or panic us. Bouncing downhill in a rocky bed, shouldering into any indentation, and then nurturing fish, mirroring a spectrum of colors, or bulking into waves that hit the spindrift beach at the inducement of the wind, it's the most protean of life's building blocks, the womb of the world. "My God, there's the river!" we will say, in pure delight at the big waterway willows, the glistering currents bounding along like a dozen otters seizing ownership of the place, as we walk within sight. Our bodies, 70 percent water (and our brains more), only mimic the earth's surface in this respect. And we want a mixed and muscular sky, bulging yet depthless, and full of totems, talismans, in the clouds: not every day but when we have the energy for it, just to know that we're alive. Rising land of course will lift our spirits too. Hills, a ridgeline, not to begin toiling right up today but the possibility of doing so, perhaps discovering unmapped crannies up there and trees as tiny as bonsai on the crest, yet dips for the eyes to rest in as we look. We already think we know too much about too much, so mountains are for the mystery of ungeometric convolutions, a boost without knowing what's on top. Awe is not a word much used lately, sounding primitive, like kerosene lamps. What's to be awed about—is this the Three Wise Men following the Star?—what hasn't been explained? Actually, I don't know what *has* been explained. If we are told, for example, that 99 percent of our genes are similar to those of a mouse, does that explain anything? Apprehension, disillusion, disorientation, selfishness, lust, irony, envy, greed, and even self-sacrifice are commonplace: but awe? Society is not annealed enough. Trust and continuity and leadership are deteriorating, and the problem when you are alone is the clutter. Finding even a sight line outdoors without buildings, pavement, people, is a task, and we're not awed by other people anymore: too much of a good thing. We need to glimpse a portion of the axle, the undercarriage, of what it's all about. And mountains (an axis, if not an axle) are harder to be glib about than technological news reports. But if you wait until your mature years to get to know a patch of countryside thoroughly or intimately, your responses may be generic, not specific—just curiosity and good intentions—and you will wind up going in for golf and tennis and power mowers, bypassing nature, instead.

No man was complete without a parrot on his shoulder, I used to think. Pirates had them—or perhaps a monkey with a string knotted around its waist—and far-flung sailors, and naturalists searching the tropics for undiscovered plant and animal species. An Orinoco toucan or an orange-epauletted Amazon or hyacinth macaw nibbled at an earlobe or chatted in their ear. At the mouth of the Congo River or the Amazon, hotels had to post a sign saying no parrots were allowed here, and the birds lived so long that in tamer harbors like the U.S.A. you might never know who had taught yours to cry, *What's that down between your legs, big boy?* In the port area of Lower Manhattan that later became the World Trade Center, I used to see foulmouthed merchant seamen's big-billed birds for sale in a cigar store that also proffered shrunken human heads with pained and puckered faces and sewn-up lips which sailors on the coffee or United Fruit banana boats had purchased from tribes such as the famous head-hunting Jivaros of Ecuador. Both the brilliant-colored parrots and the Indians' heads, suspended behind the counter by their greasy black braids of hair, had been jungle-born, except of course for the especially valuable blond-tressed heads of white women and their missionary husbands: although, buyer beware, you were supposed to be careful about fakes—maybe monkeys that had been treated and bleached.

And there was a kind of "leopard store," as I thought of it, named Trefflich's, in a brownstone at 215 Fulton Street, close to where a lot of other ships came in to dock from Joseph Conrad countries. It sold jaguar cubs, anacondas, margay cats and ocelots, aoudads and addaxes, baboons, pangolins, gibbons, adolescent elephants—importing wholesale stuff for zoos to a warehouse in New Jersey. But you could walk around the several floors, if you were with your father, and look at giant Seychelles tortoises, reticulated or Burmese pythons, black panthers peering between the slats of cargo crates, and wheedling monkeys whose organ grinder might have died. Carnival owners stopped by in the spring in painted trucks to purchase an iron cage with a sun bear already in it or rent a half-trained lion, or a bunch of monkeys. "When it comes to monkeys," a placard boasted, "we pledge ourselves to give full cooperation to all operators interested in giving the public their monkey's worth!" Beasts in makeshift confinement—an arctic wolf, a rainbow boa, a baby camel—crammed every corner, and then in season might be touring the nation's midways, living on roadkills or sick chickens the drivers stopped to pick up, the panther on foundered horses or dead dogs from a pound, the monks on fruit the public bought.

Parrots did not remain a priority for me because I sensed that they were delicate and in considerable peril, though squawking harshly and nipping fingers. Even when a fancier hamstrung them by scissoring their flight feathers, as if to bauble-ize them, they continued to emit untamable screams and like a peg-leg pirate moved about laboriously by grabbing footholds with their beaks and chimneying up or belaying down in mountaineer fashion. Their shrieks might bring the neighborhood's blue jays to the owner's window as if to try to help a friend in need, and double the noise. Then you'd see the guy abandon a thousand-dollar pet to his local flower shop, where at least it had the ferns and ficus trees for company. Or I've known a parrot or two that escaped from captivity and shimmied high into a fir tree next to the house, and even in the wintertime simply refused to come down. Up, up, the pinioned bird hitched with claws and beak, watching the hollering jays and crows circling around and screaming gleefully with them. Although of course it couldn't fly, it ate a few tart bits of bark or cone in freedom at their level. The drama continued for hours—pleas and commands from the ground, and hullabaloo from the whirling wild birds. Then a soft snow started falling, as night settled down. The native flocks—warmly plumaged and observing the newcomer's crippled condition—flew away to their sheltered roosts, while the parrot, in its bright jungle colors, climbed poignantly, stoically higher, to wait in silence to nibble needles and freeze.

I went to summer camp in the Adirondacks, helped out at an animal hospital near my home, and, with a friend's family, visited a little dude ranch in the Wind River range at Dubois, Wyoming, going out by train when I was fourteen. This showed me that whole tiers of land exist that most of us never reach; just look at, perhaps. My horse could scramble by switchbacks for a short way, like a badger galumphing. Horses were more independent-minded than a dog, preferring the open range as a grubstake to any barn and wintering there for six months as uncosseted as the elk or mule deer. The ranch hands wintered pretty tough, too—not just drank a lot but practically hibernated in snowed-over cabins, living on a wad of cash secreted in a coffee can, not a bank account, and snaring jackrabbits, eating root-cellar turnips and steaks axed off a frozen side of beef, by a hissing Coleman lantern. They lost their teeth sooner than Easterners, and the men got gimpy at an early age from being thrown or kicked. Not only the rodeo types: many ordinary wranglers were fallen on, stepped

on, in breaking horses, roping calves, rassling a steer, or had slid off
an icy road in a Chevy and limped for miles with a broken bone, help
was so damned far. The bristling, pelagic scale of the landscapes,
skyscapes, exhilarated me, plus the chance to catch sight of a cougar
by peering up a box canyon, or the coyotes that howled after dark from
the same creek bed where I had walked an hour before. In these late
1940s the Good War was barely over, evil had been defeated, but a
tremor of risk and early death still prickled the mood of many people
of middle age: veterans who wouldn't speak of what they'd done, and
for whom foreign travel had involved stifling weeks on a troop ship to
places they never wanted to lay eyes on again. They squinted and bit
their lips, thinking back. Dale, the one cowhand I got to know somewhat—who taught me to ride in a roundup and shoot ground squirrels,
and talked confidingly toward the end—was both mild in manner and
steadfast, yet lamed internally, with a cowboy's kidney disabilities and
a flat-wallet winter to look ahead to. As with Hope, I can't reconstruct
our conversations from sixty years ago, except that there were many
factualities for me to learn, glued to yearnings Dale might even help
me fulfill. Our talk was less inchoate. Childless from knocking around
the West all his life, he was sympathetic to my wish to hear stories of
mega-wildlife, trapper-hermits, gold prospecting, bigfoot myths, and
not just rehearse my saddle skills like the other dudes. That West was
already threadbare but not skeletal, and I learned that when somebody in the know recognizes what you care about, he may earnestly
try to help. Antelope, moose, and marmots—"whistlers"—we looked
for, and falling-down cabins in draws that had yarns attached to them.
Dale was slightly built, like a person who dealt with creatures so large
that heft itself hardly mattered, compared with logic and telepathy. He
sized up people quietly too, and minimized his reactions if he could,
the way you would with a haywire heifer or bull.

Act purposefully but minimally and keep your reasons under wraps, was a lesson he taught me. Not the whole formula for life, but quite a beginning, because love and openness to what you love are fragile and yet will flower if cupped and sunlit: as will a freelance toughness and survivability, when you need that. Like a certain helicopter pilot in the Brooks Range in Alaska who flew me around decades later, Dale grounded my enthusiasms at the same time that perhaps mine reinforced his. I couldn't help him face an old age of penury, but we were wistful when this summer interlude wound up. Teasing so many memories out of his mind had cheered him up, made him feel that they were worth it, and as in a relay race, he was passing along nuggets to me, not necessarily from his own life but that turn-of-the-century horse wranglers had conveyed to him. Just so, we elasticize our lives—as you'll see a tiny school of fish do in an aquarium. As quick as mercury and multidirectional, they impart a darkly silver, wriggly sorcery to the cubic inches of the tank. Instead of gallons, it becomes like having a mini-planetarium in the house, because the stars also sometimes seem to swim in the sky, not just hang in suspension there.

Pets in containers, or loose as catty companions or doggy slaves, can hardly fill in for the immensity of wind, stars, and trees, the infinity of unlobotomized animal species, the intricacy of landscapes, the galaxy of scents and shapes in natural creation, that we are losing, or just no longer sense or see. A planetarium is not the heavens, or an aquarium the southern oceans, and our own intricacy—our bristly whiskers, flaring nostrils, our fingerpads flicking in and out as ceaselessly as gills, our curling pinnae and peripheral vision and intuitive antennae, all seeking connections—perhaps demands them. Only 2 percent of Americans are farmers now, and yet the rest of us are still avid for spring's green-up and weather forecasts. Without the primeval dangers that formed us, we tune in bruising professional football or pore through the tabloids for raunchy murders, sexual triangles, and kidnappings, news of disease, greedy scandals. We actually learn skills of the chase and the feint from these, learn about insanity and bad judgment and to control our spates of rage, to cushion our marriages, downsize our fantasies, put the brakes on our Neanderthal instincts. The tabloids are appetite-rich and Darwinian. We read them for meat and war games, or watch the tube for boobs that we can't ogle in real life, and truth or consequences—robbers punished—while rejiggering our minds' chemistry with pills, replacing an aging hip with titanium, and exercising on a gym machine, or face-lifting our long-suffering skin.

But I seem to have gained, around eight, nine, or ten, the rather precious sense of continuity that knows that when you come out of the woods into a house it's only temporary; you will be going back out again. People are less amphibious or ambidextrous in this regard than they used to be. A thousand or so may have topped Mt. Everest ("Well we knocked the bastard off," Sir Edmund Hillary famously said, after conquering it in 1953), and plenty run marathons or balance on surfboards. Yet a more authentic affinity with what we call nature is being lost even faster than nature itself. Into the void slips obsessional pornography, fundamentalist religion, strobe-light showbiz (no Bing Crosby or Frank Sinatra, who blazed on forever), and squirmy corporate flacks such as the old power brokers seldom employed. If gyms don't substitute for walking, it's hard to find a place to walk, as houses line every beachfront and scissor every patch of woods with cul-de-sacs for real estate. You may prefer the ubiquity of electricity to seeing fields of stars after dark, but losing constellation after constellation in the night, and countless water meadows along uncontoured rivers, and bushy-tailed horizons, may be a titanic change. Our motors similarly wipe out the buzz and songs of insects, birds, the sibilation of the breezes that hunters used to front, always stalking into the wind and studying the folds of the terrain for how it flowed, because meals were won by knowing the intimacies of the wind. To lose moonlight, and compass placement, and grasshoppers telling us the temperature by the intensity of their sound, poses the question of whether we *can* safely do away with everything else. The ecology of solitary confinement on this planet may be calamitous: not to mention the sadness. To assuage the emotional effects, already one notices an explosion of plant nurseries, pet stores, computer-simulated androids, and television animations. We've boarded up our windows so as to live interiorly with just our own inventions—though sensing too that we are in the grip of a slow, systemic illness, somehow pervasive—as meanwhile chimpanzees are being eaten up wholesale in Africa as "bushmeat," the elephants butchered, the lions poisoned.

I knew these signature animals by the age of eighteen because I worked for two summers in a circus where we had in our charge some of the most glorious and legendary wilderness creatures. Asian elephants, Sumatran and Siberian and Bengal tigers, a cheetah, a hippo, a jaguar, pythons and boas, three lowland gorillas, a rhino, and an orangutan. My mentor then was a Mohawk Indian, from a culture that was comparably endangered. Indeed, he finished out the remainder of his years as a groom at the riding stable that services New York's yuppie equestrians who ride in Central Park, before having his ashes scattered off the George Washington Bridge into the Hudson River, which are immemorial waters for the Mohawks. But the survival of wild places and wild things, like the permanence of noteworthy architecture, or the opera, a multiplicity of languages, or old shade trees in old neighborhoods, is not a priority for most people. They are on their way out, and you simply love and love them as you, too, shuffle along. But the elephants, wrinkled in their sagging hides, appeared to recognize the tenor of events. They were not optimistic— at least I thought not—and forty years later, seeing shattered herds in India and Africa, I was surer still that they realized that the road for them shambled off downhill. Their anxiety was more than jumpy;

it seemed demoralized. Their bizarre hugeness only doomed them further. We generally discover important things late: like how very closely the great apes' genome resembles ours. This was obvious to the naked eye and won't prevent wild ones from being eaten in Africa, but makes their treatment here in captivity more appalling. And thus it was with elephants' infrasonic communications, which supplement the squeals and trumpeting we hear. It took a former whale biologist, Katy Payne, who had helped record the high frequencies humpbacks sometimes use, beyond the capacity of a human ear, to figure out that elephants also talk at acoustic, though subsonic, levels we can't detect, and that these deep sound waves travel as messages for surprising distances, from herd to herd (yet nothing like what the ocean's physics can accomplish for certain whales' low-voiced emotings).

The more complexities we come to know about a fellow being, the less cavalier we're going to feel when its kin are wiped out. Most species that disappear, of course, have never been examined or "discovered" at all. But with the jumbo kind—formerly demonized as rogues, or boat swampers and living oil wells—we have a good deal less excuse. Indeed, in the circus, decades before Katy Payne's breakthrough, I had experienced intimations that within our single herd, animals a hundred yards apart could convey their politics or frustrations by sounds below the lowest range that people heard. They would be clearly communing across the field, looking at each other, swinging their trunks convivially and swaying with eloquent body language, until after a minute or so the session ended with a strain of sound finally edging up into a low-pitched groan. I was eighteen, nineteen, not a scientist, and these insights were accompanied by a swarm of others about our giant, protean, poignant beasts—Ruth and Modoc and twenty others whose feet I liked to lie close to, testing my trust in the rapport I thought I had with their rhythms and whims. Acoustics were not the reason I was touched or central to what I was trying to comprehend, even when they stood there forthrightly and frontally, broadcasting sounds I sometimes intuited but couldn't hear.

In East Africa on two trips during the 1970s, I saw pristine herds on the vastness of the veldt, browsing slowly among the thorn trees as creatures do when engaged in being themselves. Although they were being poached, the horizons were huge, and the scale of ivory-hunting an attrition they could bear. Their humor, gait, and dignity were intact, the tutoring of the calves, the playfulness of bathing, the virtuoso trunks spraying dust when insects annoyed them, or plucking an epicurean shoot, or squealing at a stork. By the 1990s, however, when I returned twice again, the splintered groups, targeted by Somalis with Kalashnikovs, had witnessed so much butchery and anguish—their numbers more than halved—that they acted as if danger were everywhere. They drank at the water holes twitchily, hastily, and migrated between their feeding groves without the ambling ambience of old. Like the chimps I saw, they didn't just react to immediacies, as, for instance, the big cats did, but appeared to worry in advance. They weren't freewheeling personalities anymore, and it was a relief to meet a noncommittal aardvark or a snoopy jackal on the track.

Nature throbs in us through our digestive gases, sweaty odors, wrist pulse, unruly penis or bloody vulva, and nervy tics. We flinch, gasp, fuck, cluck, grin, blink, panic, run, fight, sleep, wake, and wolf a meal like animals. Our official seven deadly sins are rather animal, too, and so is bliss, I think: not only lust but that out-of-body happiness you may feel when being quite still, yet aware and self-contained. Nature is continuity with a matrix and not about causing a stir in the world, and as we destroy our links to other forms of life, it's like whittling at our heels and shins and toes. You can do it for a while until you cut a tendon, nick a bone, and find you limp. And we've now done that. Life turns into more of a riddle when not braided together with other manifestations of energy, grace, scale, and harmonics or tempo and all the rest. Humanity all alone can be constricting, and I've met more blithe spirits in frontier situations than anywhere else. They weren't the quickest conversationalists or most educated, and inevitably there were also augured souls who had fled to the mountains to get as far away from other people as they could. But as George Orwell remarked at the end of his diaries, "At 50, everyone has the face he deserves" (alas, he didn't live that long); and these guys from the era of the First World War or the Depression, living on the Skeena River or the Stikine, in British Columbia and Alaska—the Spatsizi or the Omineca, the Klappan or the Kuskokwim, the Tanana or the Porcupine—when you hollered to them from the footpath and they came out of their cabins, looked blithe. They were likely to wear long johns all year round, and light the woodstove every morning regardless of how warmly the sun might be going to shine, because you never know. Anyway, smoke and long johns discourage mosquitoes, and if you've ever been profoundly cold you won't mind being over-warm.

They were on the lookout for gold colorations in the creek beds as we walked about, and before fall got well started they would be laying in a mammoth woodpile, and extra rations under the floorboards, and boiling and re-scenting their fur traps, then, after a hard frost, throwing caribou carcasses up on the pitched roof, where they'd keep. I made sure not to take them unawares—because was this an individual who lived out here with the elements because he had abandoned everybody who had ever trusted him, or because of what he'd *sought?* With men thirty years older than me and at home with the tessitura of the wilderness in the 1960s, you didn't need to be a psychologist to arrive at some swift conclusions, mostly cheerful ones. A general competence, plus maybe the yearly salmon runs, had enabled them to ride out the six months of winter, as well as the specters that can afflict a solitary mind. If a man's smile looked to be guyed out as securely as a well-staked tent, it meant he probably grinned a lot, if only to himself, and wasn't about to blow away.

My hunches in the main worked out, and more importantly I escaped the confines of my stutter and gradually became able to talk to people as easily as to animals. Being a humanist, I was not as interested in animals but, in the Whitman mode, aspired to contain multitudes, which included being a mutt and hybrid oneself, snaky, fishy, foxy, and as Afro-Indo-European as our far-trekking forefathers. Although I was living in New York City by this time and married, and therefore swinging as if in a bathysphere into some of these roadless valleys in the far Northwest with my pack and sleeping bag, I felt at home on a moose path too. My spirit keyed into the tuning fork of old melodies—not simply the sense of trust I had acquired in Dr. Green's woods, but the narratives, I think, behind us all. In back of Gilgamesh and Beowulf, Homer, Hardy, and Melville, lie impulses of animism that personified the sweet wellsprings and ominous cliffs, the mountaintops and antique trees as godlings for our ancestors, and the fact that primates are talking to lions even today. Baboons are arguing with them on a Tanzanian plain and fathoming their reactions much as I was often doing half a century ago in the Ringling Bros. Circus. We sleep in edgy surges of a few hours that we manage to combine into a night's civilized schedule, yet would have more logic for a chimp in the forest or a baboon on the veldt, rousing from each nap to glance around for a leopard's dappled coat creeping through the gloaming.

Life is so elastic that people whose circumstances appear to be about the same may measure themselves as almost anywhere on a continuum from misery to elation, and nature herself is invoked to justify fidelity or infidelity, tolerance or violence. I've never thought of nature as a guardian angel, but rather as a polychromatic thrum you sway and hum along with and therefore are not caught by surprise by a sudden juddering in the weather, a hyena on a kill, or a soggy bowl of landscape, when you're hiking. Although never a daredevil, I didn't believe that we can live quite wholeheartedly if we are overly afraid of dying, but, on the other hand, didn't think if life gets boring you have to climb a hairy mountain. Just pick your calluses off and refresh your sensibilities. The airiest scenery I've been privileged to see was in the Himalayan foothills of Arunachal Pradesh, between Assam and Tibet in northeast India. Yet I didn't stand there yearning to scale and "top" the greenly rising and then vertiginous ridges that towered toward snow peaks like laddered but amorphous ghosts, muscular and portentous beyond the mists. I wanted to let them be. And similarly I plan not to be cremated, so that the proverbial worms can do a recycling job on me after I die, rather than be rendered into tidy, sterile minerals in an undertaker's furnace: a less juicy fate.

Now, animals live even more in the present than we do. They are geographic or hierarchical in organization, operating by rote or scented memories of previous hazards and good fortune, seeking food with smaller brains but not wistful about it, as you'll notice watching a fox glance up at suet in a birdfeeder without wasting energy in pining after a bite. Short and brutish has been a description of their lives ("brutish" being somewhat tautological), but certainly the lives of what are called the megafauna are getting shorter while ours grow longer. Some people scarcely know what to do with their bonus time—doubled life spans, plus the round-the-clock availability of artificial light—because nature doesn't deal in bonuses. The sun rises and sets when it did a million years ago, with daylight altering by immemorial increments as the planet rolls. It doesn't award you an extra hour if you have a deadline. *Can you make* it? nature asks instead, if it says anything at all. But secondly, and curiously, I think, it speaks in terms of glee. Glee is like the froth on beer or cocoa. Not especially necessary or Darwinian, it's not the carrot that balances the stick, because quieter forms of contentment exist to reward efficiency. Glee is effervescence. It's bubbles in the water—beyond efficiency—which your thirst doesn't actually need.

Bubbles are physics, not biology, and glee, if the analogy is to carry far, may be an artesian force more primordial than evolutionary. To me, it's not a marker for genetic advantages such as earning more, but an indicator that life—the thread of Creation, the relic current that has lasted all this way—is ebullient. Still, you might argue that the choosiest females select not just for strength and money or its zoological equivalents, but for the superfluous energy that humor and panache imply. The woodpecker drumming an irregular tattoo on my tin roof in the spring is not mechanistic in his ritual, as if merely to prove that he could dig big bugs out of a tree and bring them to his mate. His zest and syncopation is like when you watch two fawns gamboling with a doe, or a swaggering vixen mouth three meadow mice that she has killed to fit them all between her teeth for the trip to her den. Such surplus moments relax us and serve a tonic function—triumphal for the vixen, toning the fawns' reflexes, letting the woodpecker pause unexpectedly to listen for an answer.

The gamboling, like a kitten's stalk, prepares an animal for the hunt or being hunted, and the youngster that enjoys it most may wind up savviest. But the glee I mean is less utilitarian, more spontaneous, and a kind of elixir that needs a bit of peace to germinate. How does one account for the passive, concentrated happiness of listening by a lake to the lap and hiss of rustling water, watching the leaves jiggle, the poplars seethe and simmer? The lake is ribbed with ropes of wind and strands of sun between cloud shadows. The contours of three hills delineate the comely way that brooks feed into its blue bulk, and otters, loons, mergansers, animate it (the far mile curving out of sight), so that you'd hardly need to invent a loch "monster" for drama. And yet you can wake up nearly anywhere and experience a comparably high-pitched serenity. Glee is not complacency—in the middle of a roaring city it may seize you—and I think of it as possibly generated at life's origins, like a filament from, or footprint of, that original *kick*. Nature seems more than Evolution, punctuated or otherwise, and the Creationists may be onto something when they insist that it is an effusion of God's glory. Their god isn't mine, but glee may be a shard of divinity.

Nature, although more inclusive than fundamentalism allows for, seems to me infused with joy. Even the glistering snow is evidence, though burdensome by March, and October's dying leaves, parched by an internal trigger before the first frosts, turn gratuitously orange, red, and yellow, as beautiful as any plumage—yet what mating purpose does that serve? When outdoors with a dog, anybody can observe the gulping relish with which it quaffs evocative smells, then punctiliously may leave its own before hounding on. I have been watching colonies of animals, from chickens, mice, and garter snakes to some of the megafauna, for sixty years, and when they are not under stress you see plenty of delight and exuberance, particularly when young ones are splitting off and diligently getting a new group started. Biochemistry drives hunger and explains why animals consume one another. But what explains the elation, exuberance—this surplus snap of well-being that animals as well as naturalists feel, and people in Calcutta as much as in New York, or Arunachal Pradesh, for that matter?

Joy sprouts from squalor as well as in the middling classes, a perennial as well as a primitive emotion, as if propelled by a spin originating from the ur- or ultra-density of the Big Bang. Or should we claim that amphibians only acquired a capacity for glee after they became lizards? Or lizards only after they evolved into birds? Where and when did the perception of beauty begin? Most of us nowadays agree that the birds that sing at dawn in the spring are expressing some degree of gladness in their surging notes, not merely a mechanical territoriality. But for a person like me who considers the toads' sparkling, twinned-note, extended song on warm days in May and June to be actually the loveliest of all, the answer is not that easy. I can't swallow the notion that I—but not the toads—find it so lovely. (I also think I've seen and heard alligators and seen turtles enjoy themselves.) However, then the question shifts to whether amphibians that sing, such as frogs and toads, only began to respond to warmth and what we call beauty after they left the constancy of the water and ceased being fish. Not a sure-shot answer there either, unless you discount the evidence of your eyes when you're closely watching fish. And water is an unboxed, undulant medium. What does it mimic when it sloshes?

That crucial age when I opened up and trusted myself to nature, back in Connecticut in 1942, is about when most children start perceiving the world beyond themselves in nuanced, revelatory ways. I later tried sport hunting and gave it up, sport climbing and gave it up, preferring not to lord my ego over what I saw, as in those chill, steep rain forests of Arunachal Pradesh—like Alaska's, multiplied several times over— with footbridges woven of vines stretching across the cataracts and thatched houses perched on stilts and white peaks suspended above it all. To be immersed was sufficient, without attempting to "knock the bastard off."

If we're not immersed, we're likely to try to simulate the hubbub of a tribal encampment by collecting cats or dogs (butchering countless horses in order to feed them), or barbecue sets and fishing tackle, off-road vehicles or quirky website monikers. We'll fly in bales of greenhouse flowers from low-wage tropical countries, which are being denuded of their natural flora, to present as symbols of we hardly know what. That is, yes, for anniversaries, marriages, court-ship, holidays, graduations: but why *flowers?* Are we bees or bears, or are they somehow akin to the mysteries of glee and orgasm and why small boys stand by the conundrums embedded in the mud of a pond, then reach from the bank or roll their pant legs up and wade after salamanders, water snakes, pollywogs, and perhaps a reflection of what have you?

We reach for where we came from, our older folk a bit homesick: the nights not being starry anymore and distances not quite real. Is there anything untoward that we don't take a pill or press a button for? Nature envelops us, nonetheless, in the piquancy of cottage cheese, the giggle of thunder in the next county. Our lewdness and acquisitiveness bray to prove how recidivist we are, still with our feet in the primal muck. I live alone at the moment, and would smell piquant after a stroke, if I weren't discovered immediately. Nor, when I laugh, do I feel in the twenty-first century—I could be Babylonian. And my rapport with friends is more a refinement of ancient habituations than contemporary. Nature, when abused, may react eventually like a tiger whose tail has been pulled. We shall see, indeed, if that is the case. We will definitively find out. But in the meantime we live like those amphibians: sometimes on the dry beach of modernity and sometimes swimming in the oceans that were here eternally before.

VISITING NORAH

*T*wo pairs of marabou storks, each of them five feet tall and battle-ship gray with a pink neck and a wattle pouch, proudly posing and croaking, were raising chicks in bulky nests in the flame trees that overlooked the swimming pool at the Fairway Hotel in Kampala, Uganda. Probably because of the crowds of schoolkids learning how to swim every afternoon, they reminded me of the proverbial white and black European storks that flap over the thatched roofs of country cottages, bringing newborn human babes to each village. But marabou storks—unlike the storks of fairy-tale folklore—are carrion feeders and offal scavengers, similar to but huger than the most no-nonsense vulture, and in famine territory they of course will eat children who drop by the wayside. In the chaos of modern Africa, they have moved from the veldt and forests into the cities, wherever garbage and death and anarchy erupt. They are tolerated because, as they stalk around, gobbling refuse, rodents, fruit rinds, rotting vomit, dog carcasses, or what have you with their thick scary beaks (your eye would be a cherry tomato to them if you were lying shot), they fend off disease. But when I saw them roosting in the downtown parks, hunchbacked though formal-looking and humorless, as if watching for any homeless person who might be staggering or bleeding, they looked like undertakers to me.

Black kites and hooded vultures also circled over the city's seven hills—above its Catholic Hill, with the Rubaga Cathedral; its Muslem Hill, with the handsome Kibuli Mosque; its Anglican Hill, with the

Namirembe Cathedral; Makerere University's stately tree-rimmed rise; the separate central hill that President Yoweri Museveni governs from; the ceremonial palace hill of the Buganda kingdom; and the knobby water-tank hill, up which Kampala's drinking supply is pumped from Lake Victoria, to be distributed by gravity later on—and also the crossroads Clock Tower; the Parliament Building; the derelict railroad station; High Court; and Hindu and Bahai temples; and Nakivubo Stadium, by the odorous Owino Market, always a good place for a vulture to land. Hadada ibises, too, roosted at night in my hotel's courtyard trees, calling to one another like laughing peacocks in the evening and especially again when they flew away at dawn, crosswise—with their necks stretched out—against the sky, rising, scudding, or spiraling, and emitting the sound, *hadada*, that lends them their name, in order to begin gleaning insects, amphibians, and mice from the marshes and fields. Poverty was their friend; abandoned land was best.

This was my third visit to Kampala and my fifth to Africa. After my flight from London had circled down, however, our British Airways pilot added a personal twist to the usual parting spiel. "God bless you," he said. Uganda was emerging from the worst siege of the Ebola virus that Africa has yet experienced, and most of the Europeans and Americans on the thrice-weekly flight were no doubt aid workers of various kinds. Yet the Africans aboard were returning to the torque of a continent beset by difficulties that dwarfed the Ebola outbreak. AIDS alone lurked in twenty-five million Africans (including an estimated one million Ugandans, not counting the many who had already died), though AIDS was not really any more problematic than the enigmas of governance.

My reason for traveling to this place was personal as well as journalistic. I am a writer and professor at Bennington College in Vermont and, for a year and a half, I'd been sending money to a post office box in Kampala, tucking $20 or $50 bills every couple of months into a greeting card so that they wouldn't show through the envelope if a larcenous clerk were looking for them. The grandmother and five orphans it was intended for had confirmed each safe arrival. Now I was coming to meet them, and know them if I could.

"Mother Norah Mugga" had begun the correspondence, out of the blue, in July 1999:

> I am writting to introduce Myself to you on behalf of [my] young grand children. There are Samuel, Herbert, David, Betty and Nicholas. I am 72 years old lady and a widow. As you may be aware, in Africa we lead a hard life . . . Some of the parents died of accidents and others died of the deadly disease of Aids Scourge. As their grand Mother, I was put Under responsibility to look after them . . .

The following January, eighteen-year-old Samuel Ziwa Ssenyonjo took over the correspondence, sending report cards and the like because Norah's health had declined after a stroke. They owned a bungalow and two acres to grow food on, so their main expense was not for food or rent but, as with many Ugandan families now, school fees. Education isn't free; it costs between $25 and $500 each term, depending upon the age level of the child and quality of the school—which even at the low end of the range is an ulcerous worry in a country with so many orphans and waifs and where wages are typically a dollar or two a day.

Betty, age nine, was first in her class of seventeen at the Tween-Age Educational Centre ("What Man Has Done, Man Can Do"), and in the next semester ranked second. Herbert, three years older than Betty, was fifth in a class of twenty-four at the Kitemu Parents' Primary School, and later ninth among twenty-three. Herbert's cousin Allen (actually, eight orphans sometimes lived with Norah) was seventh in that same group, and in the next term, thirteenth. David, age ten, did not do as well, being eleventh out of a class of fourteen, and was described by his teachers as "Fair" more often than "Good." His performance at Buddo Secondary School seemed to fluctuate a bit; one term he was fifth in a class of 139, another he was thirty-eighth in a class of 113.

Samuel next put me in touch with Nsubuga Mutebi, his uncle and guardian, and Norah's only surviving son. Nsubuga was thirty-eight, the father of two little girls, and lived with his wife (also a Norah) and her fifteen-year-old orphaned sister, Harriet, near a sports stadium in Nakawa, on the outskirts of the city. They had built the four-room house of bricks and cement after he had been released from the army, using his discharge money, though the site was malarial and the interior unfinished. During his military years, Nsubuga had marched a lot between towns near the Sudan border, from which a rebel group called the Lord's Resistance Army was still staging raids occasionally. Now he worked as a driver, which meant that he owned a cell phone and therefore knew I was coming. He met me in a borrowed Toyota late that evening, accompanied by Samuel, a pleasant-looking, alert, limber teenager. Samuel was waiting to hear whether the results of the comprehensive exams he had just taken would afford him entry into the advanced phase of secondary school.

Nsubuga, round-faced and easygoing, was a conscientious son, a worrier in money matters but gregarious with his friends, a good husband—always advisable in an AIDS epidemic—and middle-of-the-road on the subject of ambition and education. I soon realized he wasn't going to ask me to try to finagle a scholarship abroad for Samuel, just to continue helping him locally. Indeed, I bought Samuel some chickens later on, for sixty-two cents apiece. The chicks—one hundred of them—would come by airfreight from South Africa, and Samuel would be able to sell them for $2 at the broiler stage (an old business of Nsubuga's, when he wasn't driving trucks eight hundred miles at a stretch for an importer). I liked their precarious eagerness, and they warmed to me too. With my kit slung over my shoulder and a green hat hiding my white hair, I looked in my fifties, they said, ten years younger than I was. I'd made the same twenty-mile night drive from Entebbe's airport to Kampala before, with the erratic strings of cubicle shops and stalls fitfully lighted along the narrow road, bikes and pedestrians at constant risk—fifty of them to every car—and the smells of sewage under the stars, but of crops and foodstuffs too, and, above all, crowds of people. *Nearer my God to thee,* my mind murmured unexpectedly, which is the gist of what I always feel upon arriving in Africa. Not that Africa is "God" but that people, creatures, vegetation are, without the static of technology and machinery.

On a terrace at the Fairway Hotel, in the equatorial balminess, we had Cokes before Nsubuga and Samuel left me. It's a midlevel hostelry where many expatriate aid workers put up, about a twenty-minute walk from the center of this million-person capital city. I had stayed here before, on two trips with a Catholic Relief Services food-delivery group into a famine region of the civil war zone in Sudan, on Uganda's northern boundary. Currently, 670,000 refugees are being fed by the World Food Program in camps within Uganda. So I assumed that the mystery of how Nsubuga's mother had gotten my name was connected to those episodes. Norah was a retired kindergarten teacher with no present income, and had told me that a stranger at her church one Sunday had let her copy my address from a slip of paper that he kept in his glove compartment. The church, St. Apollo Kirebulaya in the town of Kitemu, ten miles outside Kampala, on the Congo and Rwanda Road, occasionally drew in a few long-haul truck drivers who wanted to pray. It must have been one of these who had responded to her need and who happened to have known me years ago while shuttling emergency relief to Sudanese refugees.

I rested the next day, watching the Senegal soccer team strut about the hallways in their yellow uniforms with numbers on the front, as they psyched themselves up to beat Uganda's hapless players, the Cranes, in an African Cup of Nations qualifying match at Nakivubo Stadium. Elsewhere in the hotel, Kampala's Rotarians held hands and sang in the dining room, at their monthly reception, while the Hormonal Contraceptive Society partied with a Luganda-language singer and an electronic band. Out on the lawn below, the Ministry of Public Services was awarding its annual citations, with big gift boxes in red wrapping paper, and office-party dancing, and finally a conga line.

I talked with a Zimbabwean consultant, as we watched all this, over glasses of *waragi*—banana gin—and tonic. His job involved visiting distant villages to check on how donor money for various projects was being spent. But since Zimbabwe's troops and Uganda's army were currently fighting on opposite sides in the Congolese civil war (which also included Rwanda, Angola, and Namibia, plus Kinshasa's ragtag forces and several rebel and tribal groups), I asked him teasingly if he was regarded as an "enemy alien." A booming-voiced, large man, he said no with a laugh and defended Robert Mugabe's twenty-one-year reign as Zimbabwe's caudillo; also the recent anarchic policy condoning violent seizures of white-owned land as a proper wind-down from colonialism. He said the tacit European boycott that had resulted was unfair. Instead, Europe should police the corporations that were stripping Zimbabwe of its gold and other natural resources. Meanwhile, Ugandan army generals were reported to be looting Congolese gold and diamonds. If applied to repairing Uganda's stumbling economy, the money might have justified the lives being lost—sometimes in battles that were really over mining rights—but people in Kampala had become quite bitter over the corruption, even to the point of jeopardizing Museveni's reelection plans after a fourteen-year reign. (He did eventually win, in the spring.)

———

Next morning, Nsubuga picked me up in another borrowed Toyota—this one with a Japanese logo on the side—to bring me out to see his mother. He was trying to buy a car for his business, but the collapse of tourism, with the Ebola scare and the staggering economy and the country on a war footing, had caught him out. His day rate, about $60 for the car and gas, was the same as my room rate and the equivalent of a month's wages for most of the hotel's employees. He was low-key and congenial, however, considering the breadwinning pressures he was under, with his mother's doctor bills and the kids' school fees. His wife worked six days a week selling rice and salt at a food mart to help. He said they had escaped the HIV plague by maintaining a good marriage and paying close attention to the earliest public warnings about "Slim," as AIDS is often called in Uganda because of how it scours the body.

We rolled over several potholed, roller-coaster hills, passing a hundred walkers for every car, and sugarcane and pineapple juice stands, red termite mounds, the Obey the Thirst Pub, the Half London Bar, Divine Gift Shop, the Exotic Hotel, Success Nursery School, Didi's Amusement Park, the Oasis of Love, and the Noah's Ark School, then stopped to look at some children's wooden coffins for sale for $15 a piece, though well polished and carved (adults' were $60). Transportation was mostly by *boda-boda,* Swahili for "motor scooter," which the customer rides on the back of for a few hundred shillings (1,600 to the dollar), or the fourteen-passenger vans called *matatus* that pull in and out of traffic constantly.

We turned off the two-lane international highway in a leafy outer suburb called Buddo, on a dirt road that climbed a fertile hill, past modest bungalows almost lost in banana plantations and elephant grass, with a scattering of goats trotting about and other domestic animals plus walkers and bicyclists, and impromptu-looking vegetable plots, and birdsong whenever the car slowed. People here would hike down to the highway at dawn and catch a crowded matatu to a humdrum job in the city and maybe get home after dark, while the oldsters and schoolchildren kept the gardens going, boiled drinking water, and watched over the chickens so that no kid on a motorcycle could swoop past and grab one by the legs and sell it roasted to a trucker for a couple of bucks.

It was exciting to wind up the gentle hilltop and first catch sight of Norah's cement-and-stucco three-room house with a low-roofed porch under a grove of jackfruit, eucalyptus, and palm trees. She came out to greet me, leaning on a stick, in a yellow-flowered dress under a blue-patterned shawl. Intelligent and sweet, she looked like my own mild, kind, humorous grandmother had at about eighty-five (which turned out to be Norah's true age, when we figured it out), except for the width of her nose and the tint of her skin. Samuel was smiling beside her, again with the quicksilver quality that I liked, and shy, young Betty, who, once I was seated in the living room, knelt briefly on one knee in traditional obeisance to a visitor who had come so far. Behind this house—dark, to minimize the equatorial sun—was a mud hut that had been enlarged and cemented and was now used for storage and cooking but which Norah and her husband, Jovan, had originally built and lived in when they bought these two acres with his discharge money after World War II. They had come from Kalangala and Bubeke, two of the Ssese Islands, out in Lake Victoria (the world's second largest), marrying in 1937 and migrating to the mainland after the birth of the first of five children two years later. Jovan was drafted into the Seventh Regiment of the King's African Rifles and trained as a medic, which led to his work as a dispensary technician all over Uganda later. He established a second family in the city of Mbarara, in the west, with four other children, an African pattern not much frowned on here then, and the children visited each other till he died in 1994.

Norah couldn't walk far or talk English much because of the debilitation of the stroke, so Nsubuga led me in noticeable anguish through the plot of banana trees to the center of their little piece of property. Seven fresh, startling sarcophagi, heroic-size and starkly fashioned of cement, rested flat on the ground—the graves of Samuel's father and mother and other dear ones who had died of AIDS. He also showed me the mango trees, the beans and yams and pawpaws and cassava, the chicken shack that he and Samuel would stock, and the hundred-gallon drum that gutters on their roof fed rainwater into. I'd brought Samuel a few books—*Things Fall Apart, Abyssinian Chronicles*, Wole Soyinka, Elechi Amadi, Ngugi wa Thiong'o, Okot p'Bitek, Peter Abrahams—and he showed me his best drawings from art class, especially a splendid fish, which Nsubuga joked was appropriate because they were descended from the Lungfish clan of the Baganda people.

The Baganda king, the thirty-sixth *kabaka*, Ronald Muwenda Mutebi II, had been restored to his three traditional palaces on Kampala's hills by Museveni in 1993—his father had been overthrown in 1966—and Nsubuga, on our drives, always proudly pointed these out to me. The Baganda, like the Kikuyu of Kenya, are the dominant tribe in business and around the country's capital region, as well as the most populous ethnic group (a fifth of Ugandans), but differ from the Kikuyu in that they gained their head start before independence by cooperating with the British, not fighting against them, and generally seem more equable in their temperament.

Besides growing its famous coffee for export, Uganda ought to be a major trade center, lying as it does between northeastern Congo and the Indian Ocean as well as between Sudan and Africa's Great Lakes region. The spindly Gulu Road, running south from that border-district town a day's drive away from Kampala, should be roaring with commerce from Juba, on the White Nile—the unofficial capital of the southern Sudan—and all the natural resources there. Juba, however, has been under siege by a guerrilla army for most of the years since I visited it in 1977. To the west, Kisangani (Stanleyville), the fabled community at the great bend in the Congo River, has been racked by equally internecine warfare. So Kampala has a knot of hopeful new glass buildings, but its engines have stalled.

Yet this likeable and loosely dirty-collared, steeply built mini-metropolis centering around Nakasero Hill is endearing. The president's mansion and palace-guard quarters perch at the top, with the best hotels (the Sheraton, the Grand Imperial, the Nile, the Speke) shelved just under them. Banks and offices are at a middle level and then come the indoor, middle-class sorts of stores for dry goods, houseware, and clothes. Near the bottom lurks the frenetic bedlam at rush hour of the enormous "taxi park" at Luwum Street, where fifty, sixty, or more matatus and their hawkers are based, along with beggars, peddlers, pickpockets, and warehousemen. All the way down by the dank and fetid Nakivubo River seethes the vaster, tented babel of the Owino common market. Nairobi, in Kenya, of course has all of this chaos tripled, but Nairobi is encircled by the famished tragedy of squatters' camps, unmapped and amoeba-shaped. Ugandans, under Idi Amin's and Milton Obote's dictatorships in the early decades after independence, witnessed much crueler violence than Kenyans ever did, but because the violence emanated from the city, their impulse has been not to run to—rather, away from—Kampala in times of disaster. Kampala was so terrifying a crucible of mayhem, torture, and murder that it was not swamped with country folk, as Nairobi has been for half a century. Museveni has made the situation much better, even though his mid-March reelection was less than exemplary as a democratic exercise, and was preceded and followed by several fatal bombings. Indeed, his chief opponent, Dr. Kizza Besigye (who was favored by younger, educated voters), ran as a fresher version of Museveni. When you are in Kampala, you are not in a savage dictatorship like in Khartoum, nor in the hungry, gridlocked democratic tumult of Calcutta. Kampala is touching precisely because it is a city trembling between alternatives. Not starving, not a tyranny, and not yet choking with air pollution like Mexico City, because, except for a smoking soap factory, it hasn't a lot of industry.

Another day, Nsubuga drove me to his own home in the neighborhood of Bweyogerere on the Mombasa Road. Intermittent strips of one-story, plaster-and-cement businesses sped by: Nice Place Plastic Products, the Hot Fat Pork Joint, Maggie's Bar, and a drum maker, the Sunni Muslim hall, the Victory church. We turned off and bumped upward on a patch of trackless, slick red hardpan to a cluster of makeshift, small, mortared-over brick houses, close but catty-corner to each other, with gashed rain gullies nevertheless separating several of them, so that we were lucky that the car reached the door. We could hear other conversations and quarrels, and smell the communal privy, but Nsubuga's children, Sheila and Shakra, both breathed "Daddy!" joyfully when they saw him. (Two older ones were at his mother-in-law's farm, or *shamba*, sixty miles away—she had had twelve children, many now dead of AIDS.) I was pleased to witness this because, although I knew Nsubuga was a good man and I had taken his wife and him out a couple of times for a drink in the evening, as well as his children swimming, our friendship never achieved much intimacy. Like many people I got to know in Uganda, he was so frantically short of money that our relationship was edged with angling requests for cash. Not just the orphans living with his mother, Norah, needed school tuition, but his mother-in-law's various orphaned grandchildren did also. To finish buying the Toyota, he needed the equivalent of another $2,500, which he had no way of acquiring. Yet as he neared forty, what he thought he maybe wanted more was a little shamba of his own, to make use of the agricultural sciences that he had studied in school, before he enlisted in the army. When I asked if he wouldn't inherit Norah's two acres, he told me a bit ruefully that if his father had outlived her that would be the case, but the Bagandan tribal custom specified that a woman should leave her property to her eldest brother's oldest daughter instead—and buying it would cost more than the car.

Even with both of them working, Nsubuga and his wife hadn't managed to finish the house. The bedroom, though uxoriously cozy, was the projected garage. The narrow yellow living room, with two sofas and two upholstered chairs, a blue rug, a TV with a Spike Lee video playing on it, a small coffee table, some calendar art, a refrigerator stocked with Pepsis, and a gold wall clock, was their future kitchen. They said they had met at a wedding party twelve years before, and still touched one another, side by side, so affectionately as they talked that it seemed like an inoculation against HIV. Harriet—Nsubuga's fifteen-year-old sister-in-law who babysat for them, liked biology in school, and wanted to be a nurse if they could afford to continue sending her—was as attractive as Samuel, out at Norah's in the country, and possibly smarter. Yet, living cheek by jowl with their neighbors, the family had malarial pools of rainwater just outside that the communal outhouse drained into.

So you may wonder why, as an American traveler, I didn't simply preoccupy myself with trying to help this particular family. Well, there were malnourished street children roaming the town who had no adult relatives whatsoever left to help them. There were young Rwandan refugees, destitute and traumatized by the furnace of that next-door genocide. And the Congolese and Sudanese civil wars to the west and north, with maybe five million dead combined. On a milder note, there were the difficulties of the waitress whom I knew best at my hotel. Josephine Nantume was a single mother and—after the collapse of tourism in the wake of the Ebola epidemic and the recent kidnapping and murder of eight British, New Zealand, and American vacationers who had meant to observe gorillas in Bwindi National Park but were captured by guerrillas instead—was barely earning enough to cover her food and rent. I paid for Donald, her six-month-old son, to go to the doctor when he got feverish and started choking from bronchitis and she feared he might die of pneumonia, as well as for his regular supplementary milk. Then I hired Nsubuga to take me out along the Gulu Road to where she lived in two dark concrete rooms behind a groundnut, spice, and soda-pop store.

Donald still had a deep cough but was better, and we piled him and Josephine and Rosemary, Donald's twelve-year-old cousin who babysat when Josephine was working—all dressed in their Sunday best—into the car and drove about twenty miles for a surprise visit to Josephine's parents, in Buzzi. Her last visit had been alone on the back of a motorcycle for an AIDS funeral some time before, so this was a very special occasion. In fact, when we pulled up to the house, her parents, Kato and Nakawesa, thought the owner of the hotel must be bringing her home after an accident. But Josephine had bought sugar, rice, cornmeal, soap, and biscuits to load in our trunk to give them, and had saved about $5 so that her father could buy kerosene for their lamps or clothes for himself. Unlike so many men, he had stuck with his wife for more than forty years, and now that he was rheumatic and deaf Josephine wanted to be as loyal to him. Ever since she, at seven, had walked two hours every weekday to St. Theresa's Primary School, on the opposite ridge, she could remember him biking the eight miles to his job planing boards at a sawmill in Kawuku Town. He ached from it now, and the trip was too dangerous, with the cars tearing up behind him at warp speed. She had eight brothers, but none of them had managed to obtain more education than she had. With her $2 a day from the hotel, she couldn't pay for them to go to school. So they were each earning maybe a dollar a day as pickup laborers or by collecting firewood to process into charcoal and sell in bags to passersby along the Entebbe Road and weren't good prospects for marriage—leaving Donald as the only grandchild. She herself, at twenty-seven, wanted no more, she said, after her disillusionment with the married pharmacist twenty years older than she, with five legitimate children, who had seduced her and fathered Donald. Then he had told her she was on her own because the AIDS epidemic had left him with so many relatives' orphans to feed, clothe, and educate. She kept her hair cropped short, like a country girl's, partly to show in the environs of the hotel as she served drinks that she was not for sale, and partly to save the $4 a week that her longhaired friends spent on hairdressing.

We were in green, moist, spacious, rolling country, well cultivated yet not congested or lacking in handsome trees. And everywhere banana groves lent cover to the fields and the scattered houses built of cement, plaster, and iron sheets for roofing. Kato (the name is given to the second of male twins; he was of the Buffalo clan of the Baganda) and Nakawesa had begun their home in 1959, with bricks they'd baked, overlaid with mud and then cement when they could afford it, and an uncommon high, timbered ceiling and a proudly wooden-peaked, ceramic-tiled roof. The kitchen was a separate, open-faced structure of mud adhering to wooden poles, with mats on the earthen floor in front of the fireplace, and a pestle and mortar and a collection of cooking pots. A stack of clean banana leaves served as plates, and there were basins for washing your hands before and after eating. Josephine had quickly changed into the matronly dignity of a *gomesi* dress that made me think the pharmacist had missed the boat.

Her family was never going to starve. They had ten acres, wonderfully cared for and intricately planted with papayas, melons, and sweet potatoes, red peppers, peas, beans, pumpkins, avocados, tomatoes, eggplants, and yams, and mango, orange, lemon, large jackfruit, and little white-flowered coffee trees. The problem was that they had no vehicle to bring even their one cash crop—the banana liquor called *tonto*—to market. Cooked down, fermented, and distilled, twenty liters of tonto in a jerry can would sell for 40,000 shillings: nearly $25, if the trucker didn't cheat them. (Distilled again to eighty proof and bottled at a factory, it becomes waragi, and three-fourths of a liter sells for $5.) They had also had two cows, but rustlers had recently stolen these—probably transporting them straightaway to a slaughterhouse in Kampala. You couldn't get the police to come, even if you could afford a cell phone, because the police had no cars. And anyway, the rustlers had guns. If they came into your house, you lay face down on the floor without stirring except to give them whatever they wished (as Nsubuga, who had been through this, confirmed).

Josephine, when trying to arouse my sympathy for her father's plight, had told me that lions sometimes confronted him on his land and that he was too old for that. (Nsubuga similarly exaggerated his family's difficulties when he was asking for money, as if it were necessary.) But Kato said no, not for twenty years, and no leopards for ten, except that once a panicky cheetah displaced from a game reserve had dashed through. The wild pigs too were nearly gone; he had put his spear away. Only a few colobus monkeys, in a troop, might raid his fruit trees. Such a labor of love the place was: such variety he and Nakawesa had created in his spare time from the sawmill job.

They hugged Donald and Josephine goodbye and loaded our car with jackfruit, *bagoya* bananas, cabbages, eggs, eggplants, and sweet potatoes, mangos, lemons, passion fruit, and coffee beans for our journey back to the city. It was touching how Josephine too, given half a chance, had that ability to create a home, yet, always desperately behind on her rent, was not able to. At night, as she carried drinks to customers on the patio of the hotel, her mind was on Donald, who would have kicked off his blanket soon after young Rosemary fell deeply asleep, and might be crying unheard and coughing from the chill of having wet himself. She couldn't afford to hire a grown-up babysitter, and Rosemary stubbornly refused to take the baby into bed with her because then she would be wet and chilly too. Josephine, who was not allowed to sit down during her eight hours on duty, observed with chagrin the prostitutes who occasionally circulated and sat and drank at the tables with the *wazungu* (whites), speaking English or French or German so trippingly from long fluency at pillow talk, as well as of course Swahili and Kampala's own language, Lugandan, and perhaps their original childhood tribal lingo. They earned in a lucky night what could be a whole month's wages for Josephine.

On the other hand, a cashier at the hotel, who was also named Josephine and earned barely enough to live on, and who was required to sit at a tiny desk for eight hours, counting change for beers and barbecue, had also had a child by a married man—a businessman who was now in Tanzania. This Josephine, however, had chosen to leave her four-year-old son, Ivor, with her mother on a three-cow farm in a far western village near the Congo border, an eight-hour bus ride away. Although he was safe, loved, and healthy, she saw him only once or twice a year. Josephine Mubera (Josephine II, as I called her) was a year older than Donald's mother and had been stuck at this hotel job for ten years instead of five. She was not Bagandan but from the more foothill-and-forest Banyankoro tribe. Her own father had deserted her family early on, so that Josephine II's heartstrings were tied instead to her mother—in the country with Ivor, an auntie's and a sister's orphans, and her three unmarried sisters—but also and particularly to her three brothers, who had followed her here to the city but, like her, had been unable to pay for more education. Thus, they seemed stranded, doomed to temporary laboring jobs or pickup hustles and tempted to fall in with one of the street gangs. She was bitter about it, as well as about her own thwarted state. Four nights a week she had to sleep on a mattress behind the bar to respond to room-service calls. Even so, with her mite of a savings account, she had just opened a beauty salon and was now dreaming of a way to go to the two-year program at the best beauty school in Africa, in Johannesburg (as it was, her assistant at the shop was teaching Josephine II whatever she knew). Or alternatively, if she could find someone like me to sponsor her visa and airplane fare to America, she might persuade her relatives there to loan her enough to get the business going properly (they weren't responding by mail) or else help the smartest of her brothers with the tuition to Makerere University, about $4,000 per semester.

Instead of the hotel uniform, Josephine II wore seductive Indian shawls over her Bombay blouse, a svelte skirt, and bracelets, and scented her hair. When she first met me, she squeezed my hand and asked if I wanted her to take me home. I didn't go the sugar daddy route—in such situations I always said that I was sixty-eight and decrepit—but did gradually become her friend. I gave her money to ease her migraines and her ulcer pains, although she wasn't really seeking money for herself, and I hired Nsubuga to drive me out with Samuel to look at her salon, the Majo Unisex, in Nakawa, on the Jinja and Mombasa road, not too far from where Nsubuga himself lived.

With the garbage piled about the shopping area, kites and vultures wheeled overhead, but people walked from all directions in modest, constant numbers to buy necessities, more comfortable than in the jumbo markets downtown, where muggers sometimes stalked. Josephine's place of business was an open-fronted concrete cubicle ten feet square, with a tile-patterned linoleum floor and yellow plaster walls decorated with Dark & Lovely product posters (although the models were light skinned). It was on the second floor of a two-story rectangle set on the hardpan and facing a wholesale maize-and-sugarcane depot, a groundnut warehouse, and a dressmaking school across the dirt alley. The cubicles near hers included a photocopy shop, a bicycle parts store, a bus ticket office, a pay-for-the-telephone stall, a dressmaker, a food take-away, a Domestic Needs Market with china and cookware, and a Quez Boutique, which was her immediate competition. The roof was rusted corrugated iron, and there were other sheets of this, as well as bagged cement, for sale.

She had no hair dryers or other appliances that I could see, except two stools and plastic basins and a bucket for water, and shelving where the shampoo and oils and unguents were. The one customer during my visit, a zaftig, bored woman with a wealth of black, untidy hair, was sitting cross-legged on the floor while Josephine's assistant laboriously braided it—an eight-hour job that would last at least a couple of months and for which the charge would be $10 or $15, "or whatever she can pay," as Josephine later told me, having missed our appointment due to ongoing domestic melodramas. She was involved with an older man, a lawyer for the electricity board, who had succeeded in keeping his marriage secret from her for nine whole months and, now that she'd found out, seemed to be neglecting her. She was hurt and mad—she had only learned of his marriage because his oldest son had gotten gravely ill and, when they visited him in the hospital, had cried out "Daddy!" in his fever instead of "Uncle," as he was supposed to do. Men lied everywhere, no doubt, she said, but in Uganda it was worse, because with AIDS, the truth or lie was life or death. Her lawyer hadn't done *that*, but AIDS meant he couldn't contribute to her family's needs because he too had a clutch of half a dozen orphaned relatives to support. She'd finally met his wife—as would have been natural in the old, informally polygamous days—without much recrimination. But the tensions of survival in the saw-toothed complexity of this money economy, with so many prime-of-life deaths, had collapsed longstanding customs by which a prosperous patriarch's progeny could live on millet, cassava, jackfruit, and bananas, on separate little plots of land, and run back and forth, welcomed in each household. I asked whether having been stung once, by the businessman who had fathered Ivor and then vanished to Tanzania, and now lied to by the lawyer, she was planning—like the other Josephine, with her faithless pharmacist who was ignoring Donald—not to have another child. But she was bolder. Certainly she would, if she found a man who loved her. Children died in Africa—didn't they in the United States?—so you couldn't take the chance of bearing only one.

I hired Nsubuga to drive me the ten or a dozen miles out of Kampala to visit Samuel's secondary school, on a hill near Kyengera Town that was half an hour's walk from Norah's house. It was raw and new, nine years old, although a sign on the gate doughtily proclaimed THE STRUGGLE CONTINUES, and it had been started by the headmaster, Lawrence Muzoonga, and three partners (one already dead of AIDS) as soon as he had obtained his master's degree from Makerere University. The few yellow stucco buildings, with blue metal roofs and a scattering of trees left about the stripped hillside, handled forty-two staffers and 850 students, more than half of them girls, in the four O-level (for ordinary) and two A-level (advanced) grades that follow the seven primary school years. Lawrence, an intense, emphatic, confident young man (though disarmingly round-faced, as many Bagandans are), said that he takes about 75 percent of his applicants for an entering class of 160 and kicks out 10 percent a year for academic or disciplinary difficulties. If a student couldn't pay the $110 fee per three-month term, the school truck was available to go to the parents' shamba and pick up the equivalent in bricks, firewood, yams, maize, or whatever. A student could also work off the tuition by helping to clear the swamp that Lawrence pointed at downhill, where he hoped eventually to get their drinking water. Most were boarders, and classes ran from 8:00 to 5:30, then an hour of sports, then supper and two hours of homework, and up again at 5:30 for early prep.

Samuel's favorite subjects were art, commerce, and biology. He liked history and English less, he said, though eventually he did better in history, English, and geography on the national examinations than in the others, and graduated at nineteen from the O-levels, twenty-seventh in his class of 108. There was nothing "slow" about Samuel—just the normal impoverishing disruption of a Ugandan orphan's life. Nsubuga's wife told me that she was the one who had found each of his parents dead in their beds of Slim, four years apart.

Lawrence's manner was peremptory and somewhat off-putting as we talked in his small office, the way intellectuals in fragile, destitute Third World countries often act when talking to a rich visitor dropping in from the West, with a money belt on and a return ticket to London and New York City in the hotel safe. At thirty-three, with mostly orphans as students, he had wrung this institution out of the elephant grass, through the recent years of Slim and Ebola and Congo wars and bomb blasts—fifty-six killed and two hundred injured in downtown Kampala alone in the four years preceding my visit—plus the cult immolation fires of a church or two, as the gloss went off the peace that President Museveni had finally brought after the holocaust of the Amin and Obote years, in which perhaps half a million Ugandans had died.

In my neophyte role, I asked him whether teachers and intellectuals like him were supporting Museveni's campaign for reelection, but he impatiently said no. They were grateful that the president had introduced the possibility of free discourse to the country and sent the army either back to its barracks or into the Congo instead of brutalizing the citizenry in arbitrary street sweeps and at roadblocks. But to pander to the Western "donor nations," he had also unlocked a rampant capitalism, permitted a drastic drain of the country's resources, and fostered a climate of greed and financial corruption that was destroying the traditional community spirit, of village origin, that was Africa's virtue. So Lawrence, like many younger people I met whose idealism had not been as scalded by the violent years as that of older folks, was eager for the reforms promised by Museveni's former physician, Dr. Kizza Besigye, who was running against him and was said to be married to his former mistress. Besigye was also rumored to be suffering from AIDS, but the whispers didn't seem to hurt him in a country where that was commonplace.

The Speke Hotel, downtown, is an old colonial building that originally served as office space for the British authorities. The lobby mural shows its namesake explorer, John Hanning Speke, rifle in hand, discovering the source of the Nile at Ripon Falls at the outlet of Lake Victoria, with his train of native bearers behind him, half naked, carrying boxes on their heads. Outside the hotel, vans parked at the curb were logoed OXFAM, DOCTORS WITHOUT BORDERS, SAVE THE CHILDREN, EUROPEAN UNION, UNICEF, BUDONGO INTEGRATED CONSERVATION AND REPRODUCTIVE HEALTH PROJECT, PAN-AFRICAN BEAN RESEARCH ALLIANCE, TOTAL QUALITY MANAGEMENT, LIVING EARTH, FAMILY PLANNING. Plus, there were "briefcase NGOs" at its sidewalk café. These were the rumpled guys who flew in with a dozen gross of hearing aids or to operate on cataracts in Mbale, Mpigi, or Mbarara for twenty days, or to build a church or rent a storefront that oyster-eyed street children could flock to for a meal, and who benefited from knowing the Lord's ways: namely, that efficiency isn't actually an end in itself.

I spent several evenings at the café, mostly just eavesdropping. One day, in the opalescent dusk, I traded glances with Florence. She stared covertly and then, with a graceful, unsuggestive gesture, invited me to join her, which I did. She was a former model, now "fifty," and how painful it was "to grow old and lose your looks." I agreed, mentioning that I was sixty-eight, my mantra, and thus not in the market for sex, just stories. Of course I realized that stories would cost money too.

Florence had been married to a German TV journalist, so she knew about that, she told me, and had two "half-caste" daughters, grown now and both interior decorators, one in Denmark, one in London. Her immediate problem was that although she was living in a cousin's apartment to split the expenses, she didn't have enough money to reconnect her phone so that her daughters could call her, and she needed taxi fare to get home, which I gave her, after buying her a pack of Player's cigarettes and another drink.

When only twenty, and a student with a pittance of cash and a passport, Florence had gotten on a bus one terrifying day during the Amin regime—"Four of my brothers they killed!" she cried, drawing her finger across her throat—and passed safely through the exit controls at the Kenyan border, reaching Nairobi with a friend's address in her purse. Once there, she slept on a couch and ate little, until someone brightly thought to take her to see an American who ran a photo-shoot agency. She was a Batooro, severe in appearance, rather short, and as dark as the Congolese tribes near her hometown of Fort Portal, but with a posture of natural aplomb and straight, striking features. She still had that confident élan of a real beauty who could grab my hand imploringly like a woman who had never in her life known a turndown and was only vamping.

The American booked her for ads in the East African newspapers and inserted her into Nairobi's nightclub scene, which in the 1970s was swinging without being carnivorous. She met her German TV man just as the fashion magazines in Europe and the States were going in for safari backgrounds or African models for a startling anchor in any setting, blanching the conventional anorexic or leggy supermodels with their ebony, obsidian, or eggplant colors, more primal than Harlem's. There was a boomlet for women like her from the very center of Africa, and her American agent and German husband (she was good with both languages) soon had her posing in Switzerland against the ski slopes, or on runways in Paris, Milan, London, and New York. In New Orleans she heard live Dixieland and liked Kenny Rogers. The dark continent was so à la mode that hotels put her up for free and couturiers paid her to strut their stuff as a clothes horse in the public rooms. She wanted to show me her scrapbooks and clippings, but I believed her. The way she confided in me, listened to me, asked for favors in that great beauty manner that brooks no opposition was sui generis. The German eventually left her, inevitably; went to West Africa and a younger woman. But her daughters were safe, with European passports.

I asked Florence why, with her savvy, she hadn't landed another secure berth at a better time, while she was still lithe and magnetic. She liked white men and was still grateful to that American in Nairobi.

"Oh, yes, yes—you see, but that was my mistake," she said, smiling sadly. "I loved him. We would go to and fro, and I kept thinking he was going to come back to me." Now, like a Tennessee Williams character, peremptory but shipwrecked, she was mildly drunk and extravagant in gesture but dependent upon the kindness of strangers.

I wanted to move to another table, where a pair of Rwandan refugees were sitting, also reluctant prostitutes, who had survived the genocide and wanted only to get somehow to the peace and opportunity of London or New York and become dress designers. Florence latched onto my hand, however, imploring, in that great-beauty manner again, so I whispered a promise to her that I wasn't "going to go home with them either."

The Rwandans, Serena and her cousin Aisheba, both in their middle twenties, had scalding memories, having lived through the sneak 1994 genocide in which well over half a million people in their tiny country had been hacked to death with machetes in about three months. They had seen so much gore and dismemberment, scenes of begging and murder, impromptu amputations and castrations, bleeding and horror, that Aisheba—who was the tough one and a sort of Mother Courage, if you talked to her long—confessed that she couldn't sleep with any Africans now. The black skin produced hallucinations of wounds and stumps and bodies in piteously severed piles that swamped her. Yet selling themselves was the only livelihood Serena and Aisheba had as marginals and foreigners—beginning in the refugee camps in Burundi (which had its own Hutu-Tutsi conflict), where, being from different villages, they had fled the massacres separately, and where food was at a premium. Then, as evacuees ferried to the sprawling, improvised, emergency tent cities at Goma, in the Congo, their families virtually wiped out and both of them pregnant, they had found each other. What a joy and relief! They'd leapt into each other's arms and been inseparable ever since.

They were Hutus but had steered clear of the Hutu militias, the *Interahamwe*, that were reorganizing in the Goma camps for retaliatory raids back into Rwanda against the Tutsis to continue the civil war. The cousins had volunteered for repatriation by truck once the border was reopened and the opportunity occurred. And they insisted now on the patriotic, nontribal nomenclature of "Rwandans" for themselves as the only way to nullify the acid bath of hatred that had destroyed their country. After being resettled at home, living off bananas and cassava and keeping their heads down while the poisonous, vengeful intrigues of the aftermath bubbled around them, what they did, though, was hope for more. Leaving their children with Serena's mother and Aisheba's grandmother—the skeleton crew of survivors—they had set off as if they were sisters to try their luck in Kigali, Rwanda's capital, and make their way in the wider world. In the Goma camps they had received some medical care and basic language instruction from European aid workers, as well as regular food handouts, unless rain washed out the road. And this was when they seemed to have acquired the idea that white people were less berserk, sadistic, and treacherous (the Tutsis had previously brutalized the Hutus for years, though not on the same scale), and less inclined to turn all churches, schools, and villages into abattoirs.

Kigali didn't work out. It was still Victory City for the Tutsis (who had sheltered in Uganda too during their hard times), so Serena and Aisheba headed for Dar es Salaam, next door to the east on the Indian Ocean in Tanzania. But Tanzania at the time harbored half a million refugees in semi-permanent encampments along its border with Rwanda and Burundi. So these two were threatened and robbed, got no foothold and few customers, couldn't afford a room for long, found no friends, and returned to Rwanda after a month or so. Dar wasn't a furnace like what they'd been through, but it was dangerously swarming with penniless young men and very disheartening.

Serena, softer, prettier, more vulnerably a worrier (and pouring Coca-Cola into her glass of beer to sweeten the taste), loved to chat with her friend in Rwandan in happy fashion while sharing a pizza, oblivious of me until they would "remember our manners." Now in Kampala they were finding business slow. The Ebola epidemic had chased most of the white men away, and AIDS was scaring off in particular the civilized, companionable, generous sort of person who was not bad to spend four or five hours with. By two or three in the morning they might be released to go home with maybe a $100 bill if it had been two kindly friends employing them—expatriate construction supervisors or bush pilots or Red Cross staffers—sufficient to eke out a quiet recuperative week in their single room, cooking for themselves and swimming in a pool at a better hotel that was walking distance from their cinder-block place on a back street. When they could, they'd pay for three hours of daily group English lessons with other Rwandan and Congolese refugees. Their teacher, Aisheba said, an old Ugandan man, was becoming "like a father" to them when they talked to him after class. With no man left alive in their own families, she was frank to say they needed that. The one strong older woman was their staunch aunt, the intrepid pillar who had brought them to Kampala after the fiasco in Dar es Salaam and taught them how to appraise white men of all kinds.

This fortyish aunt, whom I never met, had just hit the jackpot. She had persuaded a Belgian not only to buy her new clothes and pay the rent but to take her to Europe. Maybe he'd marry her when her visa expired! She had given the girls her cell phone when she left and happened to call while they were sitting with me, to check how they were doing. They were about to leave for the more expensive Sheraton, where a band that might draw a crowd was going to play. They were apprehensive, delighted, but came up dry, as they told me later.

Florence introduced herself while we were still talking—she was leaving for home already—with a face that was so haunted by all she knew that Aisheba and Serena suddenly took pause. She simply asked them their names and looked at them—into them—and they shuddered a bit afterward as if envisioning the future, yet wishing too that they could know her from now on as a mentor, like the old Ugandan man, now that their auntie had flown away to Brussels. And sad because they were separated from their own children. When I mentioned that I had just become a grandfather, Aisheba told me she didn't expect to live to see her grandchildren, if she ever had any. Serena agreed. She had an unsettling habit of rolling her tongue in the front of her mouth when she didn't know what to say to me, as if she thought that fellatio was the only currency for barter she had left, after the decapitations that she had witnessed in Rwanda, the faces bashed in with a shovel, throats slit, ghastly mutilations, bound people begging for another hour of life or to be spared their eyesight or, in the agony of torture, simply for death—and then the bedlam of Goma and the brutality of Dar.

President Museveni had kept Uganda passably hospitable to Rwandans, they said, because he was from the border region himself, but if he lost this election, the lid would be off and persecution of foreigners like them would start. Although Rwanda and Uganda had been allies in the Congo war that had overthrown Sese Seko Mobutu, the two countries had lately been verging on battling each other over the diamond- and gold-mining areas they had captured. One such fight had leveled parts of Kisangani, and just now, on one of the days that we talked, Laurent Kabila—installed as ruler of the Congo after Mobutu's defeat—was assassinated in Kinshasa, the capital. Because he had turned against his former patrons in Kampala and Kigali and was fighting them both, if the Congo had had an air force, it would probably have bombed us on Nakasero Hill then and there. And like lava bubbling up, the Angolan civil war was reigniting; the suburbs of Bujumbura, the capital of Burundi, were being shelled by Hutu rebels; Sierra Leone, Liberia, Senegal, and Zimbabwe were in turmoil, and the leaders of Ethiopia and Eritrea—allies not long ago against the Mengistu dictatorship in Addis Ababa—had recently been locked in a war with each other. So when Aisheba and Serena looked to me to confirm that they should go to London or New York I said sure, wishing I could wave a wand and whisk them off to fashion school.

Men fell into conversation with me too, with stories to tell—like the taxi driver Alphonse, who used to give me rides, and whose windshield was smashed right in front of the passenger seat, where one of my predecessors had nearly gone through. He wanted to be my chauffeur. The owner of my hotel, who was a leader in the Ismaili community, had escaped being killed by Idi Amin by a couple of hours in 1972, when all the Asians were expelled. Tipped off that agents of the "State Research Bureau" were coming for him, no doubt to torture him and then slowly pound a nail through his head—which was their preferred method of execution—he told everybody that he was going to a party, but drove instead to an outdoor movie theater and thence by byways to the airport. Like Hastings Banda of Malawi, who kept a crocodile pool, reputedly to punish dissent, Amin liked to play mind games with dissidents. Another publicized method he used was to line up the prisoners and pass a sledgehammer down the file, each man killing the person immediately in front of him, on pain of a much worse death. But I tended to pay closer attention to the women, as is natural when a man is traveling alone. I went to visit Norah again with Nsubuga and relaxed among her banana trees, with a fat pet goat nibbling a peel and Samuel cleaning the chicken coop before his hundred chicks arrived. The neighbors kept chickens too, and four or five cows, and had a black, gaunt saluki for a watchdog, like an ancient remnant from the British Empire. Norah watched hospitably to see that I was comfortable, with two orphans around her skirts.

I was crestfallen several months later to hear by mail from Nsubuga that Norah had died of another stroke. And I was aghast to learn that Samuel, although he won entry into an advanced-placement boarding school, had caught typhoid and almost died. With these new friends, there always remained the tacit barrier that they were nearly destitute and I was not. So when I wanted a bit of conversational comradeship from Nsubuga or one of the Josephines, an urgent subtext of "money, money" intruded. How much would I leave behind with them when I left? Even my favorite person, the Josephine whose parents' house I'd gone to—and whose infant son Donald I had met—remarked, when I asked her whether she in turn might help a traveling American hippie if she saw one in trouble on her road, that she helped only white people who helped her. Otherwise, no, because she knew that they had a ticket for the airplane out or they couldn't have gotten a visa in the first place.

"We see two kinds of people here," she explained. "People who have an airplane ticket and people who don't."

I was reminded of this and other conversations I've had on trips to the Third World—to Yemen, India, Sudan—on September 11, when the World Trade Center towers in Manhattan were hit by two hijacked airplanes. Apart from the dismay and grief I felt, one of my reactions (like many travelers, I suspect) was that we as a nation should have foreseen it. Our amazing ignorance and monumental indifference about the developing world and its travails have corresponded, at least in my mind, to the callous and selfish attitude so many white Americans displayed toward people of color in their own country until the 1960s—which provoked race riots and civil destruction. After the catharsis of military revenge, there will need to be a kind of earthquake in the seabed of our foreign relations. Our solipsism and narcissism must undergo a sea change, toward accepting other races and religions into what has been called "the family of man."

LAST CALL

Grandparents—double-domed or double-chinned, and approval dispensers, greenback machines, emeritus jungle gyms—may be fragile in health but must avoid smelliness as a consequence, or cranky outbursts, pompous pronouncements. "Grand" is not an intensive anymore, licensing erratic behavior, but involves paying attention to and encouraging the enthusiasms children have, enhancing their exposure, their confidence in whatever those turn out to be, and backstopping a dream or two perhaps no one else can. Grandparents, in smiling almost perpetually, personify endurance, stability, humor, and connectivity, even assuming they have memory lapses, if they don't reminisce too long and manage to hold off on the geezer farts until they've waved goodbye to the car or train as it leaves and they can wobble away from the platform in privacy. Not quantity but quality matters in the memories they impart, and no spiraling souring, such as a parents' divorce can implant, is likely to occur.

Oh, and yet the drop-dead naps, total bowel evacuations, the bronchial tubes laboriously hacked clear of phlegm, and restless-leg syndrome at night, while one's thoughts crinkle like wrapping paper: in bed ten hours at a stretch, I'll find dreams constitute as much of life as what I do. On survival autopilot, they're an aid to staying above the ground—better than eating fatback and getting tiddly, as some do. I don't exercise as an end in itself or shave every day or wear a watch. Though more generous-spirited, I have less call to prove it because my phone rarely rings. I wish I could vault stairs two at a time or walk home a hundred blocks from Yankee Stadium, as I used to.

Not as much the current popular rages as those of our own generation we missed latching onto absorb our curiosity—Coltrane, Monk, or comparable figures—and keeping the backyard bird feeders full becomes important, counting species, tracking the temperature range the seeds should arm them against, as though our septuagenarian survival instincts were projected onto these nuthatches and wrens—darting sunbursts of life. So sleepy one gets!—yet talks to the dog's toothy grin about Little Red Riding Hood, and the Three Little Pigs. (His blood pressure shoots up, scientists say, whereas ours sinks salubriously down.) I dream about traveling Mongolia with a female companion, collecting reptiles, and metropolitan narratives as well, in foreign climes like Lisbon and Naples. I wish I could jazz up my molecules again like a microwave does coffee's; my trembly handwriting worries me a bit, though friends have died left and right from symptoms vastly worse than that. Beer stains on the table, smoke rings in the air, an irregular temperament: often that is how the world's work has gotten done, by shrimps and wimps, not only gaudy, bawdy musclemen. Carrots were good for the eyes, an apple a day kept the doctor away, take it easy when you're overtired, and a dog's nose should be cold. What else did you need to know about health?

Half a century after my father boycotted the Metropolitan Opera for allowing Marian Anderson to sing on its stage, thirty-five years after two bird hunters in Louisiana told me gleefully that they had "just treed a coon," and didn't mean the animal—adding that I should get my Vermont license plates out of town before dark fell—Barack Obama was elected president. I'd been at Martin Luther King's 1963 March on Washington, where nobody would have believed it was going to happen so soon, any more than those Louisiana hunters or my Kansas City father. The country had backed into the decision because of an economic meltdown and a dunderheaded opposition, but then liked what it had done, as did the world beyond. So progress leaps ahead, not simply in wiping out newspapers and bookstores. We wanted a different bottom line. As president, George Bush became a trip wire—that love of war, the tic of acquisition and aggression, de facto colonialism, and the notion that we could house limitless numbers of people on the planet's skin. Material entitlement has been supplanted as a preoccupation by the novelty of speeding gigabytes of information around, although thus far—twitter, chat, and surf—people don't appear to be actually imbibing more, but rather sound bites of gigabytes.

A general worldliness, however, has been purveyed; and playing chess with Indonesian kids across the ocean, while glancing at satellite photographs of their village or street, is terrific, if that's what the Internet was for, not our vices, or targeting missiles out of drones. Will there be mysteries left, once the earth has been wholly Googled? But grumpy old geezers have been complaining about the world going to hell in a handbasket (if only to soothe their regret at leaving it) since time-keeping began. New reading material wasn't "worth the candle." Radios were broadcasting vulgarity into homes that used to aspire to a piano in the parlor. Cars and telephones complicated the normal effort to supervise the younger element in the family. Yes, people lived longer but consequently acquired debilitating illnesses, and meanwhile the caliber of the nation's governance, the integrity of business practice, the craftsmanship of manual workers, declined, and a new sexual license demeaned religion and the parameters of entertainment.

Postcards, steamships, land-line conversations, railroad journeys, handshake agreements—I do, in turn, miss them all. And even those who don't would not glibly dismiss antiquarians who quote Madame de Pompadour's *Après nous le déluge*, if they are speaking more literally than she imagined. American elders had voiced unease at foreign embroilments and exotic diseases before AIDS and Sunni-Shia animosities began to revive a xenophobia perpetually incipient in any country of immigrants. The somersault that elected Obama shouldn't erase our recollection of other somersaults—Jim Crow recapitulating much of slavery for a hundred years after slavery's nominal eradication, or George W. Bush convincingly paraphrasing some of Lyndon Johnson's Vietnam lies less than four decades after Johnson was driven from office because of them. As a boy in Connecticut in the 1930s I saw World War I vets who had been gassed on the battlefield in France still wheezing in order to breathe; yet despite our righteous contempt as a nation for how low the "Huns" had stooped in their use of weaponry, we nuked Japanese metropolises in 1945, enormously upping the ante on how cruel war could become. Again, our scorn was boundless, in the aftermath of World War II, for how the "Japs" and Nazis had treated captives, only to vanish at directives from the highest level in Washington to grease the wheels of torture upon all manner of souls at Abu Ghraib, Bagram, Guantánamo, and other hidden holes.

The impulse to destroy that we've seen innate in generations of boys shooting turtles off logs has vastly broadened toward such jumbo portions of Creation as to raise the specter of biology leveled to primarily a forensic science. It's not farfetched. Bees, bats, amphibians, forest primates, meadow birds, pelagic fish, coral, and polar animals, at risk or worse—the upending of ecology, disequilibrium of meteorology and oceanography, desertification, extinctions at four thousand times paleontological rates, are not the sort of scale of change old grumps have previously objected to. Nature is being defenestrated in a fast-track snuffing out of half of Creation.

Amazingly late in the game, popes, presidents, and pundits began to tell us we were "stewards" of the earth. Earlier, mostly marginal or maverick figures had cared to touch on the topic, apart from a handful of well-heeled conservation charities that oversaw the status quo in our national parks, or of poster-suitable megafauna here and there. A campfire ethic of "appreciating" nature by canoeing, hiking, duck-hunting, fly-fishing, reading Wordsworth or Thoreau in college, finding balm in a walk in the woods and rural values, had seemed sufficient. Rural values were not identical to the conservation movement's (whose funding was big-city based), but I grew up collecting eggs from a henhouse, weeding a victory garden, and angling for bullheads while tenting occasionally, so I've found the speed of alteration, the totality of havoc and sprawl accompanying the pole-axing of nature, undreamt of.

Not just dogs are astonished by our readiness to piss where others drink, which, piled on the nutty new notion of fueling our cars with food, epitomizes, perhaps, our dilemma. Fish become a factory for omega oil, fowl for "buffalo wings"; the prairie's undulance produces Big Macs, a mountain's wrinkled slopes that looked a little different every morning and scented the valley below with primeval perfumes are converted to footing for McMansion patios. The pollens bulldozed by Monsanto or Weyerhaeuser, lakes soured by composted feces, bristly thickets bush-hogged, cumulatively erase the complexities that laced the horizon, as earthmovers dig the undulances flat.

The sun's spectrum still tints the sky twice a day on schedule, and the wilds entail botanical surprises underfoot. Wild means tactile, not keypad, experience, and millionaires not strolling safely past destitute persons on the sidewalk, yet not only our "better nature," either. Instead, a medley of the impromptu—napping against a boulder at the beach, then getting so intemperate about politics at a party you may not be invited back, and talking to yourself in public or private when doing so feels useful, or letting hawkweed, vetch, and Joe-Pye stalks take over half your lawn. (Joe Pye, after all, was a medicine man who helped some nineteenth-century settlers during a typhus epidemic.)

Wildness accepts the night's dreams as purposeful and rooted in common sense, though not a gold standard by which to separate repellent ideas from plausible ones. Being wild is to hurry or lag behind the bounds of politesse; but later in life these tend to fray anyway, as people bluntly voice their regrets or violate the taboo against self-pity if their health is buckling underneath them. They sleep or wake outside the conventional hours and, if it comes to that, descend into a proverbial second childhood, although the oldster's irreverence, unlike a toddler's, has been germinating for a lifetime—through promissory notes, linkups, jobs, parenthood—and is not unconsidered. His extemporizing may be irritating: whereupon, after his death, the heirs can puzzle over his safe-deposit box, whose very handle in the face of the bank's vault resembles the deceased's last, uncompromising smile. Besides mortgage papers, divorce decrees, birth and bond certificates, expired contracts and term life insurance, the contents might include an unexpected dry-oil-well deed, silver dollars from the Harding era, love missives signed with an acrostic nickname, a written resignation never spoken of or delivered to the man's employer, and a diamond ring swaddled in a square of toilet tissue. Quick phone calls prove the oil well dry, and a jeweler in the county seat says the Tiffany setting of the ring could indicate it belonged to a mother's mum. On the other hand, sentimental letters, unsigned and in a more cultivated handwriting and tone, tied with a ribbon, radiate an affinity with the ring. Did he preserve them at the bank to conceal them from his spouse?

Old guys when they retire frequently conceal money about the house, like a trump card up the sleeve, and grow white bushy beards—that late stamp of individuality for a lifelong salaryman—which you may wish you could peer behind. What did he smile at in his salad days, and how does his mouth curl now? Those tax troubles he jokes about, did they relate to an accounting overreach or a custody fight? On a bench on Main Street I sit next to a crumpled senior citizen who's on probation after a shoplifting conviction yet owns the block. Another prosperous fellow is rumored to lead a secret existence as a pedophilic sex tourist on trips abroad. Luckily I've never been saddled with forbidden temptations, but those of us who stay out of trouble—how much credit do we deserve? Beyond not harboring lawless compulsions like wanting to steal, I was fortunate in my timing. A friend of mine who enlisted in the Marines during the Korean War, while I was draft-deferred as a college student (dyslexia had plagued him in school), killed his first enemy with a trench knife, a boy whose bloody pockets contained family photographs and revealed his age to be sixteen. Later on, promoted to sergeant but more haplessly, he led his squad into a night ambush where most were immediately wiped out. Jack himself, rolling into a ball, hid weaponless and helmetless under a bush during the fading frenzy of the firefight. Huddled paralyzed, he listened to the screams of injured comrades searched out and beheaded in the dark. After a while, his hands grasped a stray helmet on the ground and he clutched it to his chest for the remainder of the night, assuming it must be his. Eventually, the North Koreans left, dragging their casualties with them, and in the dawning sunrise he noticed his arms were drenched with blood. The helmet he was hugging enclosed the chin-strapped head of his best buddy.

Haunted by his memories—whereas mine from two years after college in the peacetime Army are pretty benign—Jack needed to be retrieved by the state police when he wandered on foot down the median of the interstate one time. I know veterans who survived the carnage at Anzio or Iwo Jima, as well as a former Mountain Division soldier who, scouting Mussolini's last hideout at Salò, peered down from the ridge at the dictator himself. Yet none of them are pestered by dreams or visions like my friend—who was lost behind the wrong lines for five days on another occasion, and, another time, ignorantly shot several prisoners of war who had been prematurely released before the armistice was announced. And because our South Korean allies ran things differently, he also witnessed, from a distance, the execution on their base parade grounds of prostitutes (forced to kneel, a pistol at the ear) for the crime of contracting a venereal disease. His bumpiest recollection, however, leading him once to prepare for a bout of Russian roulette, was when he'd shot a fellow Marine who "turned sugar" during a Chinese charge. The man broke and fled from the famous bugle calls and human tidal wave, and had the contagion spread through the American positions they all might have been slaughtered. "Missing in action," the parents of such a service member were told; and into old age Jack flew the Leatherneck flag in his front yard, but also dressed up as Santa Claus for Christmas festivities: whether for ballast or ironically, I never knew.

Yet that Anzio vet most relives not the hellish combat on the beachhead there, or afterward alongside Audie Murphy at the Colmar Pocket in Alsace, but his wife dying in his arms forty years later, he says. Though not bequeathed a combat veteran's baggage of anxiety, I'm often startled by the fragility of my own emotions, my snappish short fuse or dips into despair. What's it from? I'm not nervous about death, just imbalance. One cannot control the chemistry of balance, but our expressions of condolence are ingrained in our faces as deeply as the grins of congratulation we assume companionably when hearing good news. To commune with somebody worn by grief becomes quite second nature as life goes on, and we'll recall with chagrin brusquenesses we were guilty of, which spur us to be less self-centered next time around. While adding years we do tend to learn that focus is the point, and our faces grow engraved with such versatile lines as to serve almost any eventuality, even as our powers wane. Trading comeliness for malleability, our faces betray less about the gambits we declined than what we aspired to. Jokes we thought of but never coughed up in the scrimmage of conversation; trips we dreamt of but never consummated; love affairs too timidly desired; job interviews chickened out of. A sense of humor smothered by self-deprecation may finally mark our faces with a sophisticated facade in our exit years.

"Know who your friends are" is an adage some of us seem to take forever to learn, if only because it's so much safer to mistreat friends. And cash flow becomes less of a mystery too when you're old. No sucking up to a supervisor or sniffing for a windfall, as the mathematics of paying three hundred dollars a month for glaucoma drops replaces the politics of not getting fired. When the phone stops ringing with professional obligations, one spends more time sampling this endpoint of millennia of human entertainment, hundreds of channels, and not a pretty picture in toto. Having rambled a bit, I also worry about Third World companions I've had, such as the Tibetan patriot who guided me through Sichuan Province—how did he fare in the earthquakes and police crackdown that followed? And the Ugandan middle schooler whose fees I've been partly paying—how is her family coping with the economic crises spiked by Kenya's imbroglios next door? Or a Nairobi family whose wattle-fenced yard on the outskirts of a slum was already densely planted with corn years ago against their expectation of hungry times—how are they?

Crowded like creatures in a deluxe feedlot with a menu of small-screen diversions, how will we do? Can our religions, all of which were hatched in the ample out-of-doors, retain the necessary magnetism to keep us civilized? (Alternatively, will atheists remain literate, which is what keeps them civilized?) Loving the earth as it has been, I've believed that heaven is here and the only heaven we have. Perhaps the apprehensiveness old fogies like me feel is not just garden-variety regret at losing former niceties. Yet inconsolable old folks don't last long. A seesaw of fret and equanimity serves them better. Old age is like being posted to a foreign country, where you drop and lose things, misplace names and insights, can't read signage others are guided by, slide into boredom because you're either on the skids or overexperienced but don't know which, and find a nap ignites itself after walking up a hill. Your body can become a lengthy charley horse if minor muscles weirdly assert themselves. Nor do you want to walk as slowly as you do, but your eyesight may be failing while your legs remain fairly spry. Spry and wry or high and dry can sum it up, when you sip alcohol at unexpected junctures of the day, or after a lubricious dream try jacking off. Live with a smile even if you can't spot birds other people are talking about—you've seen them countless times in the past—or are remembering generosities you didn't appreciate sufficiently when your benefactor was alive. In my case, that would include an English teacher who inspired me when I was sixteen, and a journalist, *Time*'s bureau chief in Africa, when I was forty-three. I thank them belatedly: very different men who would grimace similarly, I think, at the pass we're in, whether with regard to the state of reading now or Africa's condition.

Since my literary ambitions didn't conflict with other people's aspirations, I seem to have avoided, from the perspective of this biblical age of closure—the seventies—major regrets. Nobody would have been better off had I not been alive. And, conversely, the years were easier to navigate than I anticipated, negotiating college, publishing novels, marrying, living in Europe, generating a second career as a professor, fatherhood, writing for numerous magazines. I voted, served on juries, paid my taxes, saw my daughter become better educated than me and my mother comfortably cared for in her home until her death. Though my views were radical, I was a rhapsodist by temperament. My take on life paralleled that of circus people, as I'd known them during my formative teens—that it was perilous, under a smiling surface, risk being the entry price, and you performed your act, trusting everybody a little but no one a lot, on the assumption that ecstasy underlies both peril and perfection, then, living by your lights, moved on. Yet how does one grow the liver and lights, the lungs and ventricles for all that reading and travel, teaching and writing, plus the thousand momentary detours and miscues—life's agglomeration of shimmer and gravel? From toddlerhood to shambling along in the caveman slouch geezers revert to, we just do, defusing myriad minor misunderstandings, hustling past moonlit dells we promised ourselves to return to but have neglected to, postponing cherishing a needy niece or exploring destinations we wanted to see.

It's astonishing, the number of favorite people we lose contact with for no cogent reason. As we sleep more, our dreams may remain in the pragmatic realm—dialectical, energetic, emotionally hooked up—whereas the alarm clock heralds leg cramps and waking becomes a bit surreal. Giving up "multi-tasking" (how time flew at forty!), we employ three appendages to walk, if there's a handrail, and although we size up new acquaintances more shrewdly than before, we have less need to. Religion offers some grounding; I've attended Quaker and Congregational services on the same Sunday when I've wanted both silence and an organ concert too. Yet the sore point for those of us who believe heaven is not nebulous but right here on earth is of course that so much has been leached, bleached, desiccated, broiled, or thawed before our eyes, as if all the world's Christian, Muslim, Jewish temples were being razed as well. What's scary is humanfolk's penchant for a flattening venality, "killing two birds with one stone," as the saying goes, until there may not be any more. We who are on our last legs now can be forgiven for wondering how the continent scrolling behind us that we love is going to fare in the next umpteen years or so.

Okay, we've come to understand that damaging a nursery salt marsh to build seaside condos may hurt the local fishery, but how will knocking down rain forests to grow hamburger impact our breathing? When you tweak a spider's web, she rushes out and lets you know about it, but glacial rubble may calve precipitously because of smokestack triangulations continents apart, and the tropical fish in a pet shop may have been captured by asphyxiating half a reef's marine life on the opposite curve of the globe. Porpoises in the Gulf Stream, parrots in the Yucatán, mountains uncheapened by "conquest," two-lane highways where the landscape, not the medium, was the message, and one's sense of time, or attention span, could still twin with other mammals', not merely electronics—this is where my heartstrings were tied. And if life is holy, then ransacking it wholesale, worldwide, snaps more than just those private lines.

Bless the bivalves and beluga whales, ants and antelope, swifts and terns, the neck of the anteater and giraffe. Beaks and cloacas I lack but love because tortoises, storks, and snow geese have them. The names we have devised—corn snakes, marsh hawks, manatees, aphids, flamingos, warthogs—ring in succession like an anthem or a psalm. If heaven is on earth, we've shared it with elephants and ocelots and when we die will fertilize the duckweed and cattails with our chemicals. I've been content with that paradigm in my mind's eye, or even the notion of becoming partially limestone, so long as I remain affixed forever, as minerals or protoplasm, to Earth. Quarry or reseed me, as the dice roll, but if life is, as Emerson suggested, a seethe of ecstasy, then time in its continuum has been the seat of joy and my citizenship lies more in the humus than the strata underfoot. My allegiance is to what's alive, or was. Sea wrack, and the crab that eats a hangnail I've spit into it; the porcupine on an apple limb folding leaves into its mouth at dawn, while a nightcrawler, as pink as my fingertip, disappears into the soil under the tree before an early bird wakes up and grabs it. Giraffes licked salt off my cheeks when I worked in the circus at eighteen and discovered that sweat often coexists with pleasure but that everything should be seen as temporary, with regard to place and glee and colleagues, except I was going to love elephants at a throbbing level as long as I lived. We do our turn, hang upside down or somersault or walk a wire, then bow out of the limelight. That's the script. Yet dusk's waning illumination can be as eloquent as any other. Reds like an eft, or a rooster's comb, chicken livers or lobster shell. The sun, streaming beet, yam, carrot, or citrus colors across the sky, still has some say before the stars materialize, which we'll soon join infinitesimally as random matter once again.

Besides elephants, what will I miss? Red leaves and orangutans, barn and tree swallows, sunflowers and tiger-yellow swallow-tailed butterflies, pronghorns up a draw, and the chlorophyll that prodigally prestidigitates the greens a brown cow eats in order to make milk as white as egret feathers. Vermilion and verdigris streak the sky as the buttery coloring fades, wild turkeys roost, and the singing of the insect cadres shifts. Darkness settles slowly in a temperate zone, cutting us a bit of slack, whatever work we're at, except perhaps predators for whom it is a wake-up call—riflemen stalk deer, Lotharios women. But laborers, ungulates, and the average diurnal soul want to unwind awhile, dusk being open-ended in the sense that although you can't hike far because you can't see what's next, you may feel freer for that very reason about tomorrow. Tripping as you grope past homely furniture in the gathering dark—an old person's bump—out the window, is that wraithlike movement a raccoon sneaking toward the garbage cans or a burglar scouting? The "ruffian on the stair" is a familiar metaphor for death: yet it needn't be so rough.

Ecstasy on an Emersonian scale is not a matter of heavenly choirs, or merely orgasmic and therefore abruptly terminated. It's the moil of Brownian and microscopic motion, impulse married to activity, joy as photosynthesis or blood-pump, a tumid twitchiness, with serotonin as well as necessity the mother of invention. Glance into a schoolyard when it's bubbling, or a drop of pond water under magnification, at poplars simmering in the sunlight, their leaves a-swirl. Summer marinates us, as big bees bumble and yellowthroats witchetty-witch from the bushes and chickens peck after midges before a dragonfly gets to them. Then autumn flares; the snowscapes glister; and again next spring the snipe and woodcock whicker in courtship flight. A small striped woodpecker converts my sheet-metal barn roof into a gigantic bullhorn to rap out his territorial announcements. Ecstasy might be the rolling thunder you hear in a conch shell; or mice feet scampering in a crawl space; watching a tadpole grow feet to creep, then shoehorn damselflies down its throat with the aid of its eyes; or a caterpillar metamorphose wings. How does it feel?

The skinning of the earth, the shriveling of diversity, diminishes the reach of ecstasy as a metaphor for life, and therefore my regret at leaving it. In India and Africa, the last elephant herds I saw seemed fractured and terrified, futilely fleeing civil war, human hunger, or poachers yet again, and although not a war correspondent, I have already witnessed famine of a gravity only preliminary to what I expect lies in store. Animators, fabricators, programmers, and film librarians should have a field day as people in better circumstances retreat to simulated story lines, or memory lane.

I don't mean to sound awash in nostalgia. No birdcall is the musical equal of a clarinet blown with panache. Human beings have improved upon ordinary sound waves with Mozart and Dixieland, and in a country of the blind our era might seem an apogee, when our ears enjoy more occasions to rejoice than ever before. The trouble is, of course, it's not. To hear electronically is not the same as seeing the world via footage projected onto screens. Without the vibrancy of original vision, the freedom of all 360 unfiltered, unedited, sensual, individualized degrees, and the tang of a rapport with all manner of other forms of life—birds that wheel, grass that waves, the entire geyser of Creation—is drained. Indoors, with rock or Bach, track or gooseneck lighting, mood pills, temperature controls, exercise bikes, we can transform life into a journey of modifications, with movie personalities, dead or alive, emoting on an insect screen. When we were outrun by animals, we harnessed horses, dogs, and gasoline; envying the birds, we domesticated aerodynamics in order to invent airplanes. But the out-of-doors, which even monotheism used to acknowledge as God's original domain, is becoming so pallid a remnant of what my generation often knew, driving old Route 66 across America or its counterparts worldwide, I'm content to miss seeing its further deterioration.

That we could blacken so much land and sky in besting nature yet pay no price in consequences turned out to be an enormous wager. But the recent hullabaloo about unlooked-for "domino" penalties from heat rise and so forth is all science-scribbling—tidal and aquifer erosion, hurricane and wildfire ignition. No spiritual cost seems predicted for the impending transition from green and oxygenated planetary space—that billion-years-old sphere inhabited by all manner of other life—to cyberspace: a breathtaking change. The salmon, seals, eagles, and water birds swarming in tumultuous plenty at the mouths of rivers like Alaska's I miss already, and notice people hugging their dogs as never before, people with a finch-feeder hung on a pole in a ten- by ten-yard yard. Never mind, for a moment, whether the seas rise—will we capsize? I don't mean fail to produce sufficient fertilizer to grow protein for a humanity cheek by jowl, but our whole catamaran—animal yet ethical—as humanity.

Many people paddle just to keep afloat, but I won't miss the ubiquity of greed and grandiosity otherwise. We can cite notable political reversals, such as in Germany and Japan after World War II, or Lincoln succeeding Buchanan, or Obama elected by a nation still vividly, cruelly Jim Crow within my lifetime—yet never an environmental one, where what had become "real estate" reverts by common consent to tall-grass prairie or freelance forest. A civil war may depopulate an area to "desolation" temporarily, but has hospitable habitat ever been voluntarily emptied to accommodate other creatures? The advocacy for wildlife not confined to a zoo, botanical garden, or gazetted park is minuscule, but the gamble is monumental. To have doubled our life spans, sextupled our population, while simultaneously acquiring seven-league boots in the form of Boeing mileage, so that we bestride swaths of the world like rooms in a house—Tibet, Rome, Yemen, Uganda, in my case—is flabbergasting, a confluence of developments like a petri dish gone mad. And our frailties, from libido to greed to our constant need for both reassurance and the assistance of machinery, argue against a successful management plan.

Having relished my run, I'd be content to be granulated in sandstone next, if it comes to that, so long as my constituents remain earthbound. But self-abnegation, being usually considered a religious and therefore unpracticed virtue, does not appear likely to materialize as one sea change that might avert another. Instead: stonewalling, jawboning I'd just as soon not have to witness, plus scattershot capsule captive-insemination restoration projects for satellite-monitored species like chimps and pandas inside fenced sanctuaries where idealistic young people hug the babies for a camera. My grumpiness is not retroactive, however. I remember gratefully observing programs to save an olive ridley turtle nesting beach in India and a sandhill crane colony's breeding ground in Mississippi, for example. Public sentiment will shift toward climate and commodity conservation, and rearguard activism to preserve creatures for whom empathy is generated.

But I was a two-lane-highway man who drove with the windows down and liked surface travel, especially walking, then was content with the missionary position at night, and overall with the notion of birth and death as a round trip. The 1931 Model A Ford in which I drove to California on Route 66 in 1953 has become the 1996 Ford Escort in which I do errands in 2010. My attention span probably hasn't shortened a lot because I still tap a typewriter, thumb through reference books, kid around with bank tellers in person, and watch for nuances as in time-lapse photography, which is mostly nature's speed.

Nature is nuance, like firefly sparks and foxfire light, not bullet-train scenery. Half a dozen cedar waxwings perched side by side on a branch will pass a wild cherry back and forth along the row before one of them finally, decorously eats it. Then, surrounded by September's abundant crop, they, or an additional few, perform the playful, delicate ritual again while nattering with their lispy *tsees* and up-and-down crests, until another bolts the bit of fruit and the flock flicks off in all directions to feast in normal fashion, among the rose-breasted grosbeaks, crimson cardinals, purple finches, perhaps a raccoon family, plus red squirrels, maybe a black bear trio, and several white-flagged deer. In May, with apple-blossom petals in their beaks, the birds indulge in the same apparently celebrative communal routine again, consuming the white flowers, as a phoebe, after hawking for the early deerflies, twitches its tail quite personably, sitting in a sapling nearby. And a ruby-throated hummingbird mooches extra sugar at the tree-trunk holes a yellow-bellied sapsucker has drilled, where sweet cambium juice is oozing out. A flicker in the meantime is sampling the populace of an anthill underneath the tree, and a toad hops downhill toward the muskrats' pond to sing his trill in order to draw in a mate.

But apart from a few hobbyists, who is going to notice all this stuff? And yet if people don't, it will just vanish faster. Leaving aside the parrots and parrotfish destined for oblivion in other climes, these infinite details I have watched are central to the world I love. My smile when lying on any terminal slab may look less gratified than it should, according to the good breaks I've had, because my consternation does not relate to them, or even looking back. Instead, it's the dismay of gazing ahead.

CIRCUS MUSIC

A circus is both acrobatic and elephantine, wholesome but freakish, and that is partly why we like it so—because we are two-headed, too. A showgirl in the center ring displays her pretty legs to daddy while his children are engrossed in watching a palomino stallion dance to the band's tempo. But that, of course, is an illusion. The bandmaster, flourishing his silver cornet, is actually following the horse's mannered, jerky prance, not vice versa, which in turn is being cued by the same short-skirted lady's cracking whip. And in the old days the sideshow used to be called "The Ten-in-One" because it had "Ten Different Freaks Under One Tent for Only One Dollar! Can you beat that, folks?" as the barkers yelled. Only, I suppose, by looking inside oneself. People too fat or too small, too thin or too tall, remind us of a certain unwieldy, weird, but shrinking-violet personage whom we know all too well—as does the Knife-Thrower, the Escape Artist or Contortionist, the Tattooed or Albino Lady, hefting a boa constrictor, perhaps, and the knuckle-walking Wild Man, bearded all over, or the Living Skeleton, and the kinky but outwardly clean-cut gentleman who is wed to the swords and fireballs he swallows a dozen times a day for our entertainment. Why is it entertainment, if we're not gawking at a caricature of ourselves?

In the big top everybody wears a spiffy uniform, but if yours isn't a one-night stand and they stay until tomorrow, you'll see some of the circus people sleeping in the horse straw on the ground. And when the costumes come off, baby, don't imagine they'll remember you, no matter how hard you may think you clapped. Behind the greasepaint is quite a different sort of face and person. You wouldn't necessarily trust one of the clowns or animal handlers who give such intense pleasure to tens of thousands of children with the downright raising of even a couple; they may already have abandoned their families. Like actors only more so, circus performers are expected to be manic and depressive, and we accept the paradox that a real genius at making little kids laugh, like Danny Kaye or Charlie Chaplin, could verge on frightening them as a father. The funniness is vertiginous, and the hippodrome food too sweet. Too much is going on in the rings to absorb it all, and the physical stunts sometimes edge toward suicidal. Maybe the grisly part of the bargain is that we, the "lot lice," the Elmers, rubes, towners, hayseeds, hicks, yokels, are paying green money to watch the star troupers risk their lives. If a trapeze artist falls and hits the ground, he'll lie in front of a grandstand of utter strangers, whimpering, jactitating, and dying alone.

A circus is high and low, piccolos and trombones. The edgy tiger roars and charges, but then licks her trainer at the end, as if they had been friends all along. A clown meanly tricks his chum, dunks him treacherously in a barrel of water, and gloats for the crowd, but then the high-wire walker steals all his thunder as soon as the whistle blows. The ringmaster, though he seems the boss, is curiously not the star; the saddest puss gets the biggest laugh; and the innocence is raunchy (those leggy girls who strut their stuff alongside a whiteface Bozo so that dad has his own reasons to snicker). The clowns teach most memorably that if you trust anybody he will betray you.

We want circus people to be different from us—homeless and garish, heedless and tawdry (otherwise why pay to watch?)—yet to connect with us in deeper currents that we share. Our fear of heights and ridicule, our complicated fascination with animals (whips, but kindness), our love of grace and agility, of stylish vanity and splendid boasting, of dressing in spangles yet living in trailers and tents. As an element of rooting our children in a stable home, we nourish them with this annual spectacle of the elaborately raffish and picaresque. Therefore, we want the show people to be outlandish but never outrageous, to hide from us their perverse, larcenous, or alcoholic tendencies that may accompany the tramping life. A guy who just got out of the county jail (we hope not the Big House) for doing whatever (and we don't want to know the whatever) and then hit the road because his wife didn't want him back is coiling and flinging the ropes around that keep the aerialists' rigging up; and somehow it has become the kind of responsibility he can handle. And without quite articulating it, we want our offspring to be flexible and adventurous as well as predictable, tolerant as well as ethical, capable of flights of delight as well as down-to-earth. Also, we want circus people to know us better than we know them, in a sense: to be wise beyond what their education and social status should officially warrant in gauging human nature, and cater to and inspire our children, even though we have come to watch some of them risk breaking their necks—which is base of us—and even if they can't always manage their own private behavior. People are juggling themselves, hand-to-mouth in brassy penury in the circus, not just tossing torches or chancing an awful clawing. Then they'll live in backstreet rented rooms during the winter until they can take to the road again.

It's no coincidence that circus music is often identical to the sort of marches soldiers used to go off to die to. The stakes are high. Bravery, resourcefulness, pinpoint concentration, and self-containment are what make it work, and one reason why so many losers and handicapped souls have found their footing in the circus may be because they see in the crowds how thin a veneer conventional society paints upon our basic greed, inertia, and callousness. So why worry that you're an oddball and have to move somewhere new every other day to keep your haywire impulses under control and sublimate them into stunts? Like rich people, you have that privilege. New audience, new town, never seen you before, never'll see you again. It's anesthetic. If you screw up one of the acts today, you'll get it right tomorrow—so, no sweat, you get it right today.

"We have the fattest woman in the world, and the tallest man, and a girl who has no arms or legs, and midgets who are married! Have you ever seen a camel spit, or seals play catch, or elephants stand on their heads? A man with reptile's scales, who was once just like you! And the Good Lord made him. Can you finish your ice cream after you have looked at him?"

Good question. In the pre-television era, when much of the novel technology related to transportation, not electronics, live entertainment toured between cities by train or motor vehicle. Repertory-stage and opera companies, evangelist preachers, Chautauqua lecturers, freelance physic salesmen, vaudeville magicians, humorists, and strippers, who formerly had gone by riverboat or wagon, would troop through town—as well as the more celebrated Sells-Floto, or Sparks, or Hagenbeck-Wallace, or Sam B. Dill's, or Walter L. Main, or Robbins Bros., or Christy Bros. circuses, not to mention Ringling Bros. and Barnum & Bailey, The Greatest Show on Earth. There was Downie Bros. Wild Animal Circus, The Largest Motor Circus in the World (families and brothers stuck together in business in those days), and the famous Clyde Beatty–Cole Bros. big show, and Col. Tim McCoy & His Indian Village, or his Congress of Rough Riders of the World, and Marcellus' Golden Models (with the men's pectorals as big as the women's breasts), and Tommy Atkins' Military Riding Maids.

Fortunately, we aren't entirely bereft of a visual record of these arcane marvels. A Manhattan banquet photographer named Edward Kelty, whose usual venue was hotel ballrooms and Christmas parties, went out intermittently in the summer from the early 1920s to the mid-1940s, taking panoramic tripod pictures of circus personnel, in what could only have constituted a labor of love. He was expert, anyway, from his bread-and-butter job, at joshing smiles and camaraderie out of disparate collections of people, coaxing them to drape their arms around each other and trust the box's eye. He had begun close to home, at Coney Island freak shows, when the subway was extended out there, and Times Square flea-circus "museums" and variety halls, and the Harlem Amusement Palace. Later, building upon contacts and friendships from those places, he outfitted a truck for darkroom purposes (presumably to sleep in too) and sallied farther to photograph the tented circuses that played on vacant lots in New Jersey, Connecticut, or on Long Island, and gradually beyond. He would pose an ensemble of horse wranglers, canvasmen, ticket takers, candy butchers, teeterboard tumblers, "web-sitters" (the guys who hold the ropes for the ballet girls who climb up them and twirl), and limelight daredevils, or the bosses and moneymen. He took everybody, roustabouts as conscientiously as impresarios, and although he was not artistically very ambitious—and did hawk his prints both to the public and to the troupers, at "six for $5"—in his consuming hobby he surely aspired to document this vivid, disreputable demimonde obsessively, thoroughly: which is his gift to us.

More of these guys may have been camera-shy than publicity hounds, but Kelty's rubber-chicken award ceremonies and industrial photo shoots must have taught him how to relax jumpy people for the few minutes required. With his Broadway pinstripes and a newsman's bent fedora, as proprietor of Century Flashlight Photographers in the West Forties, he must have become a trusted presence in the "Backyard" and "Clown Alley." He knew show-business and street touts, bookies and scalpers—but also how to flirt with a marquee star. Because his personal life seems to have been a bit of a train wreck, I think of him more as a hatcheck girl's swain, yet he knew how to let the sangfroid sing from some of these faces, or simple good rolling-stone mischief, while doing justice to the ragged stringbeans, ranked in another line. These zany tribes of showboaters must have amused him, after the wintertime's chore of recording for posterity some forty-year drudge receiving a gold watch. Other faces look muddied with inchoate emotions, however, as if the man indeed had just gotten out of the penitentiary, or were mentally retarded, or could already feel the dreadful undertow of an illness like epilepsy, schizophrenia, pedophilia, kleptomania, tuberculosis, or diabetic collapse that had choked off so many fresh starts he had attempted before. You wouldn't see him in a hotel ballroom, even as a waiter. The ushers, the prop men and riggers, the cookhouse crew, the elephant men and cat men, the showgirls arrayed in white bathing suits in a tightly chaperoned, winsome line, the hoboes who had put the tent up and, in the wee hours, would tear it down, and the bosses whose body language, with arms akimbo and swaggering legs, tells us something of who they were: these collective images telegraph the complexity of the circus hierarchy, with stars at the top, winos at the bottom. Except that still below the winos were the "jigs," or Negroes, whom you may notice in uneasily angular positions as they perch semi-perilously on a wagon roof behind everybody else, up in "nigger heaven" (as expressed in movie-house terms), signifying their loose-balloon moorings in this segregated world, based on the mores of winter quarters, which were usually down South.

There may even be two bands in the picture, a black one and a white one, that might have sounded better playing together. While arranging corporate personnel in the phony bonhomie of an office get-together for a company's annual report, Kelty must have longed for summer, when he would be snapping "Congresses" of mugging clowns, fugueing freaks, rodeo sharpshooters, plus the train crews known as "razorbacks" (*Raise your backs!*), who loaded and unloaded the wagons from railroad flatcars at midnight and dawn. That was where a chug-a-lug bar fighter might wind up, in this era when "rootless" was a pejorative word, like "hedonistic" or "atheistic," and a new face in town was cause for suspicion. These ladies toted pythons, strolling around the hippodrome track, and didn't wear enough clothes; and some of the men looked as bathless as the guys from a hobo jungle who would steal your wife's apple pie that she'd left to cool on the kitchen windowsill, yet had skills you hadn't imagined. Circuses flouted convention as part of their pitch—flaunted and cashed in on the romance of outlawry, like Old World gypsies. If there hadn't been a crime wave when the show was in town, everybody had sure expected one. And the exotic physiognomies, strangely cut clothes, and oddly focused, disciplined bodies were almost as disturbing—"Near Eastern," whatever Near Eastern meant (it somehow sounded weirder than "Middle Eastern" or "Far Eastern"), bedouin Arabs, Turks and Persians, or Pygmies, Zulus, people cicatrized, "platter-lipped," or nose-split. That was the point. They came from all over the known world to parade on gaudy ten-hitch wagons or caparisoned elephants down Main Street, and then, like the animals in the cages, you wanted them to leave town. Yet if you were a farmer who thought a bear that had killed a pig was scary to come to grips with, try managing half a dozen snarling lions! Or maybe you had screwed up your nerve recently to reroof the barn? Try walking the high wire, fifty feet up, with just your wife standing underneath you in case of a slip.

When it rained, the rest of us went indoors, but show folk didn't have an indoors. They were negotiating with the mud in order to hit the road. The seat men folded thousands of chairs and "bibles," or souvenir programs. The "bull hands," the elephant men, controlled the pachyderms with a club with a hook on the end as the animals pulled out the quarter poles and the center poles and any wagons that got stuck. The transience of the circus jibed better with wild nature than the closely trimmed lawns at home—and willy-nilly a circus rolled. People with survival skills pitched in to fill the gaps. The whole grew bigger than the parts, though close to nature meant close to scandal too, as they intersect in such a phrase as "Nature calls." Nature is randy as well as rainy, smelly as well as sunny. Circus Day was uncivilized like the Fourth of July, with candied apples, cotton candy, fireworks, and special dispensation for skimpy costumes, public lust, trials of strength, breakneck stunts, colossal crowds. "It was a circus," we'll still say when some ordinary scene bursts out of control. And if your blouse stuck out farther than the next girl's, that cage boy loafing over there might decide to persuade the hippopotamus to gape her mouth for you and poke his hand inside and scratch her gums the way she liked, to make you ooh and aah at how heroic he was.

I was such a cage boy myself, with Ringling Bros. and Barnum & Bailey in 1951 and 1952, and would also pet the menagerie leopards for the right admirer. I worked for two dollars per sixteen-hour day and slept two to a bunk, three bunks high, on the train, or else could rattle through the night outside on a flatcar. The faces of the drifters I was with sometimes looked as grim and bitter as a WANTED poster, and quite at their wit's end, not having had much wit to begin with, and what they might have had perhaps dispelled in prison. They'd slammed around, with their hats pulled down over their eyes, every mother-in-law's nightmare, and knew how to jump on a moving train without saying goodbye to anybody—knew the Front Range of the Rockies, and the Tex-Mex border. And not even our rumpled banquets guy with the windblown tie—a theater-district barfly and Coney Island dime-museum habitué, who scarcely saw his own sons after they were toddlers—could have coaxed a trustful look out of them.

Up on that giddy wire or the trapeze bar—or in the Iron Jaw act, spinning relentlessly by their teeth—people did things they shouldn't reasonably do, with no ostensible purpose but showing off, while the tuba oompahed, the trombone slalomed, the clarinet climbed a rope, and the cornet hit the canvas's peak line. "Flyers" and slack-wire artists and "risley" foot-jugglers and whiteface or "auguste" clowns hoarded and pruned their skills, like the humble juggler of legend, who during the night tiptoed into the empty cathedral on the Madonna's feast day, after the wealthier citizens had long since delivered their heavy gifts, genuflected before her statue, and gone comfortably home. Alone and barefoot, he performed for her with whatever grace and dexterity he could muster. And for the first time in all of history, tears welled up in her stone eyes.

That's what we try to do, isn't it? Keep rolling, keep juggling and strutting our stuff, honoring our gods; then take a bow and exit smiling? But magic seldom happens unless a structure has been erected— whether a church or a tent—that is hospitable to it. Art is fragile, and a windless silence helps. Then depart just as the applause crests, leaving some emotion for the next act, because the thrust of the circus never stops, whether in mud or sunshine, whether the tickets have sold out or not. High stakes. The aerialist Lillian Leitzel, the most mesmerizing female performer ever, fell to her death in 1931, and afterward Alfredo Codona, her husband and male counterpart, at least on the trapeze, married an aerialist/equestrienne, but injured himself while doing a triple somersault in 1933 and never flew again. Grotesquely, he became his wife's hostler on the Tom Mix Circus—until, estranged, he shot both her and himself in her divorce lawyer's office.

Karl Wallenda, the greatest wire-walker and another compulsive, fell twelve stories off a cable strung 750 feet between two hotels in 1978, at seventy-three. But for some of these plain old Okies, Arkies, Hoosiers, Wisconsin Cheeseheads, and Georgia Crackers who got the show to run on time and then maybe drove a trailer truck all night, the gamble was compelling, too. Their trajectory ran toward alcohol and the jitters of oblivion, even though they had a seaman's way with ropes. And several gaze at Kelty's camera as if reminded of a police-station booking room, whereas the performers pose in a row in profile with their biceps bulged, or ponytail pert. "Is your body as trim as mine?" they seem to ask. "I'll stand on one hand—or one finger! I'll do a back flip from one horse to another and then lie down on the ground and let the elephant put her foot on my nose, but because we're all a family she won't crush it. Instead she'll lift me onto her shoulders and we'll chase that clown until he drops his red bloomers."

The moneymen, gimlet-eyed, with peremptory chests, let their suits, cufflinks and stickpins, their oxblood shoes and railroad men's timepieces, speak for them. They owned the tents and trucks and railroad cars, of course, but also often the lions too, despite the trainer's intimacy with them. He could be fired and have to pack his kit and never see those particular cats again. Similarly, the acrobats were not terribly suited to busking for spare change on the subway. They needed complicated rigging and a spread of canvas overhead—the whole apparatus—to gather an audience sufficient to justify risking their lives, without being clinically crazy. And a run-of-the-mill hobo, who was used to sneaking across the hazardous, lightless bustle of a railroad yard to boost himself into a moving boxcar without being detected, had probably found a raison d'être with Ringling Bros., called by show people "the Big One." In my time, if he was fired with the dreaded words "No Rehire" scribbled on his pink slip to go into the company's records, it might take the little wind that he had out of his sails. The performance, the crowds and ovations, though not directly for him, had centered and justified his shaky life.

The center poles and brocaded, bejeweled elephant howdahs might be bedecked with the Stars and Stripes, and yet one knew that the entire spectacle, unlike July 4, wasn't quite *American*. The men and women holding hands in the center ring to take a bow after manipulating their bodies on the teeterboard were probably foreigners, and might not even be married to each other—and God knows where they slept. They had somehow gelled their flightiness for professional purposes, but the idea of a new town tomorrow, a new town the next day, and consorting in a business way with freaks whose very livelihood was exhibiting their disfigurements like fakirs in an Asian marketplace (freaks inherently were un-American) was not like the Home of the Brave. What demons in themselves were they trying to anesthetize by harboring values so different from ours? We, the Elmers, the hicks, the towners, the hayshakers, had just put down good money to watch somebody shoot himself out of a cannon on the assurance that it was going to be genuine and he might really die before our eyes. But he landed succinctly on his back in the L-shaped net, swung to the ground, acknowledged our claps—and didn't then thank his lucky stars and settle down to a productive existence like ours. *Eat your heart out, rube*, was part of his message. *We'll be gone tomorrow. We'll see Chicago. We'll be in Florida. You stay here and milk your cows!*

To "the Strange People," misshapen on their little stages in the sideshow tent and peddling 10¢ likenesses of their deformities to the public, the conventional response would be, "There but for the grace of God go I." But why had He withheld His mercy when constructing them? Did their burden, as suggested by ancient superstitions, express a spiritual canker? Was external ugliness a punishment laid on the erring soul? My own feeling, while working next to them in Madison Square Garden and other arenas half a century ago, was that the object lesson ran deeper still. People were fascinated not just because of morbid curiosity and schadenfreude but because we saw ourselves incarnate in the Knife-Thrower, the Living Skeleton (or "Pincushion," or "Picture Gallery"), the Human Pretzel, the Fat Lady, the lame and wheezing Giant, and were encouraged to stare without being rude. The foxfire flicker of ferocity and awful insecurity that so frequently subverted our genial veneer lay out there exposed—much as the bum, the coward, the fussbudget, and spoilsport whom we knew all too well was embodied in some of the skits the clowns performed. (Our Knife-Thrower really got to people when, as a pièce de résistance, he "horse-whipped" pretty women who volunteered from the crowd.)

A clown or Santa Claus costume, in my experience of the individuals who wear them, can conceal a multitude of sins. But so does the attire that the rest of us hide in, using blandness to mask our shamefaced failures and maladjustments. We, too, have flat feet and big asses, chalky faces and weepy tendencies when frightened of our shadows or searching through the tanbark for a nickel we lost, a button that popped off, or a pebble that was in our shoe—we took it out but now we miss it. In the smaller tent shows the Fat Lady in the baby-doll nightie might even show it all in a curtained-off area, if you paid an extra four bits (and it was said you could insert them). In a circus you didn't have to—weren't supposed to—avert your eyes, and that may have been its ultimate kick. The guy might die, but without muttering the piety "Oh, I can't watch," we simply did.

Uzbeks rode on saddled camels. Elephants sashayed. A sway-pole acrobat almost seemed to touch the ground on each backswing, then locked his feet and slid down headfirst. A lovely woman with blonde hair hanging to her coccyx adjusted her shoulder straps, kicked off her silver slippers, and gripped a knotted rope to ascend for the Cloud Swing. Over at one side, we might not notice a self-effacing clown—not bizarrely loud now to attract attention—pulling her up with considerable care, then standing underneath in case of a mishap. But if you were observant, you realized there might be some people who had a love life after all.

The black-maned lion roared with bestial fury yet soon lapsed into contented amiability, as if he might be willing to settle in our burg. And the Albino Girl and Snake Charmer and other troupers were said to have bought cough medicine, underpants, and other personal stuff in the local stores. But just when we thought they really liked us and had been converted to our home-sweet-home values, they up and did a disappearing act. Overnight, the magic cavalcade vanished to another state, another climate. We have that gimpy, haywire gene as well, the one that makes you want to hit the road each spring while you last—a hail-fellow who knows that nothing is for keeps. You do your thing, to just whatever tattoo of music and battery of lights are available to you, survive today, sleep it off, and get up on that wire again tomorrow.

A LAST LOOK AROUND

*W*e age at different rates, just as our pacing in adolescence and later is different. Hampered by a stutter and mute with girls, for instance, I was instead precocious as a writer and published my first novel before I had lost my virginity. In fact, the publisher had to fly me east for a last-minute consultation because their lawyer, in reading the proofs of the book, discovered a passage where I seemed to be describing a sexual act that could not be depicted in 1955—only to realize in interrogating me, of course, that I had never heard or even conceived of the practice of cunnilingus. He forbore explaining, and I was drafted into the army, and my twenties became like other people's teens as far as sexual experimentation was concerned. Thus my thirties probably corresponded to their twenties, and my forties were naturally rather like their thirties: in that aspect of life perhaps my prime. It seems to make it easier now to be in my sixties, because I don't have to look back in memory very far to uncommon adventures.

Sex is hardly the only form love takes, however, and most of us become better parents, better friends as we mature. The ripening thirties and forties bring some patience and perspective. You learn to make the most of an hour with your daughter at the zoo, or lunch with an old classmate who's resettling and needs to find a job. Dawn in June, when you're my age, with the songbirds singing, and a mother merganser flies over an otter swimming ahead of your canoe, and suddenly dodges as a duck hawk sweeps out of the trees—she had been decoying you away from her knot of half a dozen bobbing babies. But down she splashes into the river, immediately diving to escape the falcon, and succeeds. Great swamp maples and willows; a wood turtle; a mallard family that appears to have eluded the falcon's notice—he's gone after a blue jay. You're with a friend who is saddled with heart trouble, and this is just the kind of spectacle that concentrates your minds. Not only the glee that you two felt when you were young and predatory like the otter and the falcon, or the mercurial delight of being alive with the sun and a breeze on the water, but the wistful awe of knowing you won't always be outdoors in a canoe during the spring in what looks awfully like God's best heaven. If it isn't, then what is?

Summer won't be endless now; nor episodes of drama and romance. The well takes longer to refill. Even walking, I pant when going uphill—a nice healthy sort of pant in my case, I hope, because I think that, in our day, our life spans, unless we drive like maniacs, are determined by our genes. My father died at just sixty-three, my mother is ninety-four, and I've always felt closer to her. People tend to gain in tolerance and grow more generous-spirited as they get older, but on the other hand, we often lose connectedness and some degree of interest in what's going on. So our generosity or tolerance is not all that expensive to us. Bring a cruel conundrum to our attention and we will certainly sympathize, but we are quite inured to the impossibility of combating injustice and to the corruption of the sort of powerful people who otherwise might try. And much as our backs slip out of whack at some small sidewise tug, so do our minds skid off the point when fatigued a little or short-circuited by a spark. I've been publishing books for forty years, and I don't have a fast-ball any more, just a knuckleball, spitball, and other Satchel Paigey stuff.

You're only as old as you feel is a refrain one hears enough that it must have some truth to it, though your oncologist might disagree. The remissions he sees uplifting the spirits of so many dying people a week short of death—when they think they are going to live on for years—could be interpreted as the exuberance of fetal angels confused by a passage toward ecstasy, or as an aspect of the anesthetic that commonly tranquilizes creatures that are being engulfed by death, whether a wildebeest in the jaws of a lion or a frog in the mouth of a snake. While in the army, I worked in a morgue and noticed that most dead people smile.

Yet we are, indeed, in some respects as young as we feel. Life is moments, day by day, not a chronometer or a contractual commitment by God. The digits of one's age do not correspond to the arrhythmia of one's heart or to the secret chemistry in our lymph nodes that, mysteriously going rancid, can betray us despite all of the surgery, dentistry, and other codger-friendly amenities that money buys. Good works don't keep you off the undertaker's slab, either. But cheeriness, maybe yes. Cheery, lean, little guys do seem to squeeze an extra decade out of the miser up above, as if feeling young were not as important as having a peppy metabolism and appreciating being alive.

Blurry eyesight, fragile knees, broken sleep, the need to pee a dozen times a day (when somebody honks at my car, parked at the side of the interstate, I assume it's a man my own age) are not inherently fun, however, although the smoothing out of temperament does help you cope. Your ingenuity, your curiosity must find a new focus, not simply exploring the world as a kid does. When I watch from my canoe a tall blue heron stalking field mice through the grass, then washing them down with minnows and tadpoles, I don't experience the surge of ambition to be a zoologist I would have felt when I was fifteen. I just want to go on seeing these intricate things next year.

Among my friends who have been notified that they were terminally ill, those who died least miserably, most gracefully, were people who could be intrigued and absorbed by the peculiar changes their bodies underwent. They didn't stop observing the incongruous handicaps, the bemusing treatments they were subjected to. The music they loved, snatches from books that had meant a lot, the news of friends who stopped in to visit, the civil war afflicting their bodies, the total novelty of dying—comprehending such a crush of sensations took all their waking time (a last hearing of *Children's Corner Suite!*) and emotional resilience. It was a voyage they stayed on deck for.

During a spell of semiblindness a few years ago, I found myself, too, registering the dismally curious stages of what was happening to me, as I gave up driving, lost the capacity to see birds in the sky, then gradually the crowns of the loveliest trees, and my friends' faces close at hand, a fascinating catastrophe. Surgery saved and rejuvenated me; I felt like Lazarus. But I learned how life itemizes exactly what you are losing. With binoculars around my neck, and then a telescope at the window, I put off curtain time. (The moon you can watch endlessly, or a lilac branch bounce in the wind, but people object to being gazed at.) As my daughter dropped in, and the leaves outside turned yellow, I was scrambling to improvise solutions: how to get a particular errand done, how to read three paragraphs by closing one eye and focusing the other closer. But would I see her face again?

I was reviewing a day at the beach I had had ten years before in San Francisco with the love of my life, stripping the rubber band out of her hair and kissing a pimple she tried to hide with her free hand, as the purple underbelly of a rainstorm rolled in, but reminded myself that since things hadn't worked out, she wasn't really the love of my life. Or was she?

Life is minutiae, and aging progresses by two steps "forward" and then one back, jerky as one's legs become. Although I was rejuvenated by millennium-type eye surgery (when nature had had it fixed for eons that people my age should quietly go blind or have heart attacks without bypasses, thus decently getting offstage and leaving enough space for younger people and other mammalians), my memory kept slipping out of gear, as if a cog were chipped, at the same time that I had more to remember in a lengthening life, and my temper grew crankier, though in fact my true balance was becoming more benign. While less in a hurry to get places, I drove worse because my mind was absent. My eyesight had been sharpened with plastic implants, but my mind coughed like an old car's motor and I would pull out into traffic without using my eyes.

My chest ached afterward a little when this happened, as it does when my waking dreams go wandering into uncataloged drawers of my memory where they have no pleasant business being. Yet I don't glance back and notice missed opportunities. Wanting so passionately to be a writer, I grabbed what I saw as the main chance at every turn, avoiding offers to become a tenured professor or a media editorialist in favor of staying freelance. Living frugally came naturally to me as a stutterer who had wondered how it would be possible to earn a living anyway. The only regret that accompanied this choice was not feeling free to have and educate more than one child, instead of the three or four I would have liked to raise if I had had more income. I've never treated anybody scurvily, at least by my lights, and don't experience chagrin of that sort, looking back. But of course I debate my two marriages, and the crossed wires that sometimes threw sparks, or other friendships that lived or lapsed. At parties, you recognize why old-fashioned women tend to be matchmakers. Couples seem so much happier than single people above a certain age; you rarely meet a widow or widower who is sighing with relief.

Marriage as the long-term pairing of men and women is such a hunter-gatherer sort of idea that its durability testifies to how primeval we still are, despite the voltage and velocities of our compression-chamber days. Our guns and murders do too, and the over-the-mountain infidelities that entertain us, our greed for swapping stacks of greenbacks ("frogskins," they used to be called) for goodies, and the special appetite for travel that seizes us, young and old. We hit the road as kids, and then again as old scouts furloughed from the city, we retire to cruise ships or

Winnebagos forty years later, feeling we've been bottled up, and forage in foreign markets, roaming for the sake of roving, watching the sun's progress as immemorial theater across the sky. But my work enabled me to travel even during my breadwinning years, in Europe or close to the Arctic or below the Sahara. I found the more you do, the more you're up to doing. Camping in the Rockies prepares you for Alaska, and Alaska for Africa. As you grow relaxed about the procedures of distant travel, you get resourceful about the details, locating a tuning fork within yourself that hears the same note in other people wherever you go. Even in war or famine or dictatorship—because we are not speaking of Pollyanna travel—your intuitions are valid because all of us have a rendezvous with death, however humble and anticlimactic that may finally be, and exotic disasters should not be incomprehensible. Like Moburu or Mussolini, we've been cruel and grandiose, have strutted, lied, and postured, known sneaky lust and shifty theft and opportunistic betrayal. The spectrum of behavior we witness in going abroad is seldom all that foreign to us.

The eye surgeon had warned me in 1992 that my blindness was going to recur and I should see whatever of the world I wanted to take in rather soon. So, at around sixty, I visited India and Antarctica, each for the first time, and returned to Africa twice. It was different because in the case of India and Antarctica I was treated to blue-ribbon, well-financed wilderness tours of sights I could never have reached when my legs were young and strong. And in Africa I was already known for a book I had written sixteen years before. The day after arriving in Nairobi, I got a call at the New Stanley Hotel from a stranger named Rob Rose, who was with the Catholic Relief Services agency and asked if I would like to accompany him the next day on a two-week trip into guerrilla territory in the civil war raging in the southern Sudan, where roughly two million people have died.

We set off by Land Rover for Kampala, in Uganda, spent one night, then ventured off quickly through disputed territory in that country's own separate, simmering civil war, up to the town of Gulu, with only one breakdown. Next morning, we continued north through the hamlet of Atiak and choppy, evacuated grasslands and acacia forests and two military outposts to no-man's-land and finally the Sudanese village of Nimule. Famine country was just beyond. The Dinka and Nuer had been allied against the Arab government in Khartoum, but now, alas, were fighting against each other as well. Their positions had consequently been shattered, their cattle and grain supplies destroyed. They'd fled to Ethiopia, been defeated there again, and retreated in starving condition back to the Nile. But the aid agencies that had been feeding them, frightened by the lethal infighting—in which three relief workers and a journalist had been shot—had pulled out.

I felt sheepish for not having foreseen more than a hint of these developments during my previous trip. Yet I was white-haired now, which changed the character of my reception, even allowing for the impact of the emergency. One elder thought I must be a "king." When I said America didn't have kings, he amended that to "millionaire," looking at my hiking boots; he was barefoot. A white-haired white man, to have come so far, must be at least a high official of the United Nations who had heard one hundred thousand people were starving here. Pathetic, short, hand-contoured little mounds paralleled the network of footpaths where we walked, each marked by ragged tokens of the famished body newly buried—a broken doll, a tiny skirt or holey sweater that had been laid on top. Dysentery or pneumonia might have abbreviated the child's suffering, but surely a potent senior figure like me, beholding such a tragedy, might intervene.

My friend Rob, half my age, by dint of sleepless and dynamic initiatives, had indeed brought fifty-eight truckloads of corn from the Catholic Relief Services warehouse in the Kenyan port of Mombasa, the first food delivery in a couple of months to the refugee encampments we visited. In my eyes, he was a genuine hero, braving the dangers here and the U.N.'s tacit boycott. But at Aswa, Amei, and Ateppi, smiling desperate children by the many hundreds ran to me, a mere itinerant journalist, to touch my hands and cheer me in the Dinka language as the godfather or patriarch who seemed to have arrived to save their lives. If only more food came!—it's been the most poignant moment in my life. Some of them, boys and girls of six or twelve, had already shrunk to skeletal wraiths, monkey-faced from malnutrition, and I saw newborns who would die without ever tasting milk. Their mothers, stretched beside them on the ground, were themselves dying and, prompted by our guides, partly raised their bodies to show me their flat breasts.

Seven women were said to have been grabbed by crocodiles on the bank of the Nile, where they had gone to try to harvest lily roots or spear a fish. Wild dates and nuts and the tufts of ricey wild plants had long since been exhausted, the rats smoked from their holes, the grasshoppers roasted. The local streams had been finger-sieved for shiners and crustaceans, and every songbird slingshotted. The very air smelled burnt. But lives were being saved by our trip. Even divided among one hundred thousand souls, fifty-eight truckloads of corn staved off the agony of hunger pangs awhile, and my white pate was winning me more credit than I deserved.

The hospital was the worst place, ringed by hungry irregular troops, the famished patients lying bedless on concrete, rationed to one cup of cornmeal per day. The nurses were so weakened they could scarcely function and were distracted by their own children's frantic straits. It seemed shameful for a well-fed man from Vermont to be touring this furnace unscathed, with boys and women rushing to him to intercede in Washington and bring it to an end. I did write about what I had seen, and did at the time shout at the guerrilla general who was thought to have helped precipitate this immediate calamity by setting up the killing of the relief workers (not realizing that white people are as tribal as anybody else), as I would not have had the confidence to do when I was young. At roadblocks I was more at ease when ordered out of the car by teenagers with Kalashnikovs, less edgy when we broke down in Uganda in lion and bandit country. I knew that mines are more of a danger than lions, and malaria more than mortar shells or the kids at a roadblock who are looking for other African teenagers to kill, not a cautious, courteous white man.

Aging is not a serene occupation, You stumble physically and tire quickly, maybe even indoors, and your mind can be tricked by threadbare circuitry into surreal or simple confusions, like the proverbial second childhood, when for a moment you don't know where you are. Not in Africa, though: you're on your toes. And I don't think of travel as a vacation. I'd love to see Venice again, but doubt I have anything to say about it that hasn't been better said. So I turn to the new phenomena of the Third World for trips, barely scratched by various hassled travel writers. I want to work out toward the brink of what I think is going to happen—the widespread death of nature, the approaching holocaust of famines, while Westerners retreat in veiled panic into what they prefer to regard as the realer world of cyberspace. (Old age will not be an enemy, in that event.)

The distractions, ruses, nostrums you used to employ to foil depression, such as sexual flings or mountain climbing, are not in the repertoire of most old guys; and their suicide rate can nearly approximate the febrile teens'. But they're also freer of sexual unease and self-esteem or money compulsions. They may lack money, yet not care as much; can better do without. And "seniors," after all, are living on borrowed time—borrowed from the unborn whose world they're using up. I'm almost twice as old as an average American's life expectancy in Colonial times. Just a hundred years ago, I'd be blind, crippled with hernias, if not already dead from asthma, appendicitis, or parathyroid disease and other stuff I've had before.

And money can become an equalizer, too. On a ferryboat from Martha's Vineyard to Cape Cod last summer, I noticed with some sympathy an oldish man standing on the deck, who the whole way across the water, and as if for dear life, hugged a sturdy, gaunt, blond, young-fortyish woman who was balancing uncomfortably against the boat's rock. Yet she patiently allowed him to do as he wished, nursely in manner if not in fact. The two young boys traveling with them looked on, amused or embarrassed, though it was not clear whose kids they originally were, his or hers. From his clinging hunger and needy passion—stock-still on the deck hugging her for forty-five minutes, except when she excused herself to go to the bathroom—she was a new and important acquisition for him. He felt thankful and lucky. Though of normal build, he looked frail and unsteady, as if he might have just had a major health scare, and was not making her a spectacle for the sake of the other passengers, but his own. Though she didn't care for the compulsive public part, on the other hand, like a good sport and with a kind of good-hearted, working-class honesty, she appeared to recognize that it was part of the deal. If you become the third wife of an ailing businessman twenty-five years older and very much richer than you, and he's recuperating from surgery at his summer home, you let him hug you round-the-clock, with or without an audience.

In my fifties, I had a sizable love affair with a woman seventeen years younger than me, a nurse who took me all over Alaska on her supervisory rounds. In chartered Cessnas, we flew to remote Eskimo or Indian villages, sleeping on the floor of the health clinic or school gym while she consulted with patients and the local nurse. Frigid, wild places where in January my eyes sometimes froze shut and I would not have gone by myself, but with her felt both bold and safe, knowing that whatever happened to me, I would not be alone. And somehow, like the Eskimos', her eyelids did not get sealed by the frosts. Nor was she winded or chilled on our strenuous walks. Whatever risks we met, surely she could wiggle me out. I remember hugging her intensely for her sex and youth, and like a lifeline to safety and my own youth. Sometimes she would pull my head next to hers and look in the mirror to see how others visualized us—was I conspicuously wrinkly and gray?—but decided no. We made love extensively every night for weeks, and the age disparity seemed to add spice. A tutor indoors, a dependent outside, I clung and pumped as if doubling my luck, my vanishing span on earth; and if I died I would be in her arms, which would make it all right. Now, I couldn't possibly do the things we did, in bed or out, flying all over Alaska, landing on rivers at hamlets where a white man was not welcome unless he couldn't be ejected because he was with the head nurse. It was delicious to bask in my friend's protection, a further frisson to fanciful sex. And chums who are eighty tell me how much more I'll lose by seventy, not to mention at their age, of the physical capacity I had at fifty-three.

But did we—we tend to wonder—capture the spirit of our times? Did we grasp a piece and participate? We know how a composer such as George Gershwin captured the expatriate zest of the 1920s with *An American in Paris* and then in the democratic 1930s wrote *Porgy and Bess*. Aaron Copland, too, not a weather vane, spoke for the thumb-your-nose 1930s with *Billy the Kid* and then did *Appalachian Spring* in the patriotic, heal-the-wounds mid-1940s. Our telescoping century, from the Edwardians through two world wars to cyberspace (my mother, who is still alive, saw the first electric lights and automobiles come to her town), has made it hard to keep current. One wouldn't even *want* to have been a flapper in 1929, a red-hunter a quarter century later, and then a bond salesman in the fabulous 1980s.

I left the city for the country in the 1980s, preferring at that point, I guess, to watch the carnival at one remove, and haven't shifted from typewriting essays to word-processing screenplays, as so many good folks have. Indeed my politics and style of dress (both shabby Ivy) have scarcely changed since I left college. I pounded cross-country during the 1950s; heard Martin Luther King deliver his radiant speech at the Lincoln Memorial in 1963; protested against Vietnam; and saw ticker-tape parades for FDR, Truman, Eisenhower, Kennedy, Johnson, and Nixon, plus King George VI and Charles de Gaulle. Didn't do drugs, but saw action enough, and didn't drop out of the domestic brouhaha until ten years ago.

I wanted to know shadbush from elderberry, dogwood from choke-cherry, bluebirds from indigo buntings, yellowthroats from yellow warblers, the French horn from an English horn, a trombone from a sousaphone, Red Grange from Red Barber, and Newt Gingrich from Joe McCarthy. We opt for what we want as daily conversation in the privacy of our minds, and whether on most days we get to watch the sunrise and listen to a snatch of the genius of Bach. It's not expensive to pay attention to the phases of the moon, to transplant lemon lilies and watch a garter snake birthing forty babies and a catbird grabbing some, or listen to the itchy-britches of the Canada geese as autumn waxes. We will be motes in the ocean again soon, leached out of the soil of some graveyard, and everlastingly rocking.

That is my sense of an afterlife and my comfort. The hurly-burly of streambed turmoil will be our last rush-hour traffic—thocketing through boulders, past perch pools and drift logs. Enough, we will say, reaching tidewater. We saw enough.

CURTAIN CALLS

*B*elieving in life, I believe in death as well, and at seventy-six look forward to my immersion in the other plane of the seesaw also. Without wishing to hasten it, in other words, I don't dread the event. The politics will be less rancid, my dentistry at an end, and the TV off. Half a century ago I happened to work in a morgue for a while and rarely noticed on a gurney a face of an appropriate age who looked sorry he or she had set sail. If this globe is the only heaven we have, I doubt the trip will be a long one. Downward into the seethe of the soil and the sea, we landlubbers become marine again. What's important is to remain tethered here as earthlings. The dead I saw had generally smiled a little as they crossed the bar: an Etruscan sort of smile, inward-turning. Etruscan sculptors maybe captured it best.

Yet I doubt inanimate energy has no relation to the synapses that have twitched our mouths a hundred thousand times into a living grin. I've spent countless hours on the banks of ponds, gazing into the amber water as flakes of dead organisms, animal or vegetable, swirled slowly toward the bottom, while living threads arose from the silt on pencil-thin currents, to whirl upward gently and incrementally as though recharged. Whether as boy or man, I was at the pond those many afternoons to do the same. It's not that simple a paradigm (or that squealing hogs are butchered so we can be energized to yell at football games), but is part of why I have few misgivings about getting old. The particulars of not watching much football or trotting around to bars, movies, galleries, don't bother me overly, although I do miss taking stairs two at a time, filling my passport with visas, and teaching at different colleges in successive semesters. Memories, thank goodness—not omissions—make me wistful, if I am. I walk slower because of diminished vision and, white-haired, cut less of a figure than younger bloods, but, twice married, with grandchildren and a cat's cradle of other memories of narratives of love, I'm not galled by missing those panting pursuits. Similarly, having glimpsed the Himalayas, though not the Andes, and visited Alaskan neighborhoods numerous times, if never Newfoundland or Iceland, I feel content with that. I didn't misuse my opportunities. Just across the road from my house is a Vermont-scale mountain I've climbed so frequently during the past forty years I can contemplate its contours from a window or pass the trailhead without feeling frustrated that I will never do so again. For four decades my retinas have engraved its heights into my gray tissue until, without needing my ashes scattered up there, I already feel geologically embedded on the indentations of the ridgeline like the guano of generations of peregrine falcons that nested on the cliffs.

Indentations are what life's all about; and I've sailed into Lisbon, Piraeus, Palermo, and Ushuaia, flown into Sana'a, Kampala, and Bombay, rattled into Mombasa and Madras on a sleeper train, walked beside the Tiber, the Seine, and the Golden Horn. I've swum in the Ohio and the Rio Grande and seen Agrigento. Wasn't that my fair share—must I see Tokyo? No: the daily skyscapes, plus some spindrift on breaking surf, and a pond in the woods should be enough. Nor do the early-to-bed aspects of growing old trouble me, because I was always a morning person, seldom a midnight drinker or sexual athlete. Indeed, I tended to limit my liaisons to people I genuinely cared about in order to avoid palimpsests, and in adventuring out-of-doors was such a cautious soul I never broke a bone, which means I don't pine for recollected threesomes drunk as a skunk. We're here to feast our eyes and hug loved ones, with our joy perhaps analogous to photosynthesis in plants—an energizing process of oxygenation that I like to imagine helps keep the Big Bang's spin to life's origins going on and on. My friend at Agrigento and on the Tiber and the Seine was married to me but later we divorced, so, after a second divorce, I'll leave a modest legacy of one daughter and her children, not a fecund array of progeny.

Yet we've had too much fecundity; it's now no virtue; it's eating us out of house and home. The strangulations of fecundity precipitate African and Asian extinctions, and there will be a worldwide avalanche of these. Death will save me from witnessing the drowned polar bears, smashed elephant herds, wilting frog populations, squashed primate refuges. Believing life has universal value, I'm worn quite threadbare from caring already—as early as age eighteen, I knew a chimp and an orangutan, and my concept of genocide never excluded them. I've been to the Arctic, Antarctica, and the high forests of Sudan (as well as a famine belt underneath), and know that the major wars of our epoch in retrospect will not have occurred in such places as Iraq but against the splendid diversities of nature, with no armistice planned or system invented for winding it down. Democracy seems no better suited than dictatorship to saving rain forests because money talks in both, and from generation to generation, rearguard battles against the devastation have been handed off. Each decisive loss is going to be forever and for keeps; and having cared for sixty years, I'm sick of elegies.

Oldsters are supposed to thumb the morning paper with satisfaction, for a soft landing in the ripening maturity of Jeffersonian democracy—not relive Vietnam or McCarthyism, wincing at millennial debates at the highest levels of government about refining American techniques of torture. Balkanized, parochial, we feel derailed as a nation, afraid we may not be rescued this time by our traditional trust that a bridging leader like Washington, Lincoln, Roosevelt will materialize in crises. Not so much the war with Islam as the end of the American Century is what we need Obama for: what will we do if we're not top dog?

I'm not "tired of London," as Samuel Johnson defined being tired of life. On the contrary, I've seldom loved New York more. And like other white-maned codgers, my aging gears engage again. At twelve I cared—the Congress of Industrial Organizations and the National Association of Manufacturers had rival fifteen-minute radio programs I used to listen to. But a less zestful confidence is embedded in America's rivalrous equations now. Union solidarity versus, for instance, the profit motive as a dogfight doesn't fit the new century as well as deeper, more ambiguous quandaries relating to what on earth we think we're doing. I've widened my allegiances beyond socialism toward Creation as a larger whole: salamanders, beech trees, not just autoworkers. Yet far from worrying less, one worries more.

On the other hand, accepting death as a process of disassembly into humus, then brook, and finally seawater demystifies it for me. I don't mean I comprehend bidding consciousness goodbye. But I love the rich smell of humus, of true woods soil, and of course the sea—love rivulets and brooks, lying earthbound, on the ground. The question of decomposition is not pressing or frightening. From the top of the food chain I'll reenter the bottom. Be a bug; then a shiner shimmering in the closest stream (want a minimal coffin, to speed the transition to multiple energies), or partially mineralized—does one need retinas and a hippocampus? Because I don't particularly want to be *me,* my theory is no. A green shoot a woodchuck might munch seems okay. I believe in continuity through conductivity: that the seething underpinnings of life's flash and filigree, its igniting chemistry, may, like fertilizer, appear temporarily dead, but spark across species like the electricity of empathy, or as though paralleling the posthumous alchemy of art.

The blasphemy of the idea that "I think, therefore I am," plus its theological counterparts, have countenanced our blitz of so much of the world one could hardly sum it up. In our billions we did it on automatic pilot, each gobbling an individual maximum, and now virtualizing a sort of substitute habitat. Yet our heartstrings don't strum only for kith and kin. That woodchuck or shiner, as if by an artesian force, can still make us grin, or a mountain ridge castellated by forests, or at the ocean, rolling combers. We don't want to drown in the combers or freeze on the mountain ridge, but their magnificence brims within us as awe, balloons in an exhilaration we may have driven for hours to experience, yet is not utilitarian except in the sense that grinning is good for us. We grin because for a moment the surf or the mountains incorporate us. We're alumni.

Put children almost anywhere and they will soon begin to play, an impulse just as artesian, though logical too, since they're in training. And if you move mice around, they'll immediately start building another nest, turning visibly more cheerful in all of their body language as they do so. But so do a flock of sanderlings bobbing along, a prowling coon if left in peace, a school of fingerlings like quicksilver in a creek: which illustrates the core of effervescence where I have placed my trust. Blake and Whitman attested to life's potential for outright ecstasy, as do our ears, if we are out during the spring. A sublevel in me seems always aware of that core of continuity, even when I'm also feeling cranky on the surface. It's the evidence that grounds me, the boom box that keeps me going.

When old, you're allowed more slack. You can nap on a park bench, spout wisecracks, go to the doctor at government expense on the arc toward "a second childhood." Flaunting the wisdom of experience from that bench becomes a great deal less fun, though, in this worst-of-centuries. I'd rather be a goldfinch eating dandelion seeds than witness, even on a TV screen, some of the scenes in store. Dhaka drowning; people eating processed algae. I won't be, you won't be, but rather than observing the gradual meltdown, wouldn't you prefer incarnation as a blue-tailed skink hunting crickets on a pine log?

As for the graph of my behavior zigzagging behind me through my places of residence like a snail's faintly luminescent trail, arrogant, dunderheaded embarrassments do prickle some of my memories, but no indelibly shameful acts. My dreams, whose imagery or story lines presumably cannot be censored as easily of what the mind bridles at remembering, confirm that. In theory at least, they might constitute a kind of St. Peter's Gate, a reckoning for old guys to confront surreally any victims they have wronged. Asleep, we are at the mercy of our subterranean minds. We can't disown the character of our recollections or the dramatis personae who berate us, such as ex-wives, old lovers enacting breakups, or children wailing. But I don't dread my dreams. Progeny, wives, parents make no staining appearance. Instead, I'm baffled by train schedules, wrong turnoffs, missed directions, a lost passport, heart-poundingly discombobulated among strangers because my ship is sailing from a pier my taxi hasn't delivered me to. Anxiety overrides regret as a motif, in car troubles I can't fix, a hotel closed for the weekend, a highway with no destination, an elevator without numbers—yet I'm thirtyish when my ineptitudes trip me up: not a boy, nor in old age. I heft my luggage and run for the right platform unhampered by shaky legs, shortness of breath, or glaucoma, as in real life would be the case. In real life I've never been this kind of doofus, either, and most of the narratives that operate as screen savers on the wall of my mind when I'm asleep are pleasanter. What's curious, however, is that my persona, in forty years, hasn't aged. Anthropology triumphs: my personality, although functioning in modern surroundings when I dream, remains fixed in a pre-industrial life span, never to reach three-score-and-ten; and, when I ask around, this is apparently typical.

My lifelong handicap of a stutter is seldom present in direct form as an obstacle, oddly enough, but perhaps is masked by the nightmares' patterns. When I panic and suffer through successive contretemps after misreading a clock (something I've never done in my actual travels), it's recapitulating a stutterer's terror of asking questions of strangers; yet he sometimes *must*. As a teenager and later I had many searing experiences on the street while searching for an address I was supposed to be at. People might duck around me as if I were a beggar or an epileptic, after momentarily pausing for the sake of good manners, then feeling taken in. Before phones were automated, four or five long-distance operators, including their supervisor, might need to tie into my pay-booth line, trying to decipher the numerals and names I had to spit out in order to place a call. Twenty scalding minutes of stammering could be consumed before their collective divination resolved the matter, yet if I wanted to enlist a passerby to read the information into the mouthpiece from a scrap of paper, he or she would generally shy away because of my shuddering posture and beseeching demeanor, muttering, "No coins!"

In dreams, the necessarily self-sufficient sense of direction I honed from the fires of those years fails me, but I do keep my cool, which, even if your off-putting disability has faded with age, is important for traveling. I've seen hunger in Sicily and Sudan; tyranny in Guatemala, China, and Franco's Spain; Hindu India; Muslim Yemen; and Brownian motion nearly everywhere. Yet I don't dream of famine or the other ordeals a traveler witnesses, or fatherhood's early delights, my parents' deaths, the spats of divorce, or a career in academia. Foiled but not humiliated, I inhabit the mentality of somebody still in the prime of life, rather than gimpy reality. For my deathbed, I anticipate a slide show of benign imagery, like my boyhood's Connecticut woods, and a collage of people I have loved.

What bothers me, though, is not my unconscious mind, which, however jittery it makes some nights, seems honorably upstanding, but my daydreams, which are not. *That* persona is fiftyish, twenty years older than the nighttime bloke but about twenty years younger than my actual age; and he's not a nice guy. Charitably, an advocate might argue that he is flailing against the onrush of debilitation via morally antsy, tail-end fantasies that seek more nooky than he has ever managed to achieve. But St. Peter would take decided exception to my harboring him. The tenor of innocence of that thirty-year-old whom I have no control over—baffled by mixed signals but who never hoodwinks or exploits anybody or is betrayed by them—is much more palatable. Since my life has appeared to me an upright one, finding my conscious mind uglier in its fabrications than when it is asleep is startling and has prompted me to reexamine my marriages, friendships, love affairs, professional relationships. A selfish waffling, more than any hanging offenses, is detectable: more omissions than commissions, in other words, and a mishmash of motivation for good behavior. When I took principled stands, how much was for integrity and how much for "authority issues" with a boss? When I stayed with my fading marriage so long, was it entirely for the sake of our child or for my wife's health insurance?

I reread packets of letters I'd received, discovering more tender generosity than I probably deserved or wanted to recognize at the time—had skated over by squinting my eyes because it could have crimped my plans to acknowledge what was being said. Yet the correspondence (this with a previous wife) continued—no angry epistles later, contested divorces, abrupt terminations. Although I'd run into a few old flames in normal circulation over the years, I placed several phone calls to people who'd been out of touch for years, plumbing for sour feelings I might have misremembered or perspectives that had changed. For instance, I reached a woman in Philadelphia who, as I'd heard from her former husband—later a postman in my neighborhood in New York—had undergone a nervous breakdown after a cross-country six months she and I had spent together in 1958 in San Francisco, while she gave birth to his baby out of wedlock. My presence had been necessary for this event because her straitlaced parents had been pressing her to have the pregnancy aborted and she didn't want the company of the biological father; their marriage afterward at the suggestion of her psychiatrist was short-lived. We had been friends before—in fact, she had relieved me of my virginity, and now sought my help. In due course I returned mother and daughter safely to Philadelphia; but had I been too peremptory, too oblivious of what the aftermath then held for her in that 1950s era, crying jags and all, in turning back to the thrust of my own life? This is what I asked, hearing her voice, decades on.

"Oh no, no, it wasn't you. Many other factors were involved," she told me with a ring of gentle fondness. "I never thought it was you." Two apiece, our subsequent marriages had ended in divorce, so there was plenty that needn't be said, but I never spent more hours beside a bed in a labor room than hers, or savored more of San Francisco's delights in the half-century since. She gave me news of the girl, living in Florida, all grown up, and that she herself volunteered in church work with battered women, but had been diagnosed with Alzheimer's disease. I commiserated over the phone without offering to trundle down to Philly to renew our intimacy. She had money from her parents to live on, and other children. What I did do, however, was buttonhole that postman, a solitary soul who had hazarded no further attachments, and encourage him to contact his daughter, not seen since she was in primary school, so he could at least obtain her Social Security number to list her as his heir. Hesitantly he did, and after a handful of halting or "weird" conversations, she agreed to let him begin flying south for visits.

My first wife expressed a justified irritation that I haven't dedicated more books to her during my career but sounded mostly exasperated with members of her own family, when I reached her, by an unfortunate coincidence, soon after the blow of the death of her father, as well as her retirement from a staff job at the United Nations. Not the most opportune time to ask for a summary judgment, though I tend to regard her as always right, her forbearance as more than I have deserved, and her help to me during the 1960s as the most selfless I ever received. She didn't remarry. Marriage may not have been her strong suit, as it wasn't mine, but we maintained affectionate relations through the ensuing decades. First spouses often should get more dedications than diplomacy permits.

My pairing that followed was with an Englishwoman on the Continent, so I tracked her down, now also recently retired from a U.N. job—I've usually gone for idealists—and snug in a flat on a steep cobbled street near Vatican City. I particularly wanted to ask whether I had been stingy when we parted at Istanbul's airport in 1965, after living together for five months on the Greek island of Samos. Like my Philadelphia friend from the 1950s, she laughed patiently. The point, she explained in a comradely fashion, was not my self-image or how many hundreds of dollars I'd given her to restart her life after our sojourn, but whether I'd wished to marry her. And no, co-dedicating a book to her ten years later had been no substitute. But, securely still single, with digs in London as well as in Rome, she wasn't caustic; only informed me that life with me had been lonelier than life without, and teased me because the Internet indicated my reviews were tailing off. She sounded so friendly, though, it required revisiting the poignancy of her correspondence to realize that she too was letting me off.

I was at my second wife's bedside for two weeks as she died of cancer, after our divorce in 1993, and suspect from our last meetings before her illness that we might have reconciled if she had not. As a marriage six times as long as, and more ironed out than, my first, its memories aren't piercing with lost opportunities recalled, and there's no sheaf of touching post-separation letters that still seem to root for me, such as my first wife wrote. There'd been anger, later muted, on my part. But in reliving culminating episodes with each of them, I can squirm to remember my ambivalence and how I censored what I took in. I never deprived anybody of better choices—of marrying who they ought to have by suggesting myself instead of him. And that may be why my partners judged my ambiguities to lie within normal bounds. Yet what *are* normal bounds—that ratio of authentic love to a mere neediness, or lust to fondness? I was cautious in these bailiwicks, not knowing the answer, and never scorched anyone by aiming for conquest. Dunderheaded behavior when linked with long-term affection will generally get you a pass.

Nor have employers, landlords, publishers accused me of deceit and abandonment. Like hoarding a grubstake to buy time to write a book, I wanted no quarrels that might sap my concentration. Pay the rent, the taxes, complete contractual commitments: a stutter pushes you to the margins anyhow. How will you land a teaching job, a chance in journalism, or simply chat up an intriguing person at a party? Even marrying, I took pains to warn the minister beforehand not to interpret my contorted expressions as signifying reluctance. I had needed to lie to an Army psychiatrist, assuring him that I usually spoke normally, so I could be conscripted to serve my country like other young men in 1955. Awake or in dreams, chaos was the fear, like my dread as a child in Manhattan that the Third Avenue Elevated would heel over with me on the platform when the trains came roaring into the station, vibrating the structure, and collapse onto the street. But when seventy additionally vivid years have passed, shouldn't one's white hairs stave off further embarrassment? What evolutionary purpose is served by continuing to burden geezers with fight-or-flight, adrenaline-pounding dreams, as if we should still be in training for primeval emergencies? Boys load up on contact sports and gory videos in preparation for defending tribe and country—but can't we insist on our infirmities? My heart and lungs would fold if I had to do some of the humping of luggage while running that my dreams require of me. Is it that our nervous wiring has yet to catch up with our doubled life spans, or that subsistence in the wilds did not entail a stage of retirement when scrabbling for status and bringing home the bacon were shelved? So I remain thirtyish in them, and those breathless shifts of tempo in the action may indeed add up to refresher training. Better a breakneck dream than breaking one's neck.

My parents never divorced and had married as virgins in their late twenties in 1931. Indeed, they knelt side by side at their honeymoon bed to pray together before deflowering each other. They wouldn't associate with people who got divorced, and my father disinherited my sister and me after we both did, so I wonder how their old-age fantasy life differed from, say, mine. My mother, bed-bound, said she had "only sweet dreams," but he sometimes read sadistic potboilers in retirement. As for me, it remains unsettling to find my sleeping brain more moral than my creepy daydreams. Asleep, I'm an underdog trying to establish a web of self-respecting circumstances I can live with; whereas awake, the narratives, though paced more tardily to accommodate reality, can resemble an outlaw's, or perhaps an adolescent's, a figment of frustration, repellent because for the moment conscienceless. But this simulacrum of myself is such a minor facet of growing old that I find the process easier than I expected, overall. From working in that morgue half a century ago, in fact, I suspect old age will dissolve like a chimera at the last, till we cross the bar transformed as "ourselves" once again.

The welts senility's indignities inflicted on our skin will be dispersed into the nearest creek sooner than the fruits of our most decent deeds, and the bio-electricity of happiness will flicker in that concluding smile I so often saw people go out with, radiating from the depths of a coma or the wee-hour banality of a hospital ward. The biochemistry of friendship can be equally a mystery, unlike perhaps infatuation, which makes evolutionary sense when it leads to copulation, or brown-nosing ingratiation, which may prove almost as advantageous. We need allies and thus want friends too, an evolutionist could say. But some friend-ships are just useful for empathy, not promotion or advancement or battlefield buddy-protection. And empathy is a mystery—a charitable outlet, not merely self-aggrandizing—and how we exult while birds arrow overhead, yelling through the winds, navigating by magnetic fields, the angularity of sun and stars, flock dynamics, and a landscape memory bank we still don't understand. We can't eat them, they're gone, yet part of us exults, much as the marbling of a moonlit sky or the scent of cedar trees uplifts our mood. This wider span of respon-siveness indicates affinities we haven't cataloged, as though already we sense we'll be repaying our infinitesimal loan from the universal energy pool pretty soon. Like the spume on top of a wave, we'll slide underneath again. The affection we sometimes feel for many other species, wild or tame, helps define or signify that "universal sympa-thy," as Thomas Mann in his last book described it. I hope to fortify foreign protoplasm, in my turn, as a root buds a stem or a tadpole a leg, without forethought.

It can just be a bug, needs to start somewhere. But why, then, care so much about the moral timbre of the life I've led? The fish or bird, or bigger bug that eats my bug, won't. I suppose if you've been a pickerel frog you ought to have been a good one, upstanding on your turf. Our last responsibility, however, is not to overstay our welcome, lingering with graspy greed into our dotage to gobble shrimp cocktails and roast lambs' legs, climate-hopping if we can afford to be coddled, in a world overbuilt, overpaved, overfished, overskinned. Haven't we "seniors" blitzed our patrimony enough? The scalded vistas testify to that; and it seems unseemly to ignore our natural shelf life to such an extraor-dinary extent—ungrateful and unflattering to the planet to resort to garish geriatric surgery or drugs to hog the stage, try to prolong our curtain calls, lest we fall not into a stream's syncopation, a tree's upward impetus, or the sea's swells, but a void. It's symptomatic of a mistrust of planes of intersection we don't understand.

I don't mean to sound Pollyanna: make light of death. When untimely, it can stink like cordite. A man once described to me how, when a grizzly bear was gnawing at him, off the Alaska Highway, the stench of the ordeal was more terrifying than the pain. I had a parallel experience, possibly, in the upper balcony at Carnegie Hall, when I found myself fighting a mindless impulse to kite my body over the low parapet, a compulsion in high places that afflicts me every year or two, though I've never desired suicide. A moment's berserk exertion could have thrown me over the thigh-high barrier, so pity for the individuals I might land on below, or even fear of the agony of the impact, didn't have much time to operate. Instead, a horrifyingly acrid stench, out of nowhere, suddenly stuffed my nostrils with an asphyxiating terror beyond the visual. I did, then, see myself spread-eagled in thin air, crumpling, falling, but the stink, incredible, illogical, was more imperative in bringing me to my senses.

In other words, against untimely death we'll thrash like a baby with all our limbs and faculties, unless we've been weathered down to slip into it naturally, after processes perhaps symmetrical to some of childbirth's, such as the bloating and eye-popping pain, plus mental recalibration, till death becomes a kind of light-and-shadow show, like sunrise slipping down a mountainside. Old guys—in the meantime—used to enjoy thumbing through the morning newspaper, until that exercise was acidified by Vietnam redux, piggybacked upon other rancor. The dead hold no opinions; and I quite look forward to that. Also, geezers, being deemed ineligible for sex, have expected a bit of a respite from cleavage flaunted in their faces, rather than every other teleprompter reader wigged with big hair, between the Viagra and Flomax ads, trying to heat up the home screen.

The centrifuge of social and technological change leaves many of us behind the curve, burrowed into temporary berths, as our habitat gets virtualized and our attention span goosed and telescoped. Old age can be as soothing as a shellfish's daily regimen, bundled with others moored to a rock, with the tides sloshing nourishment to and fro over them—except that our demolition of nature, amounting to a sort of gunboat solipsism, renders the mussel metaphor dubious at both ends. We will farm tilapia like chickens to feed the folks in Assisted Living, and the quicksilver schools of slim fish in their wild billions, as life's vast embodiment in the oceans, will be gone. It's not for me to speak for everybody and say this is a blow against God. But if joy is electric and chemical, why shouldn't it be elastic enough to permeate lives more rudimentary than ours? And if it does, and therefore is draconically shrinking, what's the conclusion to be drawn? Joy as electricity or chemistry may have been embedded within the raw spin imparted originally to us all, and like the pool of energy-in-reserve we'll sink back into as we die, must fluctuate, as pools of other kinds do.

The cascade of environmental havoc—coral reefs and flamingos dying—doesn't extend to crows, cormorants, and Canada geese, all thriving in my neighborhood (not to mention four cygnets just hatched on the pond), or the tints ravishingly streaking the sky at dawn, as Homer described. Human nature doesn't change as much as our numbers and mobility, and where we direct our eyes. We multiply, or perhaps metastasize, and will watch the flooding of Bangladesh with an insouciance callused by Darfur, Iraq, New Orleans. Round-the-clock news flashes grow corns on our consciences, as we assume we're hearing everything, although five million Congolese died in civil wars sandwiched between the Rwanda and Darfur genocides, with only negligible coverage.

But because my concept of democracy as the right to live widens beyond *Homo sapiens,* and because I knew a young orangutan when I was young, the death of his whole life-form will seem such a particularly genocidal tragedy to me—like that of chimps, the great whales, elephants, and other megafauna I've been privileged to encounter on occasion—that I want my personal extinction to precede theirs. It will anyway, but I don't want to live in a world drained of elephants and sharks and whales, where my grief over how we've treated captive apes is dwarfed when the last wild carcasses are concealed under the loads on log trucks, to be cooked as bushmeat in Kinshasa's slums. Better to be already simmering in the soil myself.

A throttled elegy wells in me when I notice a box turtle attempting to cross the road, or a venerable basswood tree (Thoreau's favorite species) slated for the chainsaw. We still treat deeds to landscape like stock certificates stacked in a safe-deposit box ready for sale, not blueprints of slivers of Creation potentially tinctured with reverence, as for a church's architecture, or simply with an embracing pity akin to reverence for all the living things that are rooted there. It's not far-fetched, however, to conceive of a sea change in how we allocate our pity and reverence in the years ahead. I believe we may tease out definitions of energy that conjure why my feeling content to welcome death is not delusional or contradictory to the catalyzing magic of waking to life in the first place. The very chalk on a blackboard sparks across the millennia like firefly light, being itself the relic of vivid life fed the lime we write with by surging riffles. And because not just vertebrates, I suspect, are galvanized by springing alive and taking form, a measure of ecstasy may also have flowed through the chalk. That's what I aspire to—in starting over, with salt in what passes for my mouth—assuming my first organisms are marine, in the sunlit ocean, mother of life. I still stoop, when walking in the woods, to stick a blue jay's feather in my hatband for a touch of élan. And I can remember what trails I climbed, in Greece, France, Uganda, or Belize, on legs routinely enjoying eighty-block walks in Manhattan, or a prance across the Brooklyn Bridge. I'd inherited my father's smile, which won me admittance to places I'd be no good in now, hitchhiking exhausting distances to visit subsistence tribes, or canning Chicken of the Sea tuna in San Diego. I'm not one who regrets defaulting on the chances of his youth now that he gets quite breathless on an upgrade.

We limp, hobble, feel our hams and sockets, but with an open schedule, sleeping as we wish, write a letter, or maybe think of writing others, crabbing a bit at people, then casually apologize, because when you're in your seventies whatever you may have said carries little real weight anyhow. I'm surrounded by a thousand books I've liked or loved but can't read them in a sustained manner with my one functioning eye, just register the titles enriching the shelves like a personal history. The riddles of light and darkness, of triangulating a working knowledge of where I am from objects I recognize and who I'm encountering from shifting contexts, is like looking at faces and landmarks underwater, but pokey and shuffling, not swimmingly graceful—improvising as in childhood.

I had humdrum disappointments, unstable emotional spells, but never in company or geography not of my choosing. No wasteland years or dishonorable discharges. I am fitfully wistful about an abortion that occurred circa 1970, but the circumstances surrounding it make me less regretful than I'd feel otherwise. Yet might this have been the son I miss? Missing him spurred me to teach better, attentive to a wide variety of college students, but rarely to envy my friends their actual sons, as these grew up. Nor did the world need me cloned. And I don't regard my two small grandsons as ego-stuffers or an apparatus for immortality. They will exercise their ingenuity under conditions beyond what we can accurately imagine and with mores under siege. Besides, an undue focus on one's own ancestors or descendants is unseemly if it demeans the poignancy marbled nearly everywhere, the dimensions of Creation, within the breadth of whose aspects our genes are infinitesimally superfluous. On the other hand, I love my grandchildren and even remember that although until middle age I paid minimal heed to my grandparents' family history (the fact that one granddad had been born in a sod hut on a Kansas homestead and the other by 1900 was logging old-growth forests in the Pacific Northwest), I, born in Manhattan to urban parents, leapfrogged back past what they were interested in to travel repeatedly to Alaska and adjoining terrain, once trailing a grizzly unarmed so closely that water was still trickling into the prints of its paws.

To me, mine was an independent tack, though nothing next to the jujitsu that may be required, as so many frames of reference become eclipsed and no form of government lately appears to operate as advertised. Drabber in air, water, and biodiversity, we may be sliding toward a planetary Lou Gehrig's disease. How many strands can you tear from a web before its tatters break? Where I live, bee trees, meadowlarks, and wood turtles, to begin with, are gone. Our push to lock in an extraordinary human longevity at the same time as countless other life spans are collapsing has produced a dicey situation; or so common sense would suggest. Such a loss of proportionality could initiate a crash in communal empathy of many kinds. Will only mavericks at first be able to detect the detonations of an ecological avalanche that will impact not just our food and water but, as all wars do, religion? Think fascism and Catholicism. Judeo-Christianity is both so people-centric as to be mute in an extinction crisis yet always ready to jettison piles of people if they don't fit the profile of the Chosen ones, and as Dhaka drowns will doubtless do this again—a scene I prefer to exit ahead of.

I saw Denali and Agrigento and, like my father before me, the Cairene and Mayan pyramids. Also a traveler, he believed that to live is to see, but died thirty years before my mother, although you'd never guess so from the peas-in-a-pod pairing of their wedding pictures. Managing the balancing act of an addiction to the adventure of travel without becoming emotionally homeless and promiscuous requires a grounding in "same-old, same-old" love, too, such as mine for the apple tree the hummingbirds nest in every spring, while toads sing from the beaver pond, and for the faces I've shared my Vermont landscape with for decades. Electric faces, sparking memories, for which I love its minor mountains more than Alaska's major specimens, and New York City above Rome. Besides, I want the company of a dog, which is not possible when vagabonding from Kampala to Beijing or Bombay. So we sit down, me and the dog—her eyes are clouding over, her hearing getting cottony—preparing for swan songs and, remembering the pye-dogs of India, the fice-dogs of Appalachia, I tell her she was lucky in this incarnation, as was I. I have quit locking the back door at night, so she can safely push it open if I don't wake up next morning. I walk as if I'm wading; you know how old people do, rotating their hips as if thigh-deep in viscidity but beetling along in a wobbly straight line, without much energy for digression.

I'm not impatient with the weather, but grateful for it; not worried about the admirable oak limb overhanging my rooftree, because I won't be here when it falls. I sign off letters "God bless" as frequently as not, though more as a sort of fumbly embrace of everybody, to wish us luck, than a conversion to a deity who either would or could. Yet love unfolds, even as my wattage sinks and I'm bent over, nodding off. Music I will miss—discrete, perfectible, and a constant companion for the past sixty years, going back to the era of the heart-breaking phrase "tickle the ivories." If heaven is on earth, it's hardly contradictory to love sunshine chevroned with tree shadows in the woods, plus the low-slung moss, a tiger-colored butterfly, the Tiffany glitter of a spider's web after a gust of rain, and the yellow-spotted salamander emerging from under the nearest log—yet feel content to die.

In the prime of life that sentiment would be absurd. When my stutter became particularly a problem, I grew hyper-alert to body language, all eyes. Or if my eyes developed difficulties, I concentrated on the acuities of memory, the antennae of hearing. Nowadays, however, I'll turn my ankle, stumbling, dim-sighted, running out of breath and therefore curiosity in the woods. I'm ready for somebody else to take a turn at doing the observing and let me join that black-and-yellow salamander under the log to wait out the emergencies. Some bug or slug (which after all is merely an escargot minus the shell) will have intercepted a speck of what was previously me, decaying and on the way to the Atlantic via a trickle toward a brook or creek, and the salamander gobbled up that humble blend of gastropod and me. Under a similar log may live a timid, coral-bellied, eight-inch snake (*Storeria*, also a favorite genus of mine), which could perform the same service, hastening the recycling process of keeping me current, so to speak.

As lightning lathes down one tree but not another, too many of my friends have already died—one from leukemia way back in grammar school; the next electrocuted at about fifteen; then a boy who cooked poison mushrooms the year we graduated from college. Others of course contracted throat or testicular cancer in middle age, or mutely keeled over at their desks after lunch high up in an office building, or tucked in bed at home. A woman I know found first her husband and later a lover dead that way. Maybe some were obese and smoked like a chimney, but others no. My father, when he learned he had gut cancer, took to sailing his one-man sloop off Maine as though the prospect of eventually joining the sea may have appealed to his agnostic sensibility, as it does (sans drowning) to my pantheistic streak. Slugs turn from blush-pink to black speckled with white during the course of their lives. And black when splotched with white, as on a panda, is an ambiguous coloration: quite cheery till you look more closely, when it can appear rather saddening or even tear-stained, Janus-faced, like a night-and-day mask, or camouflage for forests that no longer exist because they have been logged. The Grim Reaper is often depicted in Halloween parades as black and white because our bones too, under the sallowest skin or in the darkness of the grave, are going to whiten.

"Death, be not proud," John Donne famously pronounced during an unmedicated epoch that personalized death as, with our anesthetics, we seldom do. Or swing a scythe all day, cutting hay, or wring the necks of the chickens we eat, and visualize funereal specters stationed by the bedposts to crook a finger and lead us to the Underworld when "our time" has come. Haunted houses don't feature in the neighborhood sprawl of many children nowadays, nor does the resident granny who may fall asleep while babysitting and not wake up. We've got nursing homes for the likes of her and antibiotics for kids who catch what used to be called "their death of cold." And if you've loved life, are grateful for the bonus years that pharmaceuticals have provided, and believe that heaven is on earth, why would you suppose a void is going to follow all that energy? Gazing out the window, I see nothing but motion, high and low—scudding clouds, swinging leaves, right down to the millipedes (if I step outside) seething in the soil. Death, be not proud. Plant me when I die so that I can seethe with them too.

ENDGAME

*T*he fox family we fed last year must have killed our weasels. First, the vixen had come alone at dusk that spring, haggard from the nutritional demands of making milk, simply to finish any kibble left in the dog's dish. The dog was of course offended, but impotent in the house by evening, especially after we began putting out extra food, as the interloper decided not to mind being watched. Besides replenishing her strength, she might carry mouthfuls to her cubs, denned underneath the neighbors' fallen-down barn, or bury some for a rainy day under the high-bush cranberries nearby. Soon she looked less emaciated, even though shedding her red winter coat for summer made her dark-bluish skin show through. The male never chose to approach by daylight, but the amount eaten sometimes indicated he may have after nightfall.

When the pups were three months old, she permitted them to watch her eat, sitting twenty yards away, and brought them helpings, later letting them eat from the dish themselves, by order of a five-part hierarchy, interrupted by her own favoritism. If the dog barked, a car passed, or I emerged, she'd squall repeated warnings, teaching them to scramble down into the alder thickets by the stream and then the spruce woods, uphill, beyond. Our Belgian shepherd was too fat and old to catch them once they'd reached their impudent stage, but I think may have spared one or two at earlier moments, when we appeared while the vixen was training them to hunt voles in the field and she squalled that doe-like alarm. They'd reached the birches and firs to hide, but certain whimpers sounded, as if the dog—herself female—had overtaken but not bitten them, from a bitch's instinct not to kill puppies; and the fox immediately swung back as a decoy, loudly crying her squall.

They learned to pounce on grasshoppers, nip blueberries, cut off a foolish chipmunk, or grab a writhing garter snake. It was a quicksilver treat to watch the five tumble and interact, homing in on a woodchuck's scent, and as they matured, they'd taunt the dog with their agility, as a final insult hauling her dish out toward the trees. But I needed to lay down sheets of roofing tin near their hibernaculum for the remainder of my colony of snakes to hide underneath, and regretted gradually losing the family of woodchucks who for generations had lived under our own raffish barn and defunct chicken coop. Snowshoe hares, too, vanished from the vicinity, as well as our pair of weasels, which meant that last winter mice built nests among my socks and books, gnawed a sweater and a poetry anthology. I'd see their elfin figures dart from the plumbing under the bathtub to get into the kitchen. And to seed poison about only complicated matters because the dying mice, mad with thirst, jumped into the toilet and clogged it up.

I like the fact that in this hundred-year-old house two miles off a paved road in northern Vermont, the mice are still the native white-footed species, with long white tummies and acrobatic tails, using my dwelling as they might a cleft in a ledge or a hollow maple tree—not European house mice, such as infested American towns and cities centuries ago. Nor has a Norwegian house rat ever shown up in my forty years here. The gauntlet of woods must be impossible to run; even stray cats don't make it anymore. The coyotes, the fishers, the bobcats would grab them, not to mention Mr. or Mrs. Fox, who themselves would furnish a meal for the coyote pair, if either were ambushed and cornered by them while foraging. That's perhaps the main reason why the vixen and her mate denned among the abandoned farm buildings of my neighbor and me, ceding the coyote family—whose howling from the ridgetop I enjoyed nightly when I wasn't feeding her—a hunting territory concentric to hers. The coyotes, in other words, also munched rabbits, woodchucks, meadow mice, deer mice, jumping mice, and freelance miscellaneous booty like frogs and fallen apples and musk-rats, but never being tolerated as close to a house as a fox, they accepted the concentric arrangement around our farmsteads of necessity, allow-ing the fox a safety zone to raise her pups. Otherwise, not the quick, canny adults but the callow cubs would be carried back to fatten young coyotes. Their cowering, whimpering, wouldn't help them, as it had with my shepherd dog.

I don't know but what she lost one or two blunderers to predation by her larger kin even so. In any case, after that litter dispersed, our vixen sited her new den this spring down close to the asphalt, where there are more houses, garbage, domestic critters, and roadkills, but another crucial zone exists where coyotes are loath to go. The price was losing at least one pup to a car, but likely worth it, since her risky visits—undulating up our mountain notch alone through the woods (I might meet her on my walks), to wolf down whatever was set out for her, usually a mouse, after I'd switched from poison to traps—became infrequent. Red squirrels also have boldly been entering the house, more intrusive than any mouse. One woke me recently by hopping onto the arm of my chair and tapping me on the shoulder when I was napping, to see if maybe I was dead. I'd been shouting at him for stealing from the cupboards, so he wasn't begging to be fed. The fox had kept him and his ilk afraid of being waylaid on the ground if they left their big oak trees; and no fierce long-tailed weasel has appeared yet to challenge them, it seems. Close to the house he's safe from the main squirrel-hunter: the ten-pound weasel-relative called the fisher (sable, to a furrier), which likes deep woods. And the slow raccoon, nosing around omnivorously, now that the vixen's aggressive presence is gone, is no threat to squirrels, which as tree-climbers can coexist with coyotes—with people as well, because they seldom anger us; strike us as personable instead.

I miss that vulpine panache, however, that pouncer-on-a-grouse, though coyotes have more glamour, if you can see as well as hear them, which I do occasionally. Answering my harmonica, they brought their pups down off the ridge to observe my dog and me and bark a little at the two of us from a distance of thirty yards. Startling the family another time, I made a pup drop a fawn's head it was carrying. June is when they're that clumsy, but also ebullient enough to answer barred owls' calls, or ravens', or, in yapping, attempt to howl. When I acquired this property there were no coyotes, or fishers either. The most thrilling nocturnal sounds were the bobcats' screams, which are rarer nowadays because the fishers—at half the weight—are adept at catching the bobcats' smaller prey, while the coyotes—about twice as large, and especially working as a pack—do better with meat on the upper end, like a snowbound deer—whereas the poor bobcat is solitary year-round, except to breed. Indeed, it may arduously snag a deer in a drift, but have this stolen from it by a pack during the starving months; then the next week, yet again. Meanwhile, the fishers are keeping trim on porcupines, which no other predator around here has mastered the knack of killing, or else by monkeying in the trees after squirrels.

The squirrel that woke me up to see whether I was dead then chewed through a peanut-butter lid, and stole a slice of raisin bread. There's a pair of goshawks I'm hoping will catch him, if he carries his overconfidence out of doors. Hunters keep our bears from that sin, though they become bulimic, fattening on apples in the fall, and vomit under the trees. I've seen a moose, too, stop cautiously at the side of the road, look right and left for traffic before crossing, then sniff my car, if it's parked in the drive, for clues to its nature, but without lowering his rack of antlers to whack it, as you'd think he might want to. Instead, like the bears, he soon climbs the ridge for safety's sake. That red squirrel, by contrast, *wants* this house, like a hollow tree. He defecated on my toilet lid the other day; and leapt against the wall to knock down an African mask hanging there, as if to rid the place of all of its human imagery.

The next town is slated to double in populace soon, due to the construction of a new ski resort. In the jumpy atmosphere prevailing nationwide, which is both hyper-mercenary and health-obsessive, people regard real estate as more than just a dwelling or a spot to park their assets. They want a dab of garden, several healthy trees, with birds at a feeder, a breeze, and grass to mow and put lawn furniture on, which is a fancy way of lying on the ground. They want low blood pressure, no acid reflux or palpitations—longevity. Politically, in the grabby phase we're living through, this impulse doesn't take the form of widely wanting to preserve nature as a public domain. Rather, we'll tend to hire a backhoe to dig a private mini-pond and plant nursery vegetation, after chopping down whatever had grown up naturally in the vicinity before. People want muscle cars and a swatch of land to play designer on. A guy next door to where I used to live simply poisoned all of "his" frogs in the pond outside his house because they sang when they mated in the spring. He had thought he was buying silent water.

Several big-box stores are being installed on a road paralleling the Canadian border, a couple of dozen miles north of me. So that intervening stretch of farm and logging land will gradually fill up, too, and wind turbines perhaps crenellate the ridge lines—a change I wince at. Yet much more flabbergasting alterations are in store—the mowing of parts of Amazonia to grow ethanol; the melting of the poles; the desertification of more of Africa (and if you've already seen famine there, as I have, the idea of growing corn in Iowa to drive cars is obscene). Dumbfounded, conservationists are hard put to express the scope of what they feel. John Muir could save Yosemite Valley and

Rachel Carson reduce the use of DDT with eloquent polemics—but those were cap-gun battles compared to the tsunamic changes now under way. A hundred and fifty years ago, with the Great West still awaiting settlement, Thoreau proposed in an essay called "Huckleberries" that each American town should set aside a square mile or more to coexist primevally with whatever people chose to build on the rest. But what formulation could Thoreau—or Aldo Leopold, John Muir, Rachel Carson—muster in this steamroller era to divert the avalanche of crashing catastrophes? Being aghast doesn't do it.

Not just honeybees and chimpanzees are disappearing, but incomprehensibly innumerable species that have never been discovered at all. Words are needed that surpass the wails, the rage, when temples are destroyed, because this is not Yosemite Valley—this is not a cathedral whose pristine views Muir could defend, knowing he personally had all of Alaska's wilderness behind him to retreat to if he lost. Muir loved glaciers and on his hikes "discovered" some. How would he find voice for his grief at what is happening to them now? "In wildness is the preservation of the world," Thoreau famously said; and vastnesses of it existed on most of the continents then. Yet not mere cathedrals but maybe the godhead is now being destroyed. Life is an ecstasy, Emerson stipulated in his essay called "The Method of Nature"; and in American Transcendentalism heaven is on earth—there need be none further. However, if we are stripping, dicing, and deforming the landscapes, souring the oceans, and sooting the skies, we are not just wiping out cheetahs and codfish, blue whales and sandalwood trees, but undermining our very lives and afterlives.

There seems to be no baseline, as if we're in free fall. And Conservation, which used to embrace national parks and forests, wild rivers, and the like, has blurred into a new term, Environmentalism, concerned with petroleum efficiency, groundwater quality, ozone statistics, sea-level maintenance, tradewinds pollution, recycling yardsticks, climate stabilization. People want mobility, yet a hideaway "off the grid," and to have the heart muscles of a hunter-gatherer, attained in a gym, though practically living in cyberspace, but still touch the earthly verities through yoga. Meanwhile, the pace and enormity of destruction is paralyzing, as is our general indifference. The so-called robber barons, in their epoch, also had the advantage of public indifference, but theirs was an era of plenty, of surplus. Always before, we've had mountains unnamed, spare reaches of prairie untilled, oceans hardly fished, scarcely sailed. I'm hearing, however, a continuous down-curve in the volume of birdsong and its diversity every spring. Wood thrushes, like wood turtles, are rarer now. The "bittern boometh," as Chaucer said, but for how long?

The visionary poet Robinson Jeffers enunciated the situation bluntly, describing mankind in poems including "The Broken Balance" (1929) as "a sick microbe," "a deformed ape," a "spreading fungus . . . slime-threads and spores," "a botched experiment that has run wild and ought to be stopped." For many decades I've been slow to agree with him, feeling of course more empathy for people than for fungal spores or microbes—but a botched experiment, yes, I fear so. And I think by this point, Thoreau, Emerson, Aldo Leopold, Rachel Carson, Herman Melville, John Muir, would too. The word "Creation" was in common parlance throughout my young years, meaning what human innovation had not brought into being but, rather, was provided for us to start with, either by a "man upstairs" or by eons of vitality evolving before; and people, although spendthrift, felt somehow that they were embedded within it. An inherent awe or mystery was taken for granted, whereas now, I suspect, the metaphor of cancer will become commonplace, as we eat our planet's skin and soil its liquids, like a metastasizing disease. Another visionary writer, Edward Abbey, put it well, in 1970, for the new century: "We are none of us good enough for the world we have."

Will those wind-farm turbines expropriating the mountaintops wind up as a sort of Easter Island, end-of-a-civilization spectacle? "Where do the birds land when they migrate? Where are the butterflies and bats allowed to fly?" my grandmother might have asked, if confronted by our contemporary spaghetti sprawl, or the fizz of electronics facilitating the interior monologues we carry on together in a solipsism so complete it appears to eclipse the whole of the out-of-doors. Hurricane-insurance premiums do register a bit more on us than our actual demolition of habitat, although no organized religion has ever countenanced such wholesale obliteration of nature. The work of God was assumed to be a source of jubilation (as Job was told) and usually depicted in the arts by rhapsody, with appropriate obeisances to the scary side. Wildfires and mud slides will register as well, and any pandemic that breaks out of a blitzed rain forest, any pelagic thermal somersault, or crash in fish stocks—but not the loss of galaxies of less utilitarian creatures, the multiple varieties of greenery, the timbre of countless noises we've lived with for millennia—as society emigrates indoors and Creation becomes a graphic.

Are we kneecapping ourselves? Would Wordsworth, Frost, Turgenev, feel not just glassed-in and deracinated but amputated? Would Conrad and Melville have enjoyed the work on a container ship? Bird-watcher populations grow, however, as bird numbers fall, with richer folk targeting their travel to Bhutan or Costa Rica, poorer ones tacking up more feeders for the mourning doves and nuthatches that hang around. We do have a tuning fork in us that continues to vibrate to the ocean's susurrations and contrapuntal thump—to the seasons' scented swell, with birdcall ebullience and the amphibians chiming in. Quite apart from any considerations of groceries, joy blossoms for us in the sunshine, as photosynthesis does in plants. To see the curly glint of spindrift on surf, the greenly vivid pictography of moss on boulders underneath a hemlock's boughs, may make it sprout.

But why? We don't eat moss or phoebes or spindrift. And the question of delight shouldn't be moot. What deflects us from a deterministic focus solely upon consume-or-be-consumed? The magic of our retinas, eardrums, and nostrils anchors us in equanimity besides feeding us. With nature mostly shelved, can iPods do it? Nature has lent me a lifetime of flotation, to the point where I can gaze at the mountain across the way from my house that I will never climb again because of old age, and feel so thoroughly a part of it I'm not even bothered by this. Like the hawks' guano, I'm always up there.

But a penalty of an ecological education "is that one lives alone in a world of wounds," as Aldo Leopold remarked. When John Muir and Edward Abbey lost their major conservation battles, dams were constructed that they didn't want, drowning cathedral valleys (Hetch Hetchy and Glen Canyon, respectively). In other words, such campaigns could then be discrete, when nature seemed quite ubiquitous and people might still carry a rabbit's foot or split a chicken's wishbone to forecast their luck. Rivers sculpted the prairie's roll, dusk mediated the day's close. Now dusk is becoming irrelevant, in an electric tempo of 24/7, without that hour of modulation. And half the problem is that each of us notices change only by the micro-horizon of what we ourselves have witnessed. Our childhood wistfulness relates to a particular meadow with larks and bobolinks, paved over; a shoreline where terns nested, blistered instead with McMansions; a Victorian residence where cliff swallows fledged their young from mud gourds under the eaves that has been leveled for condos. The countryside we pedaled into couldn't be reached by a child on a bike nowadays, and yet this memory is so personal it may not coalesce into a larger sense of crisis.

Born in 1932, when I got my license I drove the length of Route 66 to California in a Model A Ford. But my grandfather had been born in a sod hut in central Kansas, his father a Shiloh veteran and homesteader who had rolled there by covered wagon. What *he* saw of buffalo, Indians, and lobos cannot be reconstructed. I watch maples bloom, gulls dive for porgies at the beach, and contribute money to save a remnant of the Everglades, or gaze into my dog's woodsy eyes for a glimpse of perhaps what the lobos knew, if through his more recent ancestry he hasn't been clipped like a golf green. The punch of *Silent Spring* has spraddled out to cover a multitude of toxins and settings, and none of them a worse threat to some of our best birdsong than the hamburger industry's grinding up of subtropical forests. Fifty-five years ago in the Ringling Bros. and Barnum & Bailey Circus, I took care of Sumatran, Siberian, and Bengal tigers, an orangutan, a rhinoceros, a hippopotamus, and other now-endangered animals, with no idea that within my own lifetime they would all represent relic gene pools, severely guarded in the wild, or exhibited in imitation jungles, rather than simply geographical curiosities caged in iron wagons. At the New York World's Fair in 1939, my father had installed me in a wonderfully swaying howdah on an Indian elephant at Frank Buck's Bring-Em-Back-Alive pavilion; and here I was, in 1952, in the constant presence of a herd of twenty-four. They and the red-assed, blue-cheeked mandrill were not rarities either, but supposedly commonplace in exotic corners of this inexhaustible planet that, in adulthood, you could visit—and not only if you were rich. Just ship out as a merchant seaman and jump off in Bombay or Mombasa. Dark-skinned peoples who hadn't been industrialized surely still lived as neighbors to parrots, boas, monkeys, and chimps.

As a script, this is eclipsed, except for the fanciest ecotours; and as our democracy crumbles at the edges, the jitters have precipitated a kind of land rush, quirky and behind the curve. If a bubble has popped and they've scored some severance pay or downsized wherewithal, agitated persons, after an itchy spell, with as many thousands to spend as they have fingers and toes, show up who want acreage. Here in Vermont, for such a price they can do that, if it's been logged over and grown to fireweed and goldenrod. They'll hire a bulldozer to consolidate the stones; then park a camper on a flat patch, dig a firepit in front for grilling steaks and roasting potatoes, with a card table and folding chairs underneath a tent fly they've put up as an awning, for the month of July. A padlocked cable across the entry tells you when they're not home.

"For the meltdown. My cyclone shelter," a bearded, fiftyish guy of temporarily Libertarian views explains with a grin, although he may shave the fur off when he gets another job. Probably guns are part of the fun—a Magnum or a 9 mm—because you can't shoot those off much or carry them concealed downcountry, as in Vermont. One reason we don't have lots of burglaries is that a thief should expect every householder to have firearms; and playacting at anarchy may be a pleasure for somebody furloughed to the woods from a career in government or the military. A mutual-fund manager's screen saver pictures his hut in moose habitat. "It came on a truck, but doesn't it look like Davy Crockett?"

After a divorce or bankruptcy, a sick leave that turned permanent, another burly, seedy-looking, bitter guy arrives seeking solitary absolution in a petri dish of rancid grievance and fantasy. One recent acquaintance, showing me his newly bought old farmhouse, pointed at the cellar door as we walked past: "I bet you're afraid I'm going to lock you down there?" I tactfully demurred, but became so, having thought, like most of us of a certain age, that I'd mastered the quick size-up. Does the person seem agreeable over coffee at the drugstore counter and picking up his mail at the post office, drive a plausible vehicle, and know the weather forecast? But the stuff that used to matter in a small town, like job history, paternal responsibility, loves lost or cowardly declined, drinking predilections and cancer scares, remains unknown. We had a bank holdup, and the rolling-gaited graybeard who fled was a lookalike on the security film to many of the mystery retirees round-about, who may have been fired before their pension plans were slated to kick in. His escape route, too, was not toward Canada or the inter-state but the spiderweb of dirt byways where such individuals live, with mini-mountains in between.

Regular dairy families are interspersed with them, haying in June, while pet geese wander down the roadside and sixty black-and-white Holsteins wait at the fence line to be let into the milking barn. And there are wholesome dropout couples making candles or ceramics for a livelihood, farming emus and alpacas, dyeing yarn or sewing leather, and schoolteaching or doing online accounting. Radiologists will soon be reading X-rays transmitted to them in sanctuaries such as this as well. I used to visit a neighbor's farm every evening, but economic shifts have hammered him so mercilessly that the region's future may be more typified by a stranger and his girlfriend in a yellow halter top and shorts who have bought a nearby field and hauled a self-storage container to it on a flatbed trailer they're living in. No windows or conveniences except for a globular black barbecue set and propane tank, and their belongings in fat black twist-top garbage bags stacked about. New Orleans was too low, the World Trade Center was too high, and our democracy has gone spavined. Knowing other people rusticating in vans, with a trailer lot in Florida and a dozen acres here, I haven't asked where they're from. We have hero firemen from 9/11 afflicted with a cough, and tinkering with a doodlebug, learning to split firewood and distinguish mountain ash from serviceberry shrubs. As in a Richard Scarry children's book, you might wonder what *are* all of the occupants of these housing units doing?

They could camp off-site in the state forest stretching behind my house and never be discovered, because most trippers seldom leave their cars. Southwest and uphill from me only half a mile is a ledgy outlook above where the local mother bobcat has her kittens every spring—a few hundred yards from the cleft in a pile of rocks in which, every other February, a mama bear gives birth to cubs. It is also where, on account of the spacious view over a pond and, further, undulating mountains, our Congregational clergyman chose to subject himself to an eighty-hour annual fast and "vision quest." But his hunger pinched him too badly to meditate properly, he said, so the next year he cut the fast to sixty hours, and in the third year to forty: whereupon he sought a transfer. Another man, a Roman Catholic unconnected to the minister, then picked the area of the scenic site to shoot himself, after being accused of sexually molesting a mute, paralytic nursing-home patient dying of Hodgkin's disease whom he was supposed to be caring for. He left both a death certificate already filled out and an apology for his girlfriend to find when she came back to their apartment from her own work, specifying his location; and she tied his belt around a tree at the spot, to mark her forgiveness. It's worth noting too, perhaps, that land is at such a premium, not just the bear, the bobcat, the clergyman, and the suicide have recently shared the vicinity of this ledge for important events. Catty-corner across a marshy brook and notch, yet remarkably close, as the ravens fly, is the ridge slope where the pair of coyotes raise their April pups—above but not far from a cow moose's June nursery bed, and ten flaps from the cliff face on which our ravens nest.

With wildlands shriveling and landscapes checkerboarded with ever more constricting improvisations—cleated like a football field—people tend to carom from Boise to Bangor. A beetle-browed CPA will look as headlong as Doc Holliday, his driver's license from a different state than his car's registration. At our chili stand, a heavy blonde divorcée has ricocheted from Lake Tahoe with her daughter, looking for the elixir of New England land, "to plant our roots." The owner serving them has arms freshly adorned with pastel tattoos, pink and blue, and he tells me he's likewise a newcomer. The pain of those procedures has been "therapy" for his grief at the brain damage his grown son has just suffered in an auto accident back home in Connecticut. The boy is in a coma, so he's sorry he's sunk his life savings into this crummy joint and can't be alongside him all the time. The tattoos aren't babe-and-anchor but psychedelic, as if inscribed by a technician kiting on drugs.

Which bushy whiskers are to fend off the frosts and the black-flies and which mask a man who used to juggle a multimillion-dollar budget but left a mess of broken partnerships behind? So few farmers are still actually afloat that many people dressed like farmers and driving pickups can't be—you need to glance in the back for a tool chest, tow chains, chain saw, or whatever. That fellow of indeterminate age who dawdles through the wash-dry cycle at the laundromat for an opportunity to chat with the lady who makes change could be a widower, or a genuine recluse, or a millionaire unwinding at his hideout for a week away from "Cancer Gulch" in the big city. Solitary self-medication, with the millennial refrain that "land values can only go up, right?" is very different from the back-to-the-landers of three or four decades ago, lacking the communal notion of reconstituting society, as the hippies once hoped to do. Today's mantras are crabbed, apprehensive, self-involved, as we shop around for tidy climates in gated selfishness, like a chameleon going from green to brown.

Public lands, public causes, suffer, as well as public life. But without being an optimist about the future, I still believe in the blitheness of private life. Foxfire and fireflies, or a loon's nervous giggle as it arrows overhead between two ponds, delight me. So do a woodcock's whickering, a grouse's drumming, for purposes of mating, and a toad's ethereal, extended trill, which, more than any single songbird's, seems like spring's angelic epitome—whereupon the male may clasp the female for many hours. And by late June the derisive coyotes will bring their pups down close to observe me and my dog, yapping disapprovingly so they can remember who to avoid henceforth—as do the raven parents.

The whole family flaps down in conjunction with a flying lesson for the fledglings to perch in a tree adjoining my house and indulge in a lot of censorious commentary.

My chimney swifts disappeared a quarter-century ago, and parula warblers more recently than that. But a few winter wrens, in reduced numbers, still sing as intricately as ever; and in the dappled sunlight or pewtery moonlight of the forest I'll notice a ghostly, loaf-shaped, two-foot dome of white stationed on a downed log, and wonder what it could be. Nothing white except mushrooms can survive a summer. Yet it turns out a diligent squirrel has piled poplar fluff into an orderly mass to pick through later for the tiny seeds, while watching out for a broad-winged hawk that would love to seize him. The dappled patterns of the sun's shafts bewitch me, then the pewtery moon, the barred owl's chow-house call—*Who-cooks-for- you, who-cooks-for-you-all*—and the toad's sustained, half-minute, thrilling song. (And would you claim his mate finds his proverbially jewel-like eyes less fetching than Shakespeare did?)

The bounty of wildflower colors and perfumes that magnetize bumblebees and butterflies to pollinate their plants elate us, too, although no utilitarian function is served in our case for either party, since we don't eat or propagate them, except that indirectly—bypassing Darwin—we employ bouquets for courtship and requesting coition, an odd connection, since they, the flowers, don't smell like sex. Why is their scent enticing to us as well as to insects who wish to implant eggs and grow larvae right at the source? A gift of chocolate to a woman has the logic of concentrated carbohydrates; diamonds a show of earning power; dancing demonstrates coordination and virility; clothing and accoutrements perhaps imply élan. But flowers? Besides promising a certain sensitivity to the gentler gender, they may correspond to our exuberance when gazing up at the majesty of inaccessible scenery. Then why such exhilaration at mountains too high to be hunted on?

Why these features unrelated to meat, or progeny, or proving who is the fittest? Until recently, people didn't wish to "conquer" peaks. Nor does some mechanistic evolutionary theory account for how entranced we are by sheets of falling water. Except perhaps in a salmon stream, they provide little protein, and interrupted subsistence travel. Nevertheless, like the thunder of surf, we drink in the roar. It calms us.

And why is camouflage so much lovelier than it needs to be? In terms of beauty, a cottontail's, a salamander's, a tiger's, or a python's—nature's designs—have it all over the most effective concealments military technicians have managed to devise. "Every natural fact is an emanation," as Emerson suggested: which may be the best explanation of any, because what prehistory pioneered or prefigured our sense of beauty? I don't believe we developed an aesthetic sensibility on a just-in-time basis for civilization to welcome Titian, Turner, Bach, and Mozart. Bone flutes and cave art have proven that. But autumn leaves aren't simply extraneous, like flowers, to our needs. They soon crisp into noisy litter that surely impeded hunting and augured the most grueling months of the year. So why do we admire—love—the fall colors, like thunderous sheets of leaping water of no practical benefit to us whatsoever, or a hermit thrush's solo fluting, or a modest monarch butterfly leaving the milkweed to flutter away with our good wishes toward Mexico? I doubt that we, the first Northerners to know where it goes, are the first who wished it well.

But what *did* inspire our sense of beauty? My hunch is that, like our intelligence, it's an outgrowth of a gradual refinement of existing rudiments in other creatures. Genome research and field studies are cumulatively documenting the intelligence angle. Joy in beauty will be harder to demonstrate except by an appeal to common sense. Do the species that wear the splendid plumage or coats of fur or superb scaly camouflage we admire not feel an equivalent ebullience at the sight of one another, too? Not merely lust or rivalry, in other words, but something of what Emerson expressed in his essay: that "ecstasy is the law and cause of nature." "Nature is a work of *ecstasy*," he added, the italics his. The idea that birdsong, toadsong, are a pleasure only to us strikes me as frankly absurd—or that turtles, for example, apart from appreciating one another's spots, don't gaze with gratification into a cerulean sky. As we spin in space, our joy may be a facet of the universal spate of energy which launched us all.

Not "designed" or anti-evolutionary, this theory, as Emerson put it, that "the power or genius of nature is ecstatic," is simply supplemental; and both Thoreau and he, as freelancers in Concord, accepted *On the Origin of Species* before Harvard's contemporary faculty did. Previous cultures of course had maintained a rapport, a crosscurrent telepathy, with other creatures for ages in order to hunt. Also because they served as sentinels and, beyond that, might be reverberant or versatile as spirits. During Christianity's defeat of pantheism, and then industrialization, the cleverness of wildlife and even animals' capacity to suffer were questioned, especially by mainstream science, as long as evidence to the contrary could be ignored. But in the meantime a kind of peasant grounding or savvy endured among people who truly knew about the outdoors. Even in the city, you'd see this older fellow feeling in Lower Manhattan among the immigrant folk who tended pigeon cotes on their rooftops and flew their flocks in mesmerizing circles— whirling glee—every evening after work, or sat with cats on the fire escapes like Continentals while the sun set.

The velvety rustle of fine fishing water, the dewy scent of a deer herd's favorite glen, are delights that connect to evolutionary logic. But not all that's delectable to us does: like frost flowers on a windowpane, more delicately shaped than real ones but signifying how the cold outside will bite. And when we present long-stems on Valentine's Day, are we sharing something deepseated in common with insects?

Indigo buntings, yellowthroats, black-and-white warblers give me a kick, as does the boar bear's hibernation site under a knob on the ridge facing my house, about halfway between where the ravens nest and the coyotes den. We're at close quarters here in this endgame on a pocket of state-owned forestland. His cave may be a twenty-minute climb away, above the twanging green frogs, the black-throated green warbler's *zoo zee zoo zoo zee,* the cedar waxwing's excited, lispy wheezing, the vixen's querying squall, the territorial owl, the white-throated sparrow's dauntless whistling, the wild turkey's gobbling.

Garter snakes are strongly, matriarchally communal, when you watch them, as are mice, with that bustling optimism that can make my tuning fork vibrate sympathetically, and deer, so often cheerful when together, too. As that vixen carried her young about in her mouth, how different were her feelings from a mama crocodile doing the same; or a human mother's protective hug? And when a drought ends in the desert and toothsome rains begin to fall, is just the pick-and-shovel prospector, with perhaps his donkey, happy? Do other living things only process the new conditions mechanistically? Or if antelope, bighorn sheep, cactus wrens, peccaries, and coatimundis experience a surge of gladness, does the chuckawalla, the sidewinder, the desert tortoise also? I'd certainly be sure about my toad, with his radiantly tremulous sweet song, his vocal sac bulging.

And will we wither like a girdled tree, as so many of our ancestral satisfactions are either dissolved or virtualized for indoor use? How integral are our origins? Can we simply demolish, atomize, dissipate them? What ground will we stand on? When medieval Christianity sidelined nature, it wasn't destroyed but remained as ubiquitous as bedrock. Absent that, is chaos a likely result? Worldwide, with a TV click we can view what used to be called the Levant, the Orient—drop in on Mandalay without a Suez passage—or the Amazon and Congo. Surf from a bell-voiced evangelist to pornography, or from a famine to Main Street obesity, from war footage to wastrel celebrity, in a quarter-minute. In this bubbling of images transmitted—architectural masterpieces, famous scenery—will the substance simmer and gradually evaporate, as in our easy chairs we think we've seen everything?

Vermont's endearingly recalcitrant tradition of aginners, with a three-legged milking stool strapped to their asses morning and night, talking sidewise unhelpfully to tourists, has been diluted into service industries like skiing, leafpeeping, B&B'ing. Logging and milking do go on, but even the guy with a bum left leg and busted cars in his dooryard may have a child who is deft with a computer and college-bound. Television has stripped the summer people of their mystique because where they travel and live during the winter is shown. Local kids can reasonably aspire to white-collar mobility if they stay in school, and the father can hope for a slot in a Florida trailer park if he wants a second home, too.

Worldwide, the question is room. Is there *room* for our multiplying leisure activities and longevity; the cruelty of our market economics; our implacable seining of both land and sea, lest anything escape the harvest, but otherwise fabricating a boxed reality of electronic graphics to live within? Nature has been our aquifer, siphoned from, and thus sinking, century upon century, seldom replenished even a little by anyone, not in the tropics, not in the arctic, the First World, the Third World, or our mind's eye. The electricity that powered our changes in direction and attention span is derived from fossil fuels, but scalds the present. Robinson Jeffers's 1929 simile of humankind as a vast spreading fungus of slime-threads and spores may be too laggard a blight. Blindly accelerating, we burn through entire galaxies of other life, unimaginably interlinked and unmapped—amputating ourselves from the rest of Creation, whether destroyed or still undestroyed. The risks are unfathomable. And if you don't find this tragic, open your heart.

THE GLUE IS GONE

*T*here's a flutter to society now, a tremulousness: young people studying yoga therapy after college instead of essaying graduate school, and their parents taking cooking very seriously, with Hummers in the suburbs but debt a major household topic, and several grandmothers I know unexpectedly becoming "primary caregivers" because of a divorce. The presidency seems to have gone quite slapstick, with another Texan mocking the two seaboards with an ill-considered, long-term foreign war. Yet our brains' functional areas, our pharmaceutical needs and desires, in fact our genome itself, all seem to have been mapped. We look scientifically as well as affectionately at children, we think we know so much about their stages of development (about our need for them, as well). From day care to an eventual hospice, their every twitch has been accounted for.

Yet we don't know why we are widely hated so, when America was created to be imitated and loved. Now we sometimes have to force people to love us—send in the SEALs. Our democracy, at the moment, requires other countries not to be democracies to service us with Saudi Arabian or Nigerian oil, sweatshop textiles, and electronic parts. We want authoritarian governments to preside over our suppliers, although incongruously we feel astonished at the phenomenon of "asymmetric warfare" by "those who hate our way of life." I once met a SEAL whose mother used to spit on the floor and make him lick it up, when he was small. Thus he became enthusiastic in his twenties about a career of going in for regime change. My graduating college students don't do that, but face a tougher vocational start than my own class did half a century ago. At our recent reunion, almost everyone who had functioned in a profession was glad to have practiced it when he did, not just because we were now grumpy old men but because the linkages have been dissolving in law, medicine, accounting, and so on, the ethics that, however imperfectly, have served as glue.

But death is easier, verging on the casual when we "go," with less of a mysterious or religious fulcrum to launch us up or down. It pinches when another friend departs, but his pain factor was well controlled and we don't think of him arraigned at St. Peter's Gate for a summation, and have a starkly shrinking assemblage of relatives that we acknowledge ourselves as kin to. More stratified by age and class, we're tethered to our beepers and screened e-mail instead. One hears a man with a cell phone talk first to his mistress, fobbing her off for another night, then to his wife, while fingering a loose pill from his breast pocket and swallowing it dry, screwing up his face at the bad taste. People had mistresses before, but didn't want such intimacies overheard: whereas, in this jam-packed, jittery world, who will you run into again?

We learn to skitter underneath the radar nearly everywhere, in evading rush-hour highway jams or airport security shakedowns, tax audits, or a siege of downsizing or insurance cancellations. Being alert to the conveniences of anonymity, we want the camera's eye to sweep over us without pausing, and the computer, if we're juggling plastic. We want our numbers to be in order—Social Security, passport, Zip and PIN, area code, driver's license, E-ZPass. Our divorce or retirement papers may be in a safe-deposit box, but otherwise most people trust in a backup hard drive somewhere to record their bank balance, etc., knowing hunger is for other continents. God's imprimatur has been upon us. Yet we do sense that seismic changes will be necessary to address the jumbled emergencies arising unpredictably, from watering the city of

Phoenix to salvaging Africa. We can map every yard of the Earth from space, telephone from moving cars, melt the shelves of Antarctica, sock a cancer radiologically, and get a hard-on from a pill. But it's all pell-mell, novelty as an addiction. Normality implies a permanence that people doubt, although their unease may be subterranean and perhaps they find the Lord on Sundays and tidy up.

How long does it last? What happens next? People of retirement age may be relieved to be able to indulge not only a taste for laziness but also for moral clarity. Now that they are spectators, they feel like themselves. I have a friend, a financial analyst who was on the seventy-something floor of the South Tower of the World Trade Center when it was struck on 9/11, and he survived simply by descending the stairs relentlessly, regardless of smoke, heat, debris, counter-instructions, and cries for help—hundreds of cries for help. As a black person, he found the experience not so different from the rest of his life. Having scrambled to that level of prosperity from the ghetto he'd grown up in, he had been ignoring cries for help from many directions for many, many years.

Hardball versus team play, agility versus duty, these contrasts jerk in constant tension in entrepreneurialism. But we feel even less ambiguity about our self-interest now that we are so mobile. We wonder what on earth to do. Conscience doesn't register, especially, but what is in our self-interest? Our democracy has overripened to the point where politicians poll us before they speak their minds, which creates no leaps of inspiration, but instead a circle of confusion. Agility isn't buoyancy, doesn't make us happy. This reliance on the common wisdom puts the cart before the horse because of course the theory was not that the people might somehow formulate enlightened national policies— rather that collectively, intuitively, they could best fathom who ought to be entrusted to do so.

Our responses are turning generic, too. When I see a bicyclist on the road, I'll swing a bit wider than I need to for safety's sake, not knowing who the person is but because I'm sympathetic in general to bicyclists, don't want them to feel bullied by the traffic. *In general* is how we tend to operate, in other words: in the plural, less and less in the presence of each other as flesh and blood because so much of our gabbing is done by keyboard or conversations bounced up to a satellite and back. This means we don't judge people by the honesty of their handshake or their visage anymore (Orwell's yardstick was that anybody at age fifty had earned the face he wore), or even a lifetime's reputation for integrity or its opposite, since we rarely shake hands or deal repeatedly for years with the same people now. We are zoned for housing, schooling, occupation, and so on, in hordes of interest groups, with friendship like a magic-lantern show—this one, that one hopscotching to another job on the geographic checkerboard. Nor is body language the lingua franca that it used to be. Like facial expressions, such subtleties may become vestigial, because of e-mail and what not, and go the way of the dodo bird. Nature doesn't squander energy on superfluous methods of communication.

During this transition toward more wooden faces, however, our cities' streets are sometimes incongruously transformed by domestic theater, with frowns of empathy or loverly exasperation—intimate, openhearted expressions—walking toward us on the sidewalk, not brusque at all, but inward, the feet of the person slowing as if in the kitchen or a bedroom, while he or she confides with a delicate succession of smiles into the cell phone. People are still used to the privacy of wired telephoning, and perhaps a world where you speak mostly face to face, still free to touch and kiss or poke and glare, and the voice, not deracinated by talking into ubiquitous answering machines, reverberates with a nuance of emotion the way that the eyes do. Will our voices, as well, shed spontaneity: the huskiness that betrays the tears on a friend's face across a thousand miles of phone lines and makes you automatically begin to mime your distress?

We're circling our wagons in private as well as public life—unilateralist in our gym regimens and quirky diets, in choosing pets as close companions, or soft pornography and bulky cars. Yet such a circle may add up to a zero, so that although church attendance is down, people shop around for a credo to believe in: not just Adam Smith's atavism or New Age narcissism, but an idealism marbled with faith and logic, and a limber minister to explain the details. Although I don't regard myself as dilettantish or unusually disoriented, within the past year I have received a Christmas communion wafer from Milan's cardinal in his duomo and held hands in a circle of Quakers in a library basement in Vermont. I've knelt in Methodist, Episcopal, and Pentecostal churches in America and watched Mother Teresa beatified by the pope on the steps of St. Peter's in Rome. Other visitors in these houses of worship, nibbling politely at the catechism and maneuvering in and out of half-remembered pews, also seemed to be sliding emotionally between aloofness and immersion in the happiness of being able to believe. Most of us have enough common sense to know there is some kind of God because joy wells in us perhaps analogously to photosynthesis in plants. The question is His location: inside, outdoors, in human guise, or every moist, synaptic charge? The serenity of devotion (and we do want to find that) seesaws with the allure of rebellious skepticism, plus our recent habit of surfing a surfeit of channels, abruptly moving on.

I liked the architecture of the pope's basilicas, the rationality of the Quakers, and getting hugged by the Pentecostals, with whom you could at least share a good, unshamefaced cry. But jubilation, like cynicism, can be a slippery slope, and when we switch from a fillip of reality TV or Oprah to smashmouth hockey or a soap opera or three shouting heads, our own tempo slides toward a more digital than biological mode. Professional football, for example, is edited to resemble animation, fast-forwarding the natural capacities of the body, to be replayed in further stylizations until it parallels the abbreviated summary of a fashion shoot or how speeches of potential import are diced into sound bites that aren't of a piece with real-time life. Thus, will we grow so addicted to speedy denouements and deadpan reactions that we appear like mutants to backward people who still blush on occasion or tentatively venture half a smile to express uncertainty, and part or tighten their lips in readable moods? Airport machines will scan our retinas for identification, and camera phones attempt to approximate the pungency of friendship. But will we see the picked-at nails, the pudge or scrawn, the tinge of jaundice, physical and spiritual, in the eyes that a betrayal may have left?

Advertisers, paying by the second to grab a handle on us, keep goosing the technology to crowd more images into our attention span, snapping us into and out of focus faster, as automation, on the other hand, makes us pause a dozen times a day for rote procedures that allow us clearance into our previously recorded thoughts and assets, as if we too have become decimalized. We are not digits, however, and have fuses that may blow if a disarticulation sets in. Cities have always worked because behind the imperturbability on the thoroughfares were expletives, kickbacks, impromptu generosity, and improvisation. If you had a fender bender or locked yourself out of your apartment at 1:00 A.M., a friend was going to pick up the telephone and take you in. It wasn't turned off for voice-mail screening. People cut and pasted a life out of the parade of freebies on the street. Experience wasn't virtualized from a memory bank of eclipsed realities, voyeuristic patinas, electronic simulations (although it's true that in the past half-century movies became more memorable for many people than their own humdrum lives). Information is fun, but this is a matter of distortion instead, while in the meantime our secularism powers our recent obsession with longevity, hypochondria, and the like. If there is no afterlife, by all means go for the Prozac, Viagra, Botox.

The instantaneous transmission of churned-up data may burst our eardrums for the natural to-and-fro of emphasis: what should or ought not to be in italics. Not just warfare has become asymmetric. Hired therapists lend an ear to our lamentations in place of friends, and domesticated animals are factory-farmed as squeeze toys, lovebugs. Chaos had been a frequent theme for artists since the buildup to the last world conflagration, but when the dizzy spiral turns centrifugal, it's not Chaplinesque or Dada anymore. It's not Salvador Dalí, Andy Warhol—we don't laugh or dither with Woody Allen and Federico Fellini, or wait with Samuel Beckett, because the social breakdown no longer seems to resemble the random sort of self-correcting physics of Brownian motion, a metaphor that democracy has depended on, by which deceits and incompetencies are nullified and made up for. During the 1960s three charismatic American leaders were shot and killed, yet even so, because we assumed the Kennedy and King assassinations were an outgrowth of evil, not chaos, they were bearable as tragedies, indeed bore some political fruit. The nuts and bolts of the system obliged us in that way, as, subsequently, when both Lyndon Johnson and Richard Nixon voluntarily withdrew from public life after hashing up their presidencies.

But we are seasick now. So many loyalties are being atomized, would a call for idealism permeate far through the anthill of Web sites? We are careening as a nation as if on tires that have lost their tread, bald tires that get no traction in a skid. What we have assumed about ourselves—what is ethical, perennial, versus the spam-jam sort of greedfest we are fearfully anticipating—is thrown into question. After bootstrapping an amalgam of immigrants from nearly everywhere into a superpower, we have incubated within ourselves an astonishingly dismissive attitude toward other cultures, other countries. Besides that, there's the blind faith that our melting pot will continue to cast up, whenever necessary, a leader of the stripe of Washington,

Lincoln, Franklin D. Roosevelt during any grave emergency. With the primal genius of the ballot box, popular wisdom, like some artesian force of rectitude, will well up and, balancing the alternatives, shove aside the run-of-the-hill blowhards, choosing the single individual who can coalesce a Constitution, gel a Union, or institute New Deal reforms that defuse a meltdown. You wouldn't have a Harding in the White House during the Cuban missile crisis, for instance, and George Marshall will be around, with the support of Harry Truman, if Europe ever needs to be rebuilt.

The trouble is we're not so sure right now. Democracy and dogfight capitalism, billed as free-market economics, have not been panning out for many countries, from Russia to Latin America. Remembering the galas of decolonization in Africa, the gaiety in various Soviet possessions as dictatorship fell, it's hard to square such hopes with crestfallen reality. We're not awash in AIDS orphans here; we're tinkering with boutique genetics, fertility drugs, and fretting about childhood obesity. But the constant question people ask in greeting one another—"How're you doin'?"—has acquired a provocative edge, as if any more equivocal reply than "Good!" might undermine the entire edifice of grinding commutes, multitasking laptops, exercise machinery that substitutes for being outdoors, and TV film loops winding extraneously through one's head. With sex becoming apoplectic, will we have room for global warming? Beyond that, as the king of beasts, don't we need the rest of them for scaffolding? Aren't we kneecapping ourselves, cutting our legs out from under us, by killing off everything else? What will our apishness do without grasslands and trees: spin like a monkey in a cage too small for it? Do we cradle house cats, loot coral reefs for tropical fish, and grow quaint rodents like gerbils because our family lives are splintering, or nature is shattering?

At what point—to take it to a tangent—will the churchgoer cease to regard human life as a diamond chip off the divinity, on a planet not half as green? Will we be so lonesome we finally grieve, when leafing through the tens of thousands of images of extinguished creatures, in their galaxies of shape and ritual and color—that magic roster of the dead? People will come back to the photo archives, marveling, and what will monotheism say? A society being transformed at warp speed is bound to become warped, with many of us withdrawing into a jumpy mode of privacy but the blowback of the new technologies piercing that privacy with unpredicted surveillance techniques.

Existentialism, fifty years and more ago, was kind of fun, when hedonism and pessimism still boasted of their novelty, plus the cachet of anti-fascism because the Nazis had just been unstrung. It was deemed intriguing, not frightening, that God was dead, by a movement less playful but more intellectual than Dada, after the First World War, had been. Nor was the planet speckled with hunger and civil hate like ringworm, as it is today. Decolonization was to be a straightforward process, and atheism perhaps a bit comparably liberating—whereas we would regard some peppy new idea that we are alone in the world now as adding to the delirium. With our twelve-step programs and church hopping, we're like characters in search of an Author (although meanwhile converting our trees into paper). Turn in the direction of your skid is the instruction for driving on ice. So that would mean more greed, more sex and scatterbrained flapping about, and ever-speedier transmission of data, until we slide to a halt—unless we discover that, by eviscerating nature, we have changed the rules unwittingly.

I do find at most of the houses of worship I've dropped in on an old-fashioned spirit of communing with the other parishioners that is comforting, nevertheless: of God as a current that radiates impartially through everybody, even those who try to block it off. But the days of walking to church, not driving, used to add cloudscapes, birds' songs, the weather's bite, or wildflowers and a milk snake rustling, all the panoply of green curvaceous terrain, with the grass springing up, the leaves doubling in size on the same May day when the toads, as well, begin to sing. Nature is spontaneous in that, although we know approximately what's going to happen, not when—whereas we're growing accustomed to an alternative universe of coy and spooling graphics, automated geometrics, cute-ified beasties, and a prismatic palette. If we are city folk we hear backfires rather than Hart Crane's "choiring" bridge strings, but even a farmer's tractor-altered ears may have quit distinguishing a doe's bark from a vixen's yap, when each is warning her young, or change-of-weather susurrations, running water burbling, blue jays hollering enviously at a box turtle beaking a slug. These may be the decades of unintended consequences, as when one drops a pair of eyeglasses in a field and the lenses bend the sunlight to ignite a wildfire. The droughts, floods, and hurricanes of global warming may amount to that, but as if to counterbalance our inattention to outdoor nature, the itch of indoor sex seems to have magnified into a kind of cultural epilepsy, not so much endocrinal as autistic and peevish. At the Solid Rock Gospel Church, middle-aged worshippers weep as inconsolably as if they had been virgins last night, submitting to a first Fall.

It used to be that if the town's professed freethinker happened to live next door to a local potentate of the Knights of Columbus, their families would share essentially the same ethics. But with such flux, and marriages in both camps turning squishy or ad hoc, freethinking produces, for example, a retired IBM executive I know who preaches under a hard-shell revival tent that the pernicious theory of evolution, if accepted, will cause rape to be legalized as conducive to "the survival of the fittest." All bets are off as to what your next-door neighbor may believe. Indeed, it's hard to guess who might in the longer run be fittest. Ideology, technology, and political entitlement groups have combined to create a blur. Nor would I want it otherwise; master races don't do well. And yet egalitarianism can foster myopia also, and dissolve our previous benchmarks of normalcy, integrity, without suggesting what should replace them. Will our grandchildren be able to look up on Google a tabulation of whether we lived honorably? Will it even remain a matter of pride that a given person died "an honest man"? Hometown opinion, when we had hometowns, though not infallible, assisted summings-up, which are startlingly less common now, as we mill about in search of an Author. Chaos isn't Groucho Marx or Sartre—it's scarier; and the masked anxiety inscribed on so many faces testifies to nerves being stretched past customary limits.

It's the velocity, however, that's worrisome, not some novel kink human nature has descended to. The cruelties of the ordinary school yard are simply broadcast worldwide as professional wrestling, while helicopter gunships give every Goliath a slingshot. Our moorings may have been rather diaphanous to begin with: the epicene Christ Child perched in the Madonna's lap; or the presumption that Jews were somehow singled out by God to be His own; or that there can be no other deity except Allah. But almost any canon might verge upon the suicidal now. The prophets who invented them lived in a tactile, fortuitous world under the rain and sun, with behemoths in the rivers, lions in the swales, and leprosy a commonplace along the donkey tracks. They used the stars for navigation, not just a minute's diversion, and grew or killed their food or bartered for it with those who did, and lived enveloped in the wind, the stony footing, the temperature's fluctuations, with kinship more important than a career. A matrix of mysteries then underpinned so much of religion—groundwater bubbling from a hot spring hieroglyphed with lichen, or sundogs, dust devils, a banshee gale, particular comets, the dentition of flames devouring a bush, a white peak concealed in the moon-drenched clouds, hallucinatory fumes seeping from the earth's geological navel, as at Delphi—that it must have seemed more approachable. People lived alongside sheep and goats, like an undertow from the prelapsarian currents of life, while watching massive flocks of birds, such as we can't conceive of, migrate overhead as the seasons changed. The manner of one's death hinged on more decisions than how much cholesterol one might have chosen to eat or what health insurance to pay for.

We don't quite know ourselves lately: whether in a pinch we would be brave or cowardly, kind beyond the routine courtesies or perhaps a quisling. People here don't die for a belief or even resign from their jobs on principle anymore, and social workers and the police are paid to assume some of the tasks a bystander's conscience or self-respect would once have accomplished. Their interventions oil our way so smoothly that I've seldom seen big-city faces look so brutal, or the crucifixes dangling in young women's cleavages appear more like a dollar sign. Our rancid politics, flotsam mores, the festival of covetousness being hawked by our pacesetters, our bathroom cabinets full of pills—none of these please us. But how to break through to each other? Go door-to-door like a Jehovah's Witness, telephone like a fund-raiser, inaugurate a blog? When the world was created, we weren't intended to be left alone with ourselves, according to both common sense and Noah. I was puzzled at first by the photographs of the Abu Ghraib atrocities because they reminded me of something, but I couldn't think what. Then I stumbled on a bout of TV wrestling—that staple of cable sports—and realized its pretend tortures were a burlesque of what American MPs had been inflicting on their Iraqi prisoners, which might have seemed natural to any Jesse Ventura fan. Will our loneliness, in other words, undo us? Who will we turn upon after we have finished hacking nature into slivers?

I believe in revelation and reformation—the tick of altruism versus the tock of avarice—and therefore that we can stabilize the biology of the planet once we have sickened of augering it, if our attention span and reverence for reality have not been virtualized. Too glib a pessimism would ignore how well Mozart is being performed—much better, infinitely more often, than he could possibly have dreamed. Ignore also the undiminished revulsion we continue to feel for suffering inflicted upon other people across the world; or the possibility that some gawky scientist may stumble sideways, twist his ankle, and, in falling, attain a plane of consciousness sufficiently out of kilter with the rest of us that he will plumb the question of our Author. (Or that the plants, when we have deciphered their methods of communication, will indirectly inform us of the same.) In the lasciviousness of a gun shop, men lean over the counter, thumbing their clips of fifty-dollar bills, and handle every barrel. Yet we focus more and more upon our children, as if to patch the fissuring forces. In politics we still do cherish the notion of a Jeffersonian continuum that says, "If this guy isn't doing any good, the next one will," though we wish now for a prenuptial agreement. The sheen is off war lovers and junk-stock entrepreneurs for the moment, and our celebrities have become so mercenary or chameleon that some are fading as folk heroes. The brimming, slithering ads in TV simulcolor continue to advocate a hall-of-mirrors redoubling of lifestyle choices, but the thrust seems a bit more claustrophobic.

Nature is fiber, moistened, interlaced, as sounds are, too, in the woods. Mammals can catch a warning of a hunter's stalk from the birds, or the reverse, and the whisk broom of the wind may instigate a thousand pollinations while making a few boughs sough. Yet we don't go in much nowadays for unaugmented sound, being accustomed to the modulations of engineers who titillate our ears with juiced acoustics that imply in their ubiquity, at least to me, the mush of chaos underneath. How long can fossil fuels sustain the buzz? And—engineering aside—are we really wired for it? Like painted apples in a supermarket bin, how red can we get? Will we gradually flatten, like the taste of corn and salmon, as our genes are trifled with? Or, like that car with tires with no tread, will we flip?

A COUNTRY FOR OLD MEN

*M*ore and more I've been concluding that by middle age most people in this country have sculpted their lives so they'll land about where they aimed to. The few who genuinely aspired to be rich or famous will probably become so for a spell, and those who wished for comfortable stability will find themselves with tradecraft competence, a web of friendships, grandchildren. The pleasures of versatility are their own reward for "well-rounded" folk, much like committing a couple of decades to the responsibilities of raising kids. You acquire traction and smile lines, with perhaps a well-grooved marital banter. Two by two, Noah's Ark is said to have been boarded— pairings being the easiest equation for many of us to handle, after all. And in an era of chaotic governance and commonplace mendacity and meltdown, the ambition to excel seems a bit stunted. Hoe your own row is more the message than grabbing for a brass ring, though self-expression can become as crosswise as the old children's game of pick-up sticks. While the country splits, compounding its fractures left to right, we accommodate ourselves to zany loads of debt, outland- ish overcrowding—trading trains for planes, for example, till both are drastically less fun and the roads alternatively an anthill, as blue-collar as well as white-collar families look for a hideaway, a second home.

In pick-up sticks the player plucks colored sticks singly from a pile of forty dropped helter-skelter on the table, down to the last, but without ever displacing any he isn't immediately after; if he does, the other player takes over, himself attempting to score. It resembles negotiating traffic, or the ballet of the sidewalk, threading throngs. Pedestrians finesse potential collisions by swinging slightly sideways, smiling distantly, parting the phalanx by body-language adjustments. There's nature; and then for phenomena like crowds, our second nature.

Homey imperatives such as steering kids through school, wage haggling, and good-neighborliness keep us from obsessing about what may be unraveling elsewhere: that plus our widened sense of travel— Florida, Calabria, Patagonia, Indonesia. There can be a knockabout anomie to shuttling around, and the density of our egos remains a problem, the clamoring holler to build McMansions. People wished to flaunt their first million, nibbling holes in any town, and our tribalism historically has wanted the other guy clamped underneath a heel, not just to stay in his own valley. Though tribalism lies in shards in this global epoch, the shards are still sharp, when you consider that nearly three thousand New Yorkers, dying in an act of war earlier in this decade, received a thousand times as much attention as the five million or so killed in Congo's wars.

A cross-stitch of mercenary and sexual greed has marked the opening of the new century, plus a flight toward cyber-reality, which is to say the notion that I think, therefore I am. Such an idea has seemed absurd to me since I was in college, taking a first philosophy course but spending part of each day outdoors, where the seethe of life still swamped merely thinking about it. It continues to, or every library or movie or chatroom screen. We are dragging our anchors, whatever they happen to be—landscape or literary, folklore or ethical. Dick Tracy, Natalie Wood, and Babe Ruth morph into Sweeney Todd, Britney Spears, and Barry Bonds. The new fluidity, air-conditioned, unhinged from nature, cracks open opportunities for entrepreneurial idealism as well as greed, however, in response to rolling famines, flood zones, mud zones, and the scalped forests and subsiding aquifers. Youngish activism rather than rootless self-exploration. The dwindling contexts that we operate in—whether it's water tables, tree cover, religious deference, historical reference, family continuity—makes for a kind of Queen of Hearts croquet, where the wickets, balls, and mallets all dash around in goofy, friendly-fire exchange. When Biology eventually has her say it may no longer simply be something, like cancer, we fight against; there may be hell to pay; the gamble is how much we can destroy without triggering an abyss of consequences. Extinctions—do they matter more than aesthetically? A warming climate? We truly don't know what's about to become the bottom line of that. And will the damage remain as constrained as along an avalanche track, or be multiplex? You might as well ask Thomas Jefferson or Johnny Appleseed, outdoorsmen both. If they thereupon sniffed the wind and looked for birds—*What happened? Is no space left?*—and you showed them instead the marvels inside a digital box, would they feel reassured that democracy had worked?

It has in the sense that I don't know a lot of older Americans who didn't get just about what they genuinely sought. Most of course set the bar pretty low—from modesty, timidity, inconsistency, indifference— or else were pursuing normalcies like love and family, children, friends and sports, which good humor can obtain without one doing *too* well on exams or achieving the stratospheric business success that risks a Humpty Dumpty fall. Life is going to go okay when rapport serves as well as sleepless ambition and if the person can weather the occasional divorce or job loss. Indeed, we seem to be engineered for it, and our setting the bar customarily low explains why human nature, human history, don't significantly improve. Yet by not expecting much, most of us age with considerable contentment—I've been noticing lately at senior-center lunches and church suppers—and even die with a bit of a smile, as I remember was often the case during a year I worked in a morgue in my twenties. In that era I might hitchhike across the country with a $20 bill for emergencies tucked into my shoe, whereas half a century later, when in reality I go almost nowhere, I carry at least a thousand in cash in my wallet about this small town where I live.

Why? To bribe the Grim Reaper or maybe merely an EMT as a cushion against indignity? In theory it could purchase the freedom to flag down a taxi and hire a ride of a thousand miles, or enable me to give away tons of money impulsively (not that that's in the cards either). As your legs lose their spring, money becomes mobility, whether locally or to change the climate for a season. Money can lend woof to life's warp if the weeks grow monochromatic—greenbacks are "salad" once you have filled the freezer and the furnace or looked for tolerable old-age accommodations. Women with their own careers can move out comfortably on an exasperating husband, like men seeking an autumnal bachelorhood. Nearly any mother's son descends into a constricted level of activity before buying the farm, as the saying goes. However, people don't need to join the faithful minority who acknowledge a spiritual presence in their daily rounds to make life work for them. The sunrise blazes as trumpet-colored for the doubters, and nothing prevents them from swinging their young sons and daughters up to straddle their shoulders for the morning strut to school. They can smile up their sleeves at the absurdities of the workplace, as much as any churchgoer, and wind up rather like that particular grandparent one is especially fond of.

We've got the option of duplicating qualities we admired growing up, like the generosity of a certain teacher, the loyal, lifelong craftsmanship or professional affiliations of another. Balance tends toward moorage in a safe harbor—and perhaps that smile in old age on a gurney. I've seen famine in Africa, Asian poverty, deaths in my own family, but never regarded life as not worth living for mine or other species. In hardship we squint a while, but green and cerulean are the colors of the world and lift our spirits by and by, with energy the syrup of life—which is why I've loved cities so much, Cairo and

Calcutta as well as Paris and New York. Once we've abandoned the notion of channeling Elvis or Einstein to whittle a stance for ourselves, our quotient of contentment is likely to rise. I have public benches on Main Street to sit on or can walk around to the library, not to mention the county courthouse, where I sometimes rubberneck on trial days, observing the sorrowful mishaps individuals blunder into, imagining that maybe a lady wishes to see their private parts or that shoplifting wouldn't piss off a storekeeper. The parade-ground regimentation of the legal system after an arrest is dwarfed by the byzantine tangle of rituals regarding sex and property it regulates.

I was too afraid of women as a youngster to bumble into trouble by crossing forbidden boundaries. Before then, scared enough by the Sunday-school story of the boy Benjamin, in Genesis, chapter forty-four, ensnared because a "stolen" silver cup has been deliberately planted in his belongings, that I never committed the petty thefts of candy or whatnot my classmates did. But coveting was not a major problem for me. Nor did I later want a jumbo car or house. Cultivating anonymity was better for a writer whose bread and butter was asking questions and watching others inconspicuously. With a few exceptions the masterpieces I admired had not been written by authors of peacock fame. Publishing what I wrote and keeping it in print was my aim, which over the decades I managed to do—as, without feeling like a Pollyanna, I'm inclined to think that others, in different avenues, often parallel. Not so many put all of their eggs in one basket, but that quotient rivals mine. I rarely meet somebody over about thirty who has set his sights upon a goal so front and center that he might irreversibly fail. Instead we retool, "reinvent," ourselves. Like a bird twitching its wings or a fish its tail, we switch directions in order to upgrade our prospects. Engineers describe becoming marketing executives, science teachers turn to employment as corporate chemists (or vice versa), a backhoe operator is licensed for real estate appraisals, a truck driver puts on a trooper's uniform, an office manager launches a business of her own, pumping out proposals. My father recalibrated his legal career after being refused a partnership at the firm where he had worked his first ten years; and in my thirties I realized my aptitudes were better suited to essay writing, after publishing three early novels. Flexibility is the stuff of life. Life is an arc.

At those senior lunches, church suppers, midmorning diner confabs, I hear retirees chatting about the trajectory of their lives, deepening the smile lines they already have. Hindsight logic seems half the fun. Who would have guessed you'd end up selling clothes, or as a custom carpenter or court clerk? There's no exaggerating the role patience may play in living well, or wearing a coat of the proverbial many colors—bold caution and humorous solemnity. You've talked to children and to the military, yet sometimes held your tongue, except about McCarthyism and Guantanamo. Balderdash still wins votes for popinjays, but the lag period when an environmental rescue effort, for example, can be mounted has shrunk alarmingly, voiding the chances for a new president to put the glaciers and rain forests back together or reduce sea flooding, restore the vanished galaxies of species. We prefer a president who mirrors us—a lowbrow braggart when we're in that mood, or a gallant and humane man for World War II and the Marshall Plan. Our frame of mind does need repair, but that's been true for thousands of years.

Pudgy, we sit in the senior center occasionally recounting the deaths of our spouses, round robin, for solace. How one was trying to lift his legs off the bed when the embolism took him—or a woman's heart failure, starting on the toilet, that crumpled her at the sink—and my mother, a long-term stroke victim trying to speak, whose eyes seemed to beg for death, after she could no longer swallow without choking. But was she possibly asking something else?—she wasn't able to write. Agewise, we may all be in the same boat, and yet a healthy sprinkling

of us have wrinkle lines denoting repose: not chewing over griev-
ances or kicking ass, even our own. Instead, we enjoyed a good run
and now could be an advertisement for life's beneficence, if the word
doesn't mean you can't also die of thirst in the desert. You might, but
we exerted ourselves not to.

Doing what comes naturally should prevent your children from
feeling estranged even if at some point you did get divorced; and keep
you from beaching broke on the shoals of old age, unless you never
shed a dice-or-drink addiction; and dissolve some of your midlife
mortgage anxiety. Paying out mostly balances out, and the kids who
ought to land in college eventually make it there. I believed in theory
that character is fate but have been surprised a bit, firsthand. Not to
find that hustlers beat nice guys, but that it doesn't matter; they come
a cropper, as you can read like newsprint in their faces; the length of
life unstrings them. I can go to an Ivy League alumni reunion and
meet posh fund managers who either wish they had pursued a degree
in ornithology instead of finance or are fretting about a tax shelter
gone gravely awry, not to mention a painful mismarriage. An auditor
disqualified the shelter and a judge is divvying up their assets as if to
provide for their stepchildren as well as the wife: is *that* fair? Although
grads at the Ivy gathering got a head start over nine-tenths of the folks
at the senior-center lunch, long before their seventh decade the effects
of early privilege had petered out, at least according to the emanations
of contentment versus discontent at each location. George Orwell's
last notebook jotting observed that "at 50, everyone has the face he
deserves." (Sadly, he didn't make it to that age.) And I tend to agree,
especially if you advance the criterion to the white-hair phase, when
a thousand accumulating decisions at first defined and then achieved
our goals. If subliminally we wanted to be couch potatoes, we are—or
exercised a real green thumb, cooked delicious pasta, and mastered
the organ in the corner church. Perhaps there was a mountain in the

Adirondacks whose profile stirred us to drive the Alaska Highway, and later we threw lire into the Trevi Fountain, raised Belgian shepherds, adopted a three-month-old child to enlarge our family, worked in wholesale. Whatever the destination, it turned out not to be Phil Rizzuto's or Phil Donahue's or whoever we idealized originally. Life's gauge was broader than we anticipated. Not in the sense that we batted in Yankee Stadium or chatted up celebs like Montgomery Clift; but our aims multiplied and vicarious satisfactions punctuated our days. A snatch of Scott Joplin on the radio (we don't need to have *composed* to exult); a daughter on a winning basketball team; a seagull, surplice-white but primeval in posture, that lands on the lawn to grab food left for the dog.

A certain self-selection of course takes place in who shows up for the monthly Men's Breakfast at the senior center, for instance—I sat with an ex-harbormaster and ferryman and a crane operator— or college reunions. Welfare clients aren't as likely as pensioners to come, and loners stay away, or the more deeply discouraged and unmoored. Among the Ivies, high-flying alumni who can talk about which prep school their children got into and about financial derivatives sit together, not with their classmates bemoaning the inequities of health and luck. Veterans who fifty years ago decided not to use the GI Bill to earn a college degree wound up with solid businesses and nest eggs, too, if they wished for that and followed through. But following through does not determine contentment if they also wanted beer chums or love liaisons that might derail their concentration yet engrave those smile lines people wear when reclining on their final gurney. Sly pleasures will do it, as well as the daily straight and narrow and a life of kids dashing around on summer evenings.

Integrity is rarer and doesn't tell on the face as clearly because, unlike pleasure, integrity involves cost-consciousness, even for the honest soul whose ultimate choice will never be in doubt. Stubborn sacrifice is demanded, which can mark their expressions somewhat in the way attention-seeking eccentricity might. People possessing less will brand it as a quirk. Contentment at the end of life isn't a kind of be-all, however. Orwell's criterion didn't specify what we should deserve. Discontent may be as admirable—although not self-contempt. What has surprised me is the widespread repose I've sensed in rubbing shoulders recently with old people, as one of them. In my '50s college generation, existential pessimism, counterposed to postwar prosperity, was all the rage. Yet I was a dissenter, skeptical of the skeptics because, believing in an immanent divinity, I thought life could be radiant, especially if you got outdoors. Most people aren't pantheists, though, and, accepting the cranky clichés about geezerdom, I expected they would be unhappier in old age than they've turned out. Settling for less than some of their dreams hasn't seemed such a compromise because the satisfactions from unpredicted quarters have ripened so fully, whether familial—the prodigal grandma—or just waking up each morning with no tasks to trek to.

I'd realized World War II had validated Kafka and Camus as my classmates' heartthrobs, but was instead a Whitman fan during the 1950s and ever after, loving every metropolis I encountered as well as the thunderous surf, the rolling landscape. Children are born with bursting buoyancy. Give them a few yards and they will start to play. But I didn't guess that, seventy years on, their artesian buoyancy in subdued form would remain a force. Call it cosmic gaiety, planetary photosynthesis, the Big Bang, or the green thrust. Life is thrust.

THE AMERICAN DISSIDENT

*G*oing through airport security, I've sometimes wondered what would happen if thoughts could be screened. Not that mine ever concern harming a plane, but I may have illegal ideas when looking up at the president on the TV. Dissent in its many gradations is disagreeable, doesn't win popularity contests. If you had criticized slavery or child labor or advocated women's suffrage in America at the wrong time or place, you could have been handcuffed, and lucky at that. I've been in towns in Louisiana as a young man where if I had questioned racial segregation I would have had my skull cracked; my Vermont license plates alone resulted in my being told to clear out of the parish before nightfall. The Vietnam War was divisive on a smaller scale, and I protested that lawfully, and safely too. Yet I'm ashamed to look back and realize, at seventy, that I have never been arrested on a matter of conscience. George Washington, Thomas Jefferson, Martin Luther King Jr., and lesser folk whom I admire took more risks than me. Countless people have, and I don't believe for a minute that nothing in our era is worth being insurrectional about, or even that the issues are less grave. Wherever I have been, for example, I've seen an absolutely flabbergasting amount of nature in the process of being destroyed. It will be irrevocable, but did I fear handcuffs so much that I've let it all happen without a vociferous reaction? Apparently so. Police arrest anybody they're told to; they don't care what the bone of contention is, and protesters look ridiculous anyhow, with their hollering and cardboard placards, then limply dragged to the paddy wagon. Say it at the ballot box, we tell them, pretending that a visionary minority wouldn't be a minority there as well.

William Tyndale was burned at the stake in 1536 for translating key portions of what became the King James Version of the Bible so that ordinary people would be able to read it in English. Was that too harsh? James, when he acceded to the throne in 1603, thought so, but in the era of Henry VIII neither British nor Continental Catholic opinion would have demurred, not to mention numerous worthies such as Sir Thomas More who were incensed at Tyndale's blasphemous audacity. (More himself, of course, was beheaded at around the same time for dissent of a different sort.) Dissent can be a dicey business. If it's not at least a bit uncomfortable, it's probably not real dissidence. Forty-six years passed before the U.S. government, in 1988, apologized for interning eighty thousand American citizens of Japanese descent in scuzzy barbed-wire camps during World War II, but imagine the reception that would have been accorded some hair shirt who proposed releasing or apologizing to them in his local bar decades before that? Whistle-blowers were called snitches in my youth; and reformers, soreheads who cared more about a bunch of strangers than their own families. People painted with lead, insulated with asbestos, smoked after coition, and had one for the road before leaving a party. Homosexuality was a crime, and wops, micks, Polacks, were not individuals much thought about unless you yourself were one, or had married beneath you. As for "colored people," it was nice of you to use that polite term but somewhat screwy to object to their treatment. Just for criticizing anti-Semitism (and Jews were white) I was called a Commie in school, and later my father semi-disinherited me for fear that when he died I'd break the covenant in our neighborhood, sell his house to a Jew, and precipitate a crash in his friends' property values.

Public floggings, brandings on the forehead, beheadings, ducking stools: imagine the opprobrium that must have been mounted against weak sisters who remonstrated against these customs prematurely. Did the bleeding hearts (to phrase it anachronistically) suppose that they had a monopoly on truth and a corner on virtue? Or slavery, being in the Bible—why question it? Like child labor, what could be more natural? And people nowadays who advocate the ethical treatment of animals: it must be maladjustments, "hang-ups," driving their agitation.

"Why are Mexicans called wetbacks?" I would ask.

"Because they swim across the Rio Grande."

"And why are homosexuals queers?"

"Because they're queer, dummy."

"Why are niggers called that?"

"Why, because it's short for Negro, obviously; it's a nickname."

"And Chinamen?"

"Because they're men from China."

"And why don't Negroes eat in the same restaurants as us, even up North?"

"Because I'm sure they very much prefer their own company if they drop the silverware and chew with their mouths open, or laugh too loud and talk without grammar. It's kinder, it embarrasses them if you watch."

This is old stuff; but recently—when I've written about famine in Africa—frequently, after I'd returned from Sudan, people would ask me why I had gone to witness it. They didn't come right out and inquire in all frankness whether my psyche harbored a secret ghoulish streak, because that would be discourteous, but it was their implication. In a big, booming gated community like America, why would you want to know firsthand about such things? Write a check to Oxfam, vote for a congressman who actually owns a passport, but why dwell on—surround oneself with—suffering when there's nothing to be done? "Moving on," without being rigid or judgmental about any difficulty, is the current mantra, like mood-elevating pills and meditative therapy.

Yet dissidence, being the opposite of an emollient, sometimes has the earmarks of integrity. In arguing with prevailing opinion, it may not serve the interests of the arguer: may be called unpatriotic, irreligious, adversarial, off-the-wall, loony and disloyal, irrational, neurotic, elitist or mushy, compulsive or lowbrow. Other people enjoy railing at a stationary target, and if you state a belief in something not majoritarian, you become that. Heads were knocked and demonstrators shot in mockable, in-your-face protests—with suspicious police officers and jeering bystanders—to win collective bargaining for labor and a voting-rights act. These campaigners themselves were often unpleasant personally, hard to split the difference with—and I suspect that the convections of the new century will be hotter than the last's. Dissent may then be vertiginous—although you may think, on the contrary, that the interventions of digitry will regulate not only financial probity, child-support payments, the rights of the handicapped, and the like, but everything that honor and a firm handshake used to deal with. You'll never need to know whether somebody can look you in the eye. A visionary like Joan of Arc, if one emerges, won't need to be interrogated in excruciating detail and condemned, just deprogrammed.

Originally we Americans were a revolutionary people in religion and politics—misfits in Europe or adventurers of a modest kind—and crossed a lot of deep water to try someplace new. Voting with our feet was inherently a dissent, and our democracy was raucous to start with: coonskin cap versus top hat, hillbilly or flatlander, hayseed, city slicker, bohunk or blue blood. The first generation of newcomers each had to pay its dues before the next went in for lace-curtain show, and I remember an aristocratic lady I knew half a century ago, a Mrs. La Farge, who took to calling Cadillacs "Murphy Cars" because so many Irish had begun buying them, not simply driving them as chauffeurs. "Spics" too, and she and others switched to Lincolns for a signature car.

But why ever did rich, landed gentry like Washington and Jefferson—already grandees in the New World—hassle and strike at the powers that be? Franklin Delano Roosevelt also was a "traitor to his class," but like John Kennedy, another rich liberal president later on, he didn't give away his money to the poor, any more than Jefferson or Washington freed their slaves during their lifetimes. If they'd been that revolutionary, they wouldn't have been electable. (Incidentally, the idea that a man as humane as Thomas Jefferson would *not* have slept with a lovely slave like Sally Hemings in a long-term, considerate, semi-consensual liaison—that either her color or some fleshly punctiliousness might have barred him—would astonish me more than that he did.) Indeed, what was the attraction in Christianity, a faith born of persecution and dissidence that was anti-wealth, anti-authority, and reborn in Protestant revisionism, then lately again in blue-collar fundamentalism? But although dissent is a minority position, and most of us don't want to dispute with a more powerful constituency or to challenge an injustice that hasn't injured us, it's still an exercise, an impulse, that many indulge in, at least during our late years, for reasons of self-respect, and maybe in order to square ourselves with God. We all see outrages we gloss over—whether the price of glaucoma medicine to old people or the current mistreatment of Arab Americans. We know we can still shout outside the White House (I once had the pleasure of giving a thumbs-down to Spiro Agnew in his pre-inaugural limo cavalcade as vice president in 1969, and seeing him glower back). But it's risky and consuming in a turbulent period such as this, with even jail in the offing, and requires a pileup of atrocities to override our cautious numbness. The metronome of news flashes washes out each flush of anger just as we might have begun to articulate it, so that a critical mass of protest is hard to achieve. The controversially elected president, scary attorney general, sophistical defense secretary, are beneficiaries of the din of innovation, though on both the right and left we're dubious. Things are not going well, and patriotism is the last refuge not only of a scoundrel but of confusion also.

The bubble of power has become so elusive that we don't know where it is—the Supreme Court, the voting machine, the sound-bite writer, the war room, or Dick Cheney? And our electronic novelties don't seem to clarify the ways we want to live: instead, throw us off stride. In such a cacophony, how does one dissent? How can we distinguish Tom Paine from a crank, and Joan of Arc from a bipolar street-corner haranguer in drag? Does she have to join the U.S. Special Forces, and Tom get himself on *60 Minutes?* It's not a silly question. Theodore Kaczynski, the Unabomber, was briefly heard, but by a leverage we don't want. A different love of power has muted some of the best speakers, such as Billy Graham. I heard both the Reverend Graham and Martin Luther King Jr. during their prime (Graham in the 1950s, King in the sixties), and what distinguished them from each other was not a fervency or stage charisma or mastery of oratorical skills but, rather, King's range of emotion and points of reference and realism of address, and simply what he said. Graham never uttered any sentiments that might displease a sitting president, not to mention get himself shot. His stem-winders were like a football march, canted to furnish you a buzz so that you'd stop cheating on your wife and step out of Madison Square Garden warmed for the wind. They were not sniggering and cruel, like Jerry Falwell's—whom I also heard, in his cynical prime, in the eighties, at his home church in Lynchburg, Virginia, and far afield in Alaska—but passionately midstream, like an adoring chaplain to Eisenhower, Nixon, and the upwardly mobile. For King, life was more complex, not fortissimo or full-face sunshine; it had a riddle for an underside. Falwell, on the other hand, in Anchorage, and pitched more blue-collar, sounded either tipsy or jet-lagged as he laughingly told us how to manage our nagging wives. He confided that he let *his* have her way with the houseware because outside the confines of home it was a man's world.

Dissent is a bit more like Jesus being rude in the Temple, including the chance of a walk down the Via Dolorosa if mob rule or a dictator prevails. Argumentative, confrontational, it's seldom a path to career advancement. Middle-of-the-roaders discount such a person as lopsided in his priorities, wasting energy, splurging goodwill, and venting a personality problem—as the few thorny mavericks I've known well in fact were likely to do: honesty itself in most societies being perilously close to that, and a burr under the saddle. Terrorism makes eccentricity suspect at an airport counter, and in a widening circle from there. Gone is the hippies' confident Sixties contempt for tradition, and the Seventies derision toward "breeders" and their "rug rats," or the Eighties jettisoning of idealism of almost any stripe. We fly the flag a lot now, yet what is the social compact? We've got gluts of information but are dizzy for lack of a norm. The norms of capitalism, friendship, and religion: everything is so provisional, situational, optional, such a matter of lifestyle choice that the very word "norm" is likely to victimize somebody. Our magnetic field is dislocated; gravity itself seems weakened. But weightlessness is not healthy.

The norms of loyalty, for example—how about that slightly older kid who befriended and protected you from bullies in school? Do you have the faintest idea of whatever happened to him? That early boss who was insightful and kind—is he alive? America is about climbing, which means you leave people behind, and lawyers can enforce the terms of alimony, deeds, and wills. Loyalty sounds like a sort of standstill proposition anyway: like the joke that if you want a friend in Washington, buy a dog. Your children are offspring and you may be fortunately twinned with a partner, but who else would you go to the mat for? This cleavage is extraordinary historically and anthropologically, and our tie-strings frail. In the bad old days of ethnic prejudice, people didn't shake hands with everybody, but a handshake often signified something if they did. It was like the "missionary position" in sex—much ridiculed lately, but we may miss that like a handshake fairly soon. I know a real Uriah Heep at my place of work, but would I recognize him for what he is on the Internet? I doubt it; you have to see him hunch as he scuttles on his obsequious errands. Electronically, that wouldn't show.

I'm left, right, and center, myself, because as a naturalist by persuasion, I'm therefore a political radical but a social conservative, like so many of us, from Thoreau on. Also, having grown up in the Establishment, my father a lawyer, I know that the Establishment is not entirely horned. I even wrote editorials on an occasional basis for the *New York Times* for several years in the turn-of-the-seasons slot, between Hal Borland's stint and Verlyn Klinkenborg's taking over. This meant I could attend editorial-board meetings if I wished. They were contentious, and I soon ceased to come because as a stutterer I didn't enjoy the verbal fray, but I did like Max Frankel and Jack Rosenthal, his deputy, who presided over the thrice-weekly discussions at opposite ends of the long polished table. They were career allies and neighbors in Riverdale, and rode to the office together in a company limousine, but although burning with visibly tense ambition (Jack succeeded Max as editorial-page editor later, when Max moved up to direct the rest of the paper), they were kinder, gentler *Times*men than many. There were hectic initiation rituals for me to get through, of course, but I never saw either of them be discourteous to anybody, and Jack was the best line editor I've ever had.

These were not op-ed meetings. This was where official positions were thrashed out and unsigned writing assignments made. The regular subjects like labor, business, municipal and state government, Congress, foreign policy, cultural affairs, the judiciary, had specialists, but nobody could just ride his own hobbyhorse without winning group consent or at least a median thrust that Jack or Max would enforce when the final editorial page went to press; and a foe might check its progress in the meantime. The arguments were about where and how strongly the paper ought to land, and could have national influence. We had no blacks, Hispanics, Asian Americans, or announced gays, and the slot or emphasis upon "Labor," for example, was somewhat anachronistic, given the cornice of homelessness, health care, and welfare problems looming in position to avalanche, more than strikes or union activity. We ran essentially no environmentalist editorials. I was there to write local appreciations of nature in spring—little raptures—not fight for its worldwide survival. Such an evolution lay in the future for the *Times,* just as it was left to goodhearted white liberals to take a decent position on racial issues. (Jack Rosenthal himself, for instance, went over to Newark one night to hear Jesse Jackson speak, before it was widely considered important to have done so.)

We did, in 1979, however, have feminists in the room. This was a newly centrist, suitable meat to chew on, and besides the eminent architectural critic Ada Louise Huxtable—an intellectually incisive, consummately elegant woman who usually sat next to Max or Jack as if a little above the fray and knowing where they were going to come down, anyway—we had a couple of eager advocates, such as the feisty Soma Golden, a pale, rumpled economics egghead who was gradually shouldering the good, gray fish-wrapper into enlightened opinions on women's lib. Allies sat together, and I must confess I placed myself with the white-haired or bald-headed guys facing the formidable Soma and Mary Cantwell, later a memoirist, across the table. I was forward-tilting in politics but more culturally conservative than I should have been, when the women's-rights movement was, as Emerson once said, "honoring to the age."

We weren't privy to whatever conversations Max and Jack had with "Punch" Sulzberger, their publisher. But Jack kept an aluminum mobile in his office—a sculpture depicting two acrobats balancing at opposite ends of a swaying, swinging pole—to remind him of his professional role, as he fielded calls from aggrieved or ingratiating and manipulative power brokers in the morning, then turned the phone off to work on the next day's editorial page in the afternoon. He would switch from a light-colored suit to a dark one on the day after Labor Day, no matter how hot that particular Tuesday was. The *Times* is a keel, not a rudder, and a keel is needed before any rudder. Nevertheless a great ship must turn, and we tugged at the stiff helm in diverse but tentative ways. These well-intentioned workaholics on the tenth floor were lifers at the organization—experienced journalists who as they aged wanted to stay closer to home—documenting, fortifying, and disseminating conventional wisdom, which they expressed as stirringly as they could, while altering it by inch-ward degrees. *Can we say this? How soon will we be able to say this?*—sanding it down. There was no chance of a startling, idealistic midcourse correction; our struggles were between individuals safely pre-positioned in mid-river, and nobody else could have reached the board. Max himself, as Washington bureau chief, had supposedly been scooped on the Watergate scandal by Woodward and Bernstein of the *Washington Post* because he had been sandbagged by Kissinger and was too reluctant to believe bad things about important people: an ideal background for a job at which whatever you wrote might sound anemic in a decade and bloodless in a generation. The "godfathers" of the *Times* changed, from the horrendous Abe Rosenthal (no relation to Jack), to Max when he achieved the top post, to the brilliant good guy and Africanist Joe Lelyveld, to Howell Raines, and then back to Lelyveld, but an ordinary reporter could be reassigned, or not printed at all until he left of his own accord without messy firings, if his coverage did not conform to the newspaper's views. And similarly we had no dissenters in the boardroom that I left. Jack even asked me, when his Harvard twenty-fifth anniversary rolled around, what it was appropriate for him to recount about himself in the reunion book. I liked him, told him, but was also being radicalized by the wholesale destruction of nature, and stopped doing my brief seasonal paeans to autumn, summer, and spring by and by.

Dissent is the sourdough that starts bread rising, or the reckless protest that ignites reform. But it's not for breadwinners. It's a marriage-breaker, embittering the kids; and there is wastage—peacemakers such as Rabin, Gandhi, and King killed, and lesser, luckier people vilified, pauperized, with ulcers and palpitations. The apartheid jurists who shipped Nelson Mandela to Robben Island were surely well-balanced, successful men, like the French judges who burned Joan at Rouen, and later the Roman clerics who martyred the philosopher and astronomer Giordano Bruno. Nowadays, rational officials are not aghast that we may destroy half of the world's species of plants and animals within a single human life span. And can you imagine the three enlisted men in the Army helicopter who interrupted the My Lai massacre at gunpoint—after more than four hundred Vietnamese civilians had been slaughtered by other American soldiers—receiving the Congressional Medal of Honor for their heroism, instead of a quarter century of official silence?

It's men who stand with arms akimbo who get such rewards, and people quickly become nonpersons if any cost must be paid for knowing them. You'll see it happen in grammar school, in adolescence, your thirties, forties, fifties. Integrity has its penalties, and betrayal was the usual fate of the honorable diehards I have known. It's not because there's nobody to trust, but because so often one of the definitions of people with power is that they will be people you can't trust. "Premature antifascists" was the label given by the U.S. armed forces in 1942—after the larger war against Nazism began—to the members of the Abraham Lincoln Brigade, who had sailed off to Spain in 1937 to fight Generalissimo Francisco Franco and been bombed by *Luftwaffe* Stukas, and so on. When they reenlisted after Pearl Harbor, they became objects of suspicion and were mostly confined to their bases, after having been betrayed on the whole in Spain also.

Emerson—that cynosure of American literature—was barred from speaking at Harvard for thirty years after having delivered his heretical, now celebrated "Divinity School Address"; and Thoreau, another alumnus and lecturer living nearby in Concord, was never invited to hold forth at the college at all. Their interest in Asian religions went dangerously beyond being academic, and they championed John Brown and other wild notions, Emerson even speaking before the National Women's Rights Convention in 1855. "Life is an ecstasy," he wrote in *The Conduct of Life*, which is still a revolutionary doctrine because our sense of self-interest tends to trump our immersion in it. Radiance is hot to handle. We don't want to seem guilty of not being "on the same page" as other people for too long. Then—sliding through the months—we may wonder why we have lived.

I've hardly looked in a mirror for years (don't shave using one) and, like many souls, have self-sculpted a simulacrum I carry around. Not my public identity—that disciplined old doppelgänger who knows how to maintain a facade—but the guy I hope I am, who is going to meet his maker in finishing up. Will I need a sort of splint for my spirit then, like the metal device I wore when carpal tunnel syndrome affected one of my hands? I'm more at peace than that, perhaps, and stumble more frequently when walking than in subtler respects. A mirror would remind me of the bashing I've taken, as well as some of my cynical trimmings, but it would be a distortion, too, because aging is cellular, not just a map of resentments, bafflement, or disappointment. Wrinkles simulate sagging hopes without actually signifying them, and do little to represent the spine of joy I have felt day by day (at least in the morning) for most of my life. Many people, who may seem rather bitter in middle age, by seventy are mainly grateful for having lived, willy-nilly, though quite round-shouldered from having rolled with the punches, and reticently proud of that. Nor, having absorbed those, do they think life shouldn't have blows. As Thomas Mann suggested in his last novel, we ought to live *like* soldiers without *being* soldiers; and how can you have a military without boot camp?

To be soldierly yet a partisan means dissent at times because an army kills whomever it's told to kill. Conformity and dissent are not simply a seesaw, however, because a posse comitatus and a lone maverick are not of equal power. Conventional wisdom is what incarcerated Dickens's father in a debtor's prison and hanged small London pickpockets until the 1860s. It regularly reconstitutes chain gangs in parts of our own country and allowed young Mexican children to work unconscionable hours in Texas and California. The dissenter has got to rouse himself to pay attention—and then our slumberous consciences—much as the bow-tied Boston lawyer Joseph Welch did in verbally accosting the snarling Senator Joseph McCarthy during the McCarthy red-scare congressional hearings in 1954, with TV cameras rolling and Welch's clumsy wording affectingly unrehearsed: "Have you no sense of decency, sir, at long last? Have you left no sense of decency?"

Cameras have become a precondition for effective acts of conscience. Otherwise Police Chief Bull Connor in Birmingham, Alabama, could have kept on knocking down Negro demonstrators with fire hoses, and the Buddhist monks in Saigon would have had no international audience when they incinerated themselves to protest the puppet regime of Ngo Dinh Diem. But broadly speaking, dissenters include the itchy folk who staff food pantries and shelters for the walking wounded in our blistered society. If doubts didn't nag them to action, the blisters would become calluses. Just as laughter can be a form of dissidence, so is seriousness—whereas conformity, like a frat boy, smirks out of one side of its mouth so that nobody will notice. Reverent in the pew, it spits out in the parking lot and pees between the cars.

We do have this tradition of free speech (monks martyred in Tibet weren't filmed by the Chinese press), and of a civil response to passive resistance that made it possible for Martin Luther King, and Gandhi in British India, to practice a symbolic disobedience without being immured forever in prison, or left for dead by the police. A Gandhi in French Algeria, Soviet Russia, Milošević's Serbia, or Sharon's Palestine would not have been let off as lightly. Although the average citizen does not red-letter our constitutional guarantees (he might punch the bastard instead or fire him for his nutty political views), lawyers do remember, and many a cop the morning after, and some college graduates and most autodidacts. I certainly have views my neighbors wouldn't agree with—somebody has to or we'd still be living in trees; I'm sure posterity will see it my way, don't you agree? A good number of us are closet dissidents and know what's wrong with the world better than more worldly folk do. We're not Galileo or Giordano Bruno, but anybody winning more of life's rewards than we are is probably selling out to some extent, don't you think? Tom Paine died ridiculed by the likes of John Adams and virtually destitute, and Joan in burning agony at Rouen in 1431. One judge was imprisoned for having raised objections to her trial, and a friar, Pierre Bosquier, overheard bemoaning her being burnt alive—after abjectly and publicly recanting—was only sentenced to eight months on bread and water.

Most of us would not have demurred that far; the danger would have frightened us. We'd have said she had it coming, like John Walker Lindh and other confused, petty idealists of today. Joan was major, not minor, but so ambiguous in her person and inspiration that a blurred but firmer parallel might lie in our responses nowadays to the titanic tragedies we are beginning to witness that, as an obverse, may live as long in history, like the AIDS pandemic, the plague of African famines, the worldwide holocaust we are inflicting on other forms of life. To each conflagration we don't react. Obese, and tending a lawn or window box, we are indifferent. Television footage would "bomb" if it showed a lot of skeletal orphans or hundreds of species blinking out in the tropics. Nor would real carpet bombing go over well if it were filmed from the ground, not by the aircraft's Nintendo gadgets. Nor would we want to hear the screams of various Muslims being drawn and quartered with electric shocks at our behest in obliging Third World dictatorships. We want to believe instead in a sort of rapt rhetoric—one nation under God, libertine in pursuing happiness but also after goodness. Unfortunately the privilege of free speech doesn't promise that you're going to say anything new, such as defining goodness. But nine out of ten of us have a rough idea of how we conceive it to be. And we know that dissent is innate to both honesty and altruism, that there are laws and higher laws. To be upright is not just keeping a Sabbath or paying one's union dues. (Some of the old agnostic Yiddish poets used to cluster together in New York's housepainters' union.) Accruing integrity is a process, not charted, and when the chips are down, you might wind up fighting fascism prematurely, or volunteering like Thoreau, a century ahead of other Americans, to go to jail for a principle.

Next to nobody quite practices their religion, and we know that raw democracy would be so intemperate it must be bridled. Yet horse's asses do attain high office and then delegate to other horse's asses more power than all but half a dozen of the politicians who have been freely chosen by the electorate. Thus we find ourselves in thrall to chumps like Robert McNamara, who later apologize for what they've done. Power can ramify exasperatingly in a democracy, when few officeholders could be elected if they said precisely what they meant. We assume they're partly rascals on a stage—makeup and make-believe. So our jury system may embody grassroots democracy better, even though the lawyers can be expensive, because an anonymous twelve does decide the verdict as they wish, without having passed the hat. And in that context we distrust holdouts, much like individuals who make our street look bad by not mowing the lawn. But with such exceptions, in a democracy we tend to harbor a soft spot for the proverbial minority of one who has unpredictable thoughts. His ego or punctilio can displease us, like the habit of unbending fussiness and carping, the pose of dissent as a monocle. Yet it can also be as invaluable as reading glasses in deciphering falsity. And falsity is what we wind up not wanting—not by the end.

Aung San Suu Kyi, of Myanmar, asked for an encyclopedia to help see her through a decade of captivity. And how trivial a recompense is her distant fame for so many years of silent, grinding confinement. More germane is bearing witness for her people. She is the celebrated one among tens of thousands of nameless prisoners of conscience worldwide, new sufferers continually replacing those killed or released. We know what the jailers are probably like, and the common tattlers and conniving Vichy Frenchmen and -women who would sell your hideout for a hundred dollars—and the tame press that would not remark much on it. Brutal, go-along wage slaves are scattered everywhere, and slick flacks as well. We recognize the verbal cowardice that occasionally enables us to hold on to our own jobs. (I mean, suppose, as a writer, I'd said I have known a good many Jewish-American journalists who displayed a "dual loyalty" toward Israel and America in writing about the Palestinian conflict. It would have been professional suicide.)

I don't have a lot of faith in the truthfulness of power or the fairness of public opinion. But if you skim off the scum who everywhere float into turnkey and mouthpiece jobs, I think that ordinary folk over

the long run are suffused with a kind of benign, almost blithe asser-
tiveness that is the engine of democracy when it works. For hundreds
of years sniveling pickpockets needed to be hung from a gibbet before
the clergy, and the mothers and fathers of other school-age boys, took
enough notice to raise a tentative, uneasy complaint. The thumbscrew
and rack were abolished too (though I doubt there is less torture—
just as no doubt a thousand-fold as many small boys die much more
slowly and painfully of famine now than were strangled on Tyburn
Hill). But reforming the atrocities we inflict upon nature will be more
problematic. When a critical mass of damage has been done, it will
be as if we had stopped hanging small boys only after there were no
more small boys.

Dissent is essential—it coughs up germs and clarifies the spirit—
whether or not you are too late. And don't quail at getting excited; why
not put in an exclamation point, the way the militants who founded
the conservation organization Earth First! did? That's part of what
life is about. Giordano Bruno was burned at the stake with a torture
device clamped to his tongue so that he couldn't speak the truth as he
saw it to the crowd in the Campo di'Fiori as the faggots were lit, not
in order that he wouldn't hurt anybody's feelings there. Yet dissent is
a tool of kindness, on the whole. We don't want the mentally retarded
executed, illegal immigrants dying of thirst in the desert, sea turtles
wiped out for the sake of shrimp cocktails, Predator drones perfected
to the point of being able to assassinate anybody, based on their DNA.
We dissent from cruelty and greed, solipsism and nihilism, from war-
lovers and eye-gougers (that is, people who gouge the landscape our
eyes feed from).

But you can't dissent in earnest if you have no intimations of what
you believe. Then it's simply temperamental. A double negative—not to
admire sequoias or cathedrals, but say don't destroy them—will vitiate

your claim. Death, for example, will be as much a mystery to me as to anybody. I don't expect it's either Christ or merely biochemistry (and can't guess what poor creature, in this century, one might like to be reincarnated as). I believe it will be more than death, or bare-bones rest, however. And that puts a fire in my belly to preserve the mysteries and decencies and beauty and complexities we have.

EAST OF EVEREST

$\mathcal{B}$ack to the future, I thought, heading for India again, that kaleidoscopic subcontinent now closing on a billion people, the squeeze of human beings fissured by religious righteousness and rapacious capitalism, with incongruous juxtapositions of seething hustle and mystic symbolism, ten and a half hours' worth of time zones away from New York City. You have to like the idea of people—the chattering crush and possible divinity of myriads of them—to enjoy India. All those separate envelopes of rushing, self-important, self-involved dignity: the cut of the headcloth or glint of the sari denoting caste, class, or whatever. People in galaxy numbers have a whole-is-greater-than-the-parts reverberation, at least for me. I'm usually elated by crowds, whether in New York or Cairo, London or Calcutta—the glee, élan vital, and energy. Even amid vistas of poverty, I tend to think I see meaning. Generosity in squalor.

I was headed, however, for the state of Arunachal Pradesh ("Land of the Dawn-lit Mountains"), a salient of Indian territory in the foothills of the Himalayas extending eastward between Myanmar and Tibet. China, in fact, contests Indian sovereignty in this border region, home to some two dozen animist hill tribes, and invaded in blitzkrieg style in 1962, when Arunachal Pradesh was constitutionally part of the neighboring Indian state of Assam. Eighteen years earlier the Japanese, under General Renya Mutaguchi, had also invaded Assam, to try to sweep the British out of India. You need an internal visa to enter Arunachal Pradesh (it was opened to foreign tourists only in 1995), and tribal insurrections continue to harass the army and plague the police in Assam, where traditionalists want autonomy. At Guwahati, Assam's capital, shortly before our arrival, Bodo rebels blew a hole in the bridge across the Brahmaputra River and, separately, derailed an express train loaded with Guwahati passengers for New Delhi, with great loss of life—all in the name of secession for "Bodoland."

The approach by jet to Bombay from the Arabian Sea still affords views of a lovely diadem of yellow lights—not boastful or bombastic in its wattage like a Western city, but tentative, evocative, and home-made, sort of a glowing crescent. The passengers clapped as we landed safely, as they often do on Third World flights. Then we waited for an hour in a rattletrap bus before transferring five miles to the domestic airport, and five hours there. I was pleased, though, because my friend Trudy and I began meeting the surge of souls you do while on the road in India. A young engineer who was returning to Bangalore after attending a conference in Cincinnati. A cruise ship steward just back for six weeks of home leave in Cochin after six months of sailing in Alaska and the Caribbean. A couple of American Hare Krishna pilgrims en route to an ashram, and a shaky forty-something Canadian who had come in search of, as he said, "Nada." Also a middle-aged Goan woman who had been living comfortably in London but was now returning to India for the first time in eight years because she had begun to suspect that the half-million-pound estate her family had donated to charity was being converted into a moneymaking scam.

Our next stop was Calcutta, that proverbially dying city and yet India's intellectual and artistic capital. As in a parable, squalor and joy cohabit, while almost everyone over the age of ten swims hard against the tides and density to obtain their daily pound of rice. If you think people are a chip off the old block, embodying a spark of divinity— God's holy chosen tribe straddling like Gulliver the Lilliputian natural world—how many can be too many? India's situation, seen broadly, looks more optimistic than this particular frenetic megalopolis of refugees and street-dwellers collapsing from accrued procrastination and dystopian dilemmas, nearing three hundred thousand souls per metro square mile, and any spare dirt patch ditched for a rice paddy or dug out to grow carp. By the millennium India's population may triple from what it was at independence in 1947; Calcutta's also, though Calcutta's infrastructure is desperately asthmatic now. Yet the lift my spirits got in Calcutta is memorable because it seemed sanguine.

The next morning we had time to see the city's wholesale flower market, down under Howrah Bridge—cantilevered, ramshackle, ungainly, and said to be the busiest in all the world. Two million people a day somehow manage to cross it, afoot or squeezed into an assortment of vehicles—omnibuses, gypsy cabs, auto-rickshas, regular rickshas, mopeds, pedicabs. In the muddy warren of alleys below and south of the bridge, lorry-loads of flowers had been distributed overnight and were being sewed into red religious garlands for temple offerings, feasts, fests, marriages, and burials in a hundred tiny establishments, then tossed into bicycle carts and handcarts for delivery. The brown shoals of the Hooghly River were stained red and yellow from the masses of petals washed in by the rains, plus yesterday's discarded flowers. Where stone steps went down, a lot of people were bathing in it also, though there was floating flotsam and offal. The mix and flux of flowers, people, and offal is of course India's curse and blessing: what distinguishes it from "us."

Another flight took us 325 miles northeast across Bangladesh to Guwahati, the administrative and trading center of Assam. It's a sprawled-out, comparatively prosperous little riverbank city, cupped under choppy green hills. The government hotel overlooked the Brahmaputra River, which was wide as the Mississippi even at this driest time of year, with a small temple to Siva on an islet in the middle, and a black-and-white stork stalking the shore. There were dugouts on the Brahmaputra too, and cormorants diving, harrier hawks and pariah kites scouting about, and vultures sailing high and martins scooting low. In the morning in the garden I saw an owl, and mynahs, common as robins, and drongos, magpies, gray-necked crows, and turtledoves. Cool, majestic trees decorated the promenade above the waterfront, and peddlers shook nuts into your hand for a rupee or two. Below, a dozen people were washing their clothes, soaking the garments and pounding them on a drift log. Several sampans were floating leaflike out on the vast river, each with a loaf-shaped little shelter in the middle and propelled by a man with a pole standing at each end.

The Brahmaputra flows 1,800 miles from inner Tibet, beyond the Himalayas, in a great loop around to the mouth of the Ganges via the plains of Assam, having drained in the meantime about 626,000 square miles by way of twenty-four major tributaries. Assam's fertility is much enhanced as a result. Two-thirds of its farmland is planted with rice, and the other best cash crop is harvested from the plantations of tea, though it also produces a sixth of India's petroleum. So the three minor insurrections that were in fitful progress in the state at the moment—and noticeable to us as graffiti in Assamese or bold headlines in the local papers (or else because any vehicle deemed drivable by the military had been seized for transporting soldiers)—were apparently not about hunger, but ethnic pride. The frontier with China, a much larger flashpoint, is north of Assam through the layered mountains of our Arunachal Pradesh and guarded by roadless outposts that the army's helicopters supply. The Brahmaputra is famous for torrential canyons and pugnacious tribes where it crosses wildly through the main chain of the Himalayas from Chinese territory—dropping, for example, six thousand feet in a curving canyon in just two miles, right at the border, but already more than seven hundred miles from its source. Yet here on the plains, it looked hugely sedate.

We set out for our adventure, six Americans and Gautam Malakar, our Delhi-based guide, in a stubby blue bus toward the city of Tezpur, a district center six hours upriver on the north bank, which had been the limit of the Chinese advance in the 1962 war. (The Chinese troops withdrew later that year under international pressure, and the border dispute remains unresolved.) Mostly rolling rice country, diked, ditched, and closely cultivated in checkerboard plots, with family fish-ponds occupying slight depressions amid the paddies, it was more of a breadbasket than claustrophobic. There were banana and betel-nut plantations as well, and we passed a sizable paper mill that was being fed with truckloads of bamboo poles and sal trees. Also the village of Nelli, where Gautam said three thousand Muslim immigrants from Bangladesh had been slaughtered by Hindu locals fifteen years ago.

As we got into higher terrain, the tea plantations began. These were extensive, but some of the hilltops were still wooded naturally, and the paddy fields presented a wide, pretty quiltwork of grays and greens. Scattered humpbacked brown cattle or black buffalo browsed the stubble in the fallow stretches, with dark tick birds and white egrets accompanying them, or straggling, peppy files of goats. A troop train rattled alongside the road for a while, the commanding officer leaning out the door in his military tunic and white pajama pants.

More and more tea plantations replaced the gridwork rice paddies as we climbed away from the Brahmaputra. On our ribbon of road there were two-man handcarts, one-man handcarts, and occasional battered, wheezing trucks painted like carnival wagons, blue with gaudy yellow designs and tinselly tassels hanging over the windshields. Periodically a broken-springed bus barreled by, careening to a stop if somebody walking raised a hand. Wicker fish traps were set in the streams.

After the town of Gohpur there were no main arenas of cultivation, just forested ridges rising into Arunachal Pradesh. At the clamorous border our skinny, lorry-pitted road passed through the small hustlers' towns of Banderdewa and Naharlagun. A billboard greeted us at the roadblock where police checked our papers: ARUNACHAL PRADESH AWAITS TO YOUR ARRIVAL WITH ITS ENTHRALLING VALLEYS. Either our papers were not in order or some "efficiency money" (as bribes are called in India) had to be paid, because we went to a sort of truck stop for barbecued goat meat and Godfather Super Strong High Power Beer while negotiations progressed. Eventually the police chief's brother got hired as our temporary guide.

Arunachal Pradesh (population one million), formerly known as the North East Frontier Agency, became India's twenty-third state in 1987. The regional capital, Itanagar, is an ugly, energetic community land-locked among roadless mountains and largely cut off from the rest of the state it's supposed to govern. We shared the dining room of the best hotel with the Minister for Tax and Tourism, who was bellowing drunk, but after supper we drove across town to the comely new yellow-roofed Buddhist monastery atop one of the city's hills. It had recently been dedicated by the Dalai Lama, and the day before we visited, twenty young boys had arrived for their novitiate. They were visibly excited to be assuming the duties of apprenticeship—patrolling the lovely, freshly painted temple counterclockwise in shifts, with prayer flags flying over-head, launching a prayer to heaven with every tremble and flip. Later, they would be sent out individually with begging bowls to subsist for a year on the charity of strangers. Every religion, it seemed to me, should fly prayer flags at its temples and send priests out for long walkabouts to fathom something of the way other people live.

It's not how Americans travel, however. Our group included a likable Fifth Avenue dentist and his school-board-chairman wife. Another man was a Pittsburgh business executive; he was with his Florida mistress, he had been a prep-school roommate of Jack Kennedy's and said he hadn't slept in a sleeping bag since he was twelve or been in a place he couldn't get out of by helicopter before. We had a staff of ten to care for us: Gautam, a Bengali from New Delhi; four Sherpas from Nepal; three Assamese from Guwahati; and Michi Reni, an Apa Tani from the hill town of Ziro.

Because of the lack of roads, we needed to loop back into the lowlands of Assam for an hour or two in order to reenter Arunachal Pradesh and go farther, climbing along a series of river gorges brocaded in shimmering green. The previous night our little bus had been suddenly requisitioned for moving troops around (we weren't told why or where), and as replacements we'd gotten three shaky, breathless cars, which soon began suffering breakdowns, giving us time to spare in villages such as Licky. The bamboo-slat houses had overhanging thatch roofs, and the villagers Tibetan faces, not oriented yet to smiling at tourists. Over the next ten days, in fact, we saw only one other party of tourists, a group of Austrians. Being well east of Nepal, and even of Sikkim and Bhutan, Arunachal Pradesh is not a launching pad for mountain-climbing attempts, and politics of the old style had kept it unfrequented—not nuclear bluster, so much in the news recently, but skirmishing rebel bands, tribal fights, and the Chinese infantry along the border. It's also not a druggy hangout, and there are no places to shop, no airports for a quick entry or exit. In every town where we slept over, policemen checked our faces against our passport photos, forgetting that satellites do the spying now.

I'd been in many mountains before, but not the Himalayas. Vertiginous cuts and gorgeous gorges succeeded each other, as we wound round and round, up the watersheds, with serrated ridgetops always rising above us no matter how high the road climbed. And these were the mere foothills. All we'd ever see were foothills, exhilarating and awesome but, at six thousand feet, only a fourth as high as the farthest ranges. The dirt road was slippery where recent washouts had occurred; the only source of wage employment seemed to be in repairing it. Otherwise, people fed themselves by stump farming (slash-and-burning) or subsistence hunting—the men with old Enfield rifles, the boys with slingshots, their quarry including musk deer, wild boar, songbirds, monkeys, turtles, and miscellany such as caterpillars. The bulky wilderness cattle known as mithuns—which are domesticated gaurs, the wild oxen of India, like shorthaired buffalo thriving in the steepest rain forest yet tame when led back to the village to serve as a bride price or funeral sacrifice—were to be seen occasionally, like big black-skinned innocents grazing amid the riot of ferns, vines, rushes, grasses, and sedges, on sidehills pitched at sixty degrees. There had also been some sporadic logging of old-growth trees in the region, but this had just been halted by an environmentalist lawsuit in New Delhi. We saw an army helicopter laboring north to supply a frontier post a hundred miles beyond the nearest road.

We were aiming for Ziro. The Apa Tanis, twenty thousand strong, are regarded as perhaps Arunachal Pradesh's most prosperous tribal group. Even before their first contact with Europeans—H. M. Crowe, a British tea planter of redoubtable temperament, ventured into their territory in 1889—the Apa Tanis had shifted from hunting and gathering to an agricultural economy. They occupy an anomalously level plateau of about twenty square miles five thousand feet up in these otherwise tumultuous mountains, and intensively cultivate it. In the past, though demonstrating less prowess as individual warriors than such neighbors as the Nishis and the Hill Miris, they outnumbered them locally and had more cohesion, raising big families in crowded bamboo villages, and so were able to defend as well as grow an abundance of rice, while their adversaries lived sparsely off wild meats and plants like the sago palm.

In muddy Ziro, we camped next to an experimental orchid farm run by the World Wildlife Fund. (There are hundreds of native species.) But in traditional hamlets like Hang, we saw older Apa Tani women wearing wooden plugs in their nostrils and latticed blue facial tattoos, originally a custom that discouraged raiders from kidnapping them.

The Apa Tanis trade rice for livestock and cotton with neighboring tribes and are good weavers. By legend, they originated their patterns by imitating a spider's web, or the shimmering ripples on the Kali River, or a butterfly's beauty, or a snake's paisley skin, or the symmetry of a fish's scales. The loom is a simple one, and the woman sits cross-legged facing it, leaning back against a strap that holds it straight.

Next morning, on the road to the Tagin tribal stronghold of Daporijo, we saw forktails, rollers, and tits; saw fields of millet, maize, sugarcane, pumpkins, ginger, and gourds. The watercourses were not apologetic. They crashed, bashed, and plummeted by the logic of physics. No dams or levees, and the treacherous road tiptoed in tenuous switchbacks high above the torrents.

We first passed through the homeland of the Nishis. "Nishi" means "hill men," and this tribe lives in a scattered fashion. Being aggressive, individualistic hunter-foragers, its members usually forgo the governance of headmen. The men sported talismanic hats that appeared somehow to contain a whole indigenous world. The basic frame was of wickerwork and musk-deer skin, but sewn to the front of that was a sizable tuft of black-bear fur in place of the customary podum, or knot, of their own hair that many tribes wear, with a brass skewer through it. Above the bear fur was a huge red-dyed hornbill's bill, projecting forward. Attached to the top of the cap but instead extending back were an eagle's muscular fingers and riveting talons. And a cluster of classy peacock feathers hung down in back. These Nishis wore short, sheathed swords.

After we stopped at one point and scrambled up a mucky rise, we provoked the hilarity of several startled ladies in saris, at work on a steep hilltop with pestle and mortar, or a backstrap loom, by asking through Michi, our narrow-faced Apa Tani translator, if we could tour one of their houses. Big bamboo porches led into the dimly airy interior, ventilated and lit by the spaces between the polework on the sides, and all tied with vines. Though tree posts and logs supported the crosshatched stiltwork below, and though the floor itself was closely laid with halved bamboo poles to furnish a flat surface, the structure moved, nestlike, according to the wind or the influence of our shifting weight. The four or five separate hearths in roomy compartments were partitioned by cane curtains and fireproofed by a mud foundation laid on top of the bamboo floor. Over each little fire there was a blackened canework sling that held the stored food—newly harvested rice that was drying and meat being smoked. The rafters functioned as a closet or as dresser drawers; clothing was hung at a convenient height on them. And on the side wall were a few nails where you'd see a winnowing basket or a cultivating implement or a quiver of slender bird arrows in a bamboo stem or an animal skull.

With Michi's help we chatted, having climbed so sharply through the mud to meet them. Pigs ran around, and a dead goat hung on a fence. The boys wore slingshots round their foreheads, and some men were cutting house posts with bush knives trimmed with monkey fur. Nearby a woman was mixing sand and cement to bolster a small dam at the outlet of a forest spring. Sometimes, she told us as she worked, the villagers took drums and pounded through the forest, driving a congeries of wildlife—frogs, hares, rodents, wild hogs, and deer—into a trap amid the palms, creepers, wild banana, nahor, tita, and silk-cotton trees.

The bottle-green Kamla River demarcated the end of the Nishis' territory from the beginning of the Hill Miris', though after we had crossed the bridge there wasn't an immediate difference to be seen. Unlike the Apa Tanis, who had placed their crowded villages on oddments of the least cultivatable land so as to maximize the rice crop, the less numerous, more warlike Hill Miris and Nishis had been primarily concerned with security when they set their settlements on hilltops, a long haul from water but a hard knoll for a band of raiders to get at.

Now that headhunting and local skirmishing have ceased and the tribalists have been pacified (as recently as four or five decades ago, encyclopedias described Arunachal Pradesh as scarcely explored), with a couple of languid soldiers posted in every town that the road goes through, these defendable hamlets remain simply glorious vantage spots. Far-off vistas of cloud forest and plummeting slopes spread everywhere, both higher and lower than you, with the slash-and-burn quilting of farm work just occasional: rice, millet, yams, corn, wheat, potatoes, tobacco, peppers, in subsistence parcels. Otherwise, many varieties of bamboo and sal, poma and toon trees, walnuts, chestnuts, pines, spruces, oaks, rhododendrons, and vigorous undergrowth enrich the scenery.

Traditionally, the Hill Miris are said to believe that they found their home by following flights of birds south from Tibet and that, apart from the Sun-Moon Creator God, the most powerful spirit is Yapom, the deity of the forests, who may assume quirky but ominous human form. Hill Miris are flamboyant—the women with beaded necklaces and metal bracelets and earrings, the men bearing on their chests a leopard's or a tiger's jaws with a mirror in the middle and wearing a decorated cane helmet, sometimes with an entire tiger's tail dangling down. We saw one man flaunting an eagle's wing across his chest, and other men with cobra skins draped around their necks and boars' tusks on their heads. Unfortunately, large cats such as tigers are vanishing from Arunachal Pradesh, and it was only the old men who had been able to kill one of them as a rite of passage. The young men either wore the smaller leopards' jaws or else were reduced to using the jaws of mere wildcats the size of an American bobcat. Gautam told us that the Hill Miris are still an aggressive tribe, and they did object to being photographed, with several older men stalking severely out of camera range. Women standing in their dooryards dodged away.

Two gorges were set catty-corner underneath us in this clamor of mountains striped with streaming clouds. Burial in such a setting, as the Hill Miris do it, is performed by members of the opposite sex. Then several stuffed monkeys are placed on a platform above the grave of the person who died, outfitted for the trip to the netherworld with little pack-baskets of food and tubes of rice beer and miniature tobacco pipes stuck in their mouths, as servants for the soul.

We camped on the bluff of the Tagin tribal town of Daporijo for two nights, at the confluence of two splendid rivers, the aquamarine tributary Sippi and the earthier Subansiri. It was more than scenery—it was positively paradisiacal, though the town is the site of an army base: the Ninth Assam Rifles. We saw crag martins stunting below us over the water, and ravens, forktails, white-breasted kingfishers, black drongos (like blue jays), yellow bulbuls, mergansers, a blue whistling thrush, pied wagtails, and a falcon darting, cruising, high above. The Subansiri appears to be lonely and majestic, a sublime, graceful river assembling thousands of square miles of Himalayan watercourses after their tumult is mostly done. All that drenching rainfall, the vertigo of the massifs of the mountain range, collected into just this one of many tributaries of the grander Brahmaputra, curving in quiet python coils toward the Bay of Bengal.

Daporijo had a concrete market street with assorted stalls and flickering electricity. We set off in the morning to visit some Tagins, up a gorge of the Sippi, in the next-to-last village, Nintemuri, that can be reached on four wheels. In two places the mud road had washed out next to horrific precipices where we skidded dangerously. The Tagins, like the Hill Miris and Nishis, were hunter-foragers who are thought to have crossed the Himalayas from Tibet and, also like them, until recently were little known to the outside world. And vice versa—in 1953 a group of Tagins ambushed a government exploration party, killing forty-seven of its 165 members. They wear round cane hats and build square bamboo houses; hunt barking deer, mountain goats, crocodiles, snakes, wildcats, and hares; lead mithuns about by a woven-vine rope; wear a black-root woven cape that looks like bearskin and sheds rain; and hang straw effigies on a bamboo frame in front of a shrine to ward off malignant *wiyus*, or spirits, which are subsidiary to the benignly indifferent Sun-Moon god, called Daini-Pol.

Verrier Elwin himself, the British explorer-author who, inspired by Gandhi, was the principal champion or protector of these hill tribes after India's independence, wrote that the Tagin area was "the most formidable, the most desolate, in a way the least rewarding country I have visited. . . . The climate is abominable; the people are undernourished and tormented by diseases of the skin; the tracks are impossible." And the mountains were indeed molar and uninviting, the weather lawless. The V-cut of the valley cleaved the views in each direction very short and left little space for cultivating terraces. At Nintemuri, some Tagin men were amused to say that their grandfathers had shot arrows at the first survey helicopters that went over in the forties. Michi, in chatting, added that his own Apa Tani grandfather had helped fight the first military expedition that showed up near Ziro in the 1950s, having penetrated their territory from Assam, after India won its independence, with a mission to establish a national hegemony. Too young to be in the forefront, he'd stood behind the warriors, preparing and handing forward arrows—though many of them were killed by machine guns or taken away as prisoners.

The bridge over the Subansiri River was a funnely rattletrap of metal and boards that had recently fallen out under a bus with eight-two people on it and drowned them all. It did us no harm, but another bridge we crossed that day, going toward the town of Along, tore up the undercarriage of one of our cars and halted us for a bit. The steel-and-wood structure was falling apart. Loops of loose wiring and jumbles of nails stuck out from the rusting girders and busted planks.

We were crossing from the territory of the Tagins to that of the Gallongs and from the drainage of the Subansiri River to that of the Siang, the Arunachali name for the upper Brahmaputra itself. The tributaries of each river had carved giddy, green, orchestral valleys that deserved the august name "Himalayas," and we wound like bugs along the vast margins of these, from pass to pass, then down again. And begin again.

When the Gallongs—like the Nishis, Hill Miris, and Tagins—were still regarded as fearful cannibals and bestial murderers by the people of the farming floodplains between Guwahati and other populous towns beside the big lowland Brahmaputra after it has straightened out, they were not known by their present names, but as Abhors or Daflas, "savage" appellations bestowed on them by agricultural Assamese, who had long cultivated the protection and good opinion of the English and previous conquerors. And for years, into the middle of the twentieth century, they intimidated intruders, killed the occasional unwary explorer, and maintained a local pattern of hunting, raiding, and sometimes slavery, unsubdued.

The British first came partway up the Siang in force when the Japanese tried to invade Assam during World War II. Then, after Independence, the nationalistic expeditions became more punitive and punctilious. Down in Tirap, for instance, three hundred villagers were massacred by the Assam Rifles in 1954. And several roads were quickly built after the Chinese invaded India in 1962. The Gallongs, however, seem rather milder, more assimilated, a less bristly people nowadays than the Tagins, Hill Miris, and Nishis.

From Daporijo to Along—home of the Gallongs—was a long, rainy haul. Clouds sopped the mountainsides, up, up around hairpin turns, fishhooks, switchbacks, with valleys set at a tangent like gargantuan elbows, and a peak peeking out at almost moon-height, way beyond. Or we'd skid through a streambed, a pony-size galloping cataract, if the road had washed out, and almost over a drop-off, where the forest, perhaps through sheer, seething density, bound by its cat's-cradle creepers, had still managed to cling. Only birds had much fun negotiating these. The horn on one vehicle failed—as dangerous on mountain curves as losing your headlights at night (which we also once did).

We were just skirting all this immensity, threading the edge. When one of our cars broke down again, we walked uphill awhile to a well-watered settlement of lush fields and banana trees terraced on a slope. I saw a leopard's prints on the track, and a bear's prints, and heard so much birdsong, noticed so many butterflies, smelled the fragrance of so many flowers that it was clear these people had obviously struck a good balance between slash-and-burning for crops and maintaining the overall web of life.

The Gallongs grow grapefruit and oranges, do backstrap looming and mortar-and-pestle milling, but boast an occasional TV aerial on houses close to their capital, or an ornate porch railing and some hanging plants to dress up the primitive bamboo architecture. In the village of Pangin, spread in leisurely fashion along a bench above the Siang River, we saw smoked squirrels and monkeys hanging next to the hearths, and millet and maize fields galore. Yet also jalopies and pickups, and several young men who had been to the city.

But the principal boast of Pangin is its two hundred-yard-long cane suspension bridges, in the splendid pre-Contact engineering tradition. The Siang cuts a good working trench through this part of the valley, so it can rise thirty feet without flooding the mossy ground where the big trees grow. The bridges, constructed of coils of cane, are slung all the way across like a swaying, looping-down, open-topped, V-shaped tube going from one huge tree to another. Bamboo poles are laid end to end on the bottom to provide a bouncing sort of footing, and cane ropes, horizontal but also webbed vertically, furnish handholds at about chest-height, plus a gingerly sense or partial enclosure. You climb up along a huge split log to the jump-off point and look down the narrow incline, which jounces slightly in the wind and slants scarily up again to the stubby platform on the tree over on the other side. Two people can barely slide past each other, if that becomes necessary, holding the vine rails and treading the pole floor.

Forty or fifty feet underneath us were four slim bamboo fishing rafts, each poled by a single man, who combined with the others to set a net and drive fish into it by banging the water. The river was at its most placid stage, despite the daily rains we had had, so a little later Trudy and I stretched out on a drift log on the wide gravel beach for a spell of privacy, letting the tour group move on and watching the tiptoe traffic of women carrying pack baskets of grain or loads of bamboo across the elastic bridge over us. Some little kids came down the bank, questioned us about America, and waded with spears after fish or threw stones at them and scanned the bushes for a bird they could hit with their slingshots. The young men who had been fishing approached us with curiosity as well but asked whether we were afraid. We said no.

"The people here are innocent," one told us. "In Calcutta they would rob you." He moved off without doing so, but when we saw him beating a screaming dog not long afterward, and after Trudy had shouted at him to stop to no avail, I decided we'd better get back nearer the road. This was country where people like us might have been shot full of arrows as recently as when I was in my teens.

I went and sat for a while later on at the mud hearth fires of two lean patriarchs in their longhouses. One was a priest, also the son of a priest, as he told me through Michi. He had decided to become a priest twenty-five years ago, when he felt his own calling, and had been trained by another shaman. When I asked if he healed sick people with herbs, he told me no, just prayers and animals that he sacrificed. The twisting fingers of firelight, the silence except for our murmuring voices and the wind brushing against the bamboo house-frame, the smell of smoke and forest meats (the canework hammock hanging over the fire, where meat and rice were stored, looked practically fireproof, it had so hardened with soot), made me relax my wristwatch-and-monotheistic rigidity.

I live in the woods without electricity anyway for a third of the year, but that is like wading in a swimming pool, next to the ocean of lifelong habituation of people who live by the sun, stars, and fire-flicker from birth to a quiet grave. The spirits of tigers and hollow old trees and the muscling-in weather and mountain massifs are no more implausible than Jehova of the Pentateuch—though in knee-jerk fashion we repel the thought that nature might be more than geophysics, that it might also be spirit and whimsy. Our own spirit can have no counterpart short of heaven, we think. It sprang full-blown into existence only with us.

The priest was probably fiftyish, though his wiry figure and face looked older by Western standards. His wife and daughter sat cross-legged across the stewpot-size fire in the breezy room, with the sky in its night costume outside. He said, through Michi's translation, that the tiger was the biggest spirit in the forest, among the animals, though if you killed a bear or a leopard you would have to do *puja*, too, lest its spirit haunt you. The trees large enough to have a spirit were malign as well. They were being cut, so when the forests were logged off commercially and the wildlife killed, it would simplify things in the sense that constant propitiation might be at an end. But the undergirdings of the culture, of course, would be gone also. His negotiations were all with the world as it was before agriculture and industry.

The other patriarch, in another bamboo house with a busy, tidy fire as its centerpiece—the ends of two burning logs touching each other, controlled by how far he pulled them back or pushed them together—had worked for the British as a hod-carrier in the 1940s, when they had established a tentative military post at Pasighat, a week's walk downriver on the Siang, about where it changes to the Brahmaputra. (In far Tibet it is called the Yalutsangpo or Tsangpo.) And whereas in the cities there is a tendency to remember Calcutta's Netaji Subash Chandra Bose as a hero who raised an Indian liberation army to fight against the British alongside the Japanese in World War II—exalting him even above Gandhi, who was too pacifist for contemporary tastes—remote tribal peoples such as the Gallongs remember the British more as protectors than oppressors, as they try to resist being swamped and nullified in contemporary India. He spoke in this sort of vein, as I enjoyed again the whickering silence, just the fire's ticking, and the night birds outside. He and his wife muttered to each other in normal voices that were much softer than my ears could easily take in.

The labyrinth of giddy valleys and soaring high country of Arunachal Pradesh harbors twenty-six major tribes, of which we had encountered only five on the scant road system. We continued east toward Pasighat—maybe the finest drive of all, with the road running a thousand feet up along the Siang's jungly gorge. One's retinas could hardly register the green and white water boiling way down below and the stupendous opposite flank going up to regions that the clouds obscured or sailed alongside. The river twisted like a striped reptile, swelling and rolling—constructing cliffs, flooding meadows. After hours of wild, wonderful grandeur we saw, with reluctance, the gap where the Siang forks onto the plains, and a Brahmaputra ferry waited.

BARLEY AND YAKS

China used to be a word for crockery in the West, but now has become at once our banker, our competitor and yet supplier, and, as a dynamo, incipiently our cloud-befouler. Sixteen of the world's twenty worst cities for air pollution smoke there, and the Gobi's winds do blow. When you land at Beijing's airport you may cough claustrophobically and think you need cataract surgery, the vistas appear so milky. Then the landscape unrolls as you're traveling—continuously huffing and puffing, steaming and smelting—with people, people, hurrying and laboring minutely at extracting or earthmoving, but without the tapestry of liberties and spiritualities you'll see in India. Fearing the ideological somersaults of the past, they live in the present, a bit robotically. Echoes are discouraged, memories dropped. On the other hand, a nation bursting at the seams with what is approaching one-fourth of humanity, of course, cannot be categorically disliked—all those live-wire youngsters, spooning lovers, hobbling oldsters—and Sun Yat-sen's portrait had replaced Chairman Mao's in presiding over Tiananmen Square during the 2007 Golden Week spring holiday when I visited. The police presence was not oppressive and rumor had it that his visage might someday adorn some of the currency, as China's concept of the context in which Mao's 1949 revolution occurred evolves and broadens.

The country didn't nearly implode, like Russia did at first, in moving from forced collectivization toward a market economy, or need its natural resources to rescue it, as Russia did its oil fields. Instead, a dialectic flexibility, broiled through decades of Hundred Flowers cultural purges or Great Leap Forward convulsions and doctrinal flip-flops, punctuated by horrendous famine (all telescoped into half the time the Soviets had employed for their experiments), helped goose its phenomenal recent growth. Greed became admired rather than a capital offense. Yet these switchbacks have fostered a more prudently unironic attitude among middle-aged Chinese than characterizes any other dictatorship I've been in. Having watched not only dissenters, but advocates who, devastated after the next course correction, opted out, most Chinese have accepted being noncommittal as the normal mode, even when this neutrality is expressed through a hectoring tone—since hectoring, oddly enough, has remained the method of discourse throughout the past half century. I dropped in on a World Trade Organization conference at my hotel and noticed how distinctly forcefully China's delegates spoke, no matter how little objection could be raised to whatever they were saying.

The past has been erased, the present is mistrusted, and the future feared, as the cliché goes. Indeed, for example, many of the Buddhist temples that were razed in earlier sociopolitical tempests or during the 1959 conquest of Tibet have been reconstructed for purposes of tourism—yet without dormitories for the monks, who otherwise might be able to bring their actual religious spirit to life. Building cranes, enormously angular, loomed above Beijing, and cement factories fumed on any road or rail route I took out of this great boomtown. In the park adjoining the Forbidden City, each trash can had been assigned by the police to a particular homeless person to wrangle a living from. The man my friend Tenzing and I talked to was thirty-six, looked fifty-six, a yak herder from faraway Gansu Province, who said the local police there had disabled one of his hands with a knife during a false-arrest scuffle—which broke up his marriage and his livelihood—and then granted him no redress. After journeying to Beijing to appeal his case, he'd been refused a pension but permitted the right to recycle the bottles and cans from this one garbage barrel for his sustenance, and to sleep, winter and summer, under a nearby bridge. Couldn't I, he asked, find him a job herding yaks in the United States?

It's hard to find a translator because, although the Chinese study English in school, most of their teachers, too, have never spoken to a foreigner, or at least not an "Ocean Person," the slang term for somebody who isn't Asian. To do so during the Marxist years could have prompted an arrest, in the unlikely event such a chance even arose. So from embarrassment or vestigial caution, educated folk don't regularly initiate conversations or volunteer their help in the manner common when one is traveling elsewhere. Religious input—whether of the Taoist, Buddhist, Confucian, Christian, or Muslim variety—was also consciously scrubbed out of the body politic decades ago, as well as the ethic of simple help for victims of injustice or privation, as counterintuitive to survival. Therefore displays of hospitality or kindness are rare; and I understood why a college student of mine in the U.S.— though majoring in the language—had returned from a summer trip to China saying it had been awful; he was "a slave" for a while in a village where he'd run out of money, and worked with his hands for a businesswoman for only rice for his belly, until a European couple happened to pass through and rescue him.

Thus for a combination of reasons the best translators, apart from a few professionals, tend to be outlaw Tibetans who learned their English illegally in India while attending the Dalai Lama's school— having accomplished the perilous crossing of the Himalayas on foot for a couple of weeks, while hunted by detachments of the Chinese army, into Nepal. The return journey, years later—whooshing across a jungle river, harnessed to a hidden cable and equipped with false papers, then maybe smuggled farther underneath the packages in a mail truck—would be scary also. People not shot but captured, of either sex or any age, are kicked like a human football by the soldiers in a concrete room until they bleed from every orifice, and then starved to skin and bones for six months in prison in the "re-education" process.

In any case, the experience is transforming. A brown bear rises on her haunches for a gander at the little band of escapees sneaking across the shoulder of her snowy mountain, then wading hand-in-hand through the terrifyingly neck-deep braided channels of the Brahmaputra River. After trading some of their clothes to nomadic Nepali herdsmen for food during the final stretch of the hike toward a bus ride to the storied freedoms of Kathmandu, they reach New Delhi, and Dharamsala, or Bangalore. Tenzing is a generic name I am employing for various Tibetans who assisted me, including one who finally did break through after being caught the first time and beaten within an inch of his life, then jam-packed in a cell for months with a university student who had been turned in by his own professor, who'd walked into his dorm room unannounced and spotted a book by the Dalai Lama on the table. Both boys could scarcely walk when they were released.

So, you wind up with pickup translators who speak English like an Indian and are living in a ten-dollar-a-day Beijing hotel, or on two dollars a day in Chengdu, the capital of the province of Sichuan—to which I now caught a sleeper from one of Beijing's wonderfully efficient old train stations, though my compartment mates—a mother, her small daughter, and the grandmother (this family the dependents of a Xerox company district manager)—were harassed by the railroad police because the little girl was now one meter tall and didn't yet have a separate internal passport. The deluxe train, like Beijing's subway, its central boulevards of banks or ministries, its zoo and main amusement park, was like a cleaned-up version of the Western standard. But with no fallow patches of real estate outside, cotton or truck gardens were planted wherever colorless blocks of bare-bones cement housing didn't adjoin another spuming surge of industry.

We chugged up into the Min Mountains, crossing several of the Yangtze's feeder headwater valleys—the Jialing and Jiaojiang river watersheds—a lonely, lovely, severely grudging, bristly, Colorado-style, hardscrabble ranching country of cul-de-sacs short on grass but rich in rock pitched toward the sky. Soon, however, each budding watercourse was being dredged along the downslope for factory sand or roadbed gravel, as we descended to the mining pits, refinery furnaces, brick-yards, and power plants of another busy city. Wheat and apple trees grew on the terraces, till rice and sugarcane, soybeans, corn, sorghum, tobacco, and pig and fish farms replaced them in the lowlands, with water buffalo at work, and mimosa, cypress, and banyan trees or cotton fields interspersed by housing blocks for the dense labor force, but much more regimentedly than in an Indian landscape.

Chengdu, in Sichuan Province, a leading upbeat little city, was never conquered by the Japanese during World War II, nor its ameni-ties subsequently leveled by Red Guard gangs. In the Tibetan quarter, I ate yak dumplings and drank buttered tea in an upstairs restaurant where heretical thoughts could be muttered—an ochre-clad monk was eating there. Tibetan salt, herbs, and hides used to be carried the two-hundred-fifty miles south to Chengdu by middlemen, who traded Chinese rice, sugar, and tea for them at the end of a yak trail out of the mountains near Jiuzhaigou; and I heard stories about the Chinese conquest of Tibet during the 1950s. Doomed clan chieftains had ridden out of their villages with a couple dozen cavalry, waving their swords and bolas against the machine guns. Or, equipped perhaps with muzzleloaders and defending a defile so narrow that the invad-ing tanks couldn't clank through, Tibetan snipers had picked off the Chinese infantry while their women and children huddled safely in a pocket notch behind them. But never having seen an aircraft (there are still Tibetans who have not), they'd left air power out of their calcula-tions, whereupon MiGs or helicopter gunships swept in and strafed their families, sheep, and yak herds catastrophically. The last holdout patriarch martyred himself and his two sons when their bullets ran out while besieged in a cave among the crags. But one son did survive, so his proud descendants are somehow marked with the same neck scar his father's shot had left.

My informants, Tenzings all (that common Tibetan name has become more famous in its Sherpa incarnation in Nepal, the Sherpas being a people of Tibetan language and culture who are said to have originated in and migrated from the Min Shan some centuries ago), sat chatting on a bench beside a goldfish pool while I visited a historical museum with life-size statuary of ancient Chinese warlords, each hugely mustachioed and ostentatiously well fed. When I asked whether the Chinese soldiers raped the Tibetan girls they captured close to the border into Nepal, the Tenzings told me no, they were only whipped, but that the Nepalese soldiers on the other side might grab and rape them before turning them loose. They said their own families in the mountains still had muzzleloaders, however, bought from Muslim gunsmiths whose families had forged them from time immemorial, and who knew how to make nothing else. The Uygurs of Xinjiang Autonomous Region—adjoining Tibet, but also over against Tajikistan, Kyrgyzstan, and Kazakhstan—have a current rebellion simmering against the Chinese regime because they enjoy the advantages of resupply from neighboring sympathetic co-religionists with Kalashnikovs.

The Chinese periodically lighten up on the Tibetans, however, allowing them three children per family, for instance, instead of only one, as with the ethnic Han, who comprise 90 percent of the nation's population. LESS CHILDREN, LESS PROBLEM, says a ubiquitous billboard. But another admonishment sounds more urgent: CHILDREN ARE NOT A TOURIST ATTRACTION—lest the toxin of child prostitution spread from nearby countries like Thailand and Cambodia, which are blighted by it. Even so, a woman who is officially summoned to the district hospital to have her tubes tied after bearing her quota, but then loses a child, may want to raise the money to visit a distant clinic sub rosa and try to get her fertility restored. Families believe that an infant can die if a spirit, and not necessarily even a malign one, merely passes too quickly through the room: that its vulnerably unseated soul may be swept along.

A subway was under construction through Chengdu, but the breezy parks and college campuses, pedestrian nooks and refurbished temple architecture (though skeletally manned) and quirky shops and restaurants would probably hold their own. Leaving Chengdu's fertile plain, we drove north through Dujiangyan, Wenchuan, Maoxian, Zhenjiangguan, and Songpan, mostly above the gorges of the Min River, which was being industrially stripped of its bed to manufacture concrete and dammed for more hydroelectricity, pluming absolute thunderclouds of dust from a sequence of emptied agricultural riverine communities. Jackhammers, bulldozers, and earthmovers were operating around the countless tunnels under construction, with one lane left for traffic. The uprooted villagers had staged several spontaneous demonstrations that had blocked this road until they were smothered by army troops, the driver told me: because in a People's Republic any public protest can be construed as mounted against, not a corporate project, but the interests of the country's entire populace, and therefore the dissenters deserve to be regarded as treasonous.

As we mounted past the hundred miles of denuded blast zones and hair-raising hairpin turns with ten-ton lorries rounding them, toward thinner watercourses and an alpine climate, the industrial possibilities diminished and we began seeing fruit or walnut orchards, flocks of sheep and goats, and, by the walled trading center of Songpan, gnarly-roofed Tibetan villages with yaks moseying shaggily in the meadows. North from the Huanglong highlands, we could glimpse snow-tufted mountains and the kind of passes between them that legends sprout in. Spirits—beneficent, indifferent, or malicious—inhabit all such regions and the passes are thoroughfares for them as well as for people. But certain passes are so heavily and swiftly trafficked during the night that a human traveler or herdsman caught halfway through by a storm or bad planning, who falls asleep, may lose his life's spark—which can be blown out like a candle flame by the wind of the spirit's passing. He'll be found in daylight, unbruised, unfrozen.

And despite the venerable yak-train trail going by, where Tibet's salt, sheep's wool, and mountainside medicinal herbs and furs were bartered for Chinese rice, sugar, wheat, and tea in Songpan, it was barley, which grows in the Tibetans' own harsh climate, that was their staff of life. Still is, my Tenzings said. They harvest the barley kernels into yak-skin sacks, then store as much as a five-year stockpile in great log caches almost the size of their houses against hard times. To grind a two-month supply into flour, each family—using in turn the village's water wheel—first pours a quantity into a large dry frying pan lined with sand, which is later strained off and can be employed again. After three minutes on the flames, the grains begin to pop into floral form like mini-popcorn and leap up toward your face as you stir the batch with a bamboo whisk; and it is these you grind, daylong, in shifts at the water wheel. The flour alone, stored dry, will keep for about a year, or may be fermented for three months into a wine—in nine, into a kind of brandy or whiskey, which, if aged for another nine years, reaches a peak.

Barley, lacking gluten, bakes as an unleavened flatbread, soured with yak milk, but mainly is eaten as porridge, together with other staples like cheese, or with turnips, beans, cabbages, potatoes, or onions, grown in season and stewed or sautéed along with meat once a day. To prepare the meal of porridge, or *tsampa*, whether at home or while camped after scrambling across the steppe with a hundred browsing yaks, you fill your big wooden bowl halfway with hot tea, then add half a handful of yak butter to melt in it, and crumble in another half-handful of cheese. Meanwhile three handfuls of barley flour have been gently boiling and now are kneaded into a richly moist mixture to create an edible warm dough that you nibble in small pieces with more buttered tea as a beverage. Calves have gotten the skim milk and bean stems—or the goats and pigs have, if a family's youngsters feel like chasing them, because the nearest escarpment can be a three hours' hike straight up. Yaks, by contrast, may be as tame and slow as the water buffalo domesticated by the Han Chinese at lower elevations, and worth four hundred dollars apiece to ride and plow with—ten times a sheep's value, plus possessing the added advantage of furnishing eight times as much meat. This is important to Tibetans, who are not vegetarians but leery of the actual act of killing, which they believe people will answer for in a difficult, hallucinatory death. Thus having fewer scenes of slaughter to remember is better. The brother of one of my guides had just sold his entire herd of sheep in order to be free of the burden of slaughtering them for income, and not to a butcher but to another shepherd for less money.

Tibetans didn't hunt a lot or pursue predators for fun or eat waterfowl or fish, as a rule, and so when the Chinese conquered Tibet in their 1959 blitzkrieg, resettling countless lowland Han in its territories to dilute the traditions, religion, and character of the region, it was like a paradise at first of duck-shooting and fishing for the newcomers. In many villages the work inevitably was no longer focused upon herding yaks and growing barley but skewed toward logging the forests or commerce. When I asked, in a community of ethnic Han that has been superimposed among the Tibetans in the Saba Valley, if the senior members could recall where they'd been transplanted from, their friendly faces suddenly went blank.

"We don't remember."

They kept 108 penned pigs, however, the same number as there are beads on a proper Buddhist prayer string. Numbers are important. Any cluster of Tibetan villages will boast a fortune-teller schooled in reading not only the stars' basic alignments but the permutations into which dice fall when repeatedly questioned. Up a notch, perhaps, from the dice-thrower will be the local shaman, who has learned the properties of a whole arsenal of herbs, and where to search each of them out, plus the alchemy of spells: how to cast them or break them. Individuals train and apprentice for both of these vocations, and may be tempted into venality or malice in the matter of spells, for instance. But there is also the rarer phenomenon of men who are genuine healers—inspired—born with the gift—who can't be hired, like some of the shamans, to practice, for example, blacker arts. They simply try to heal people, blowing drops of water on them from their palms, or flicking it with a finger or a quill, to make them well. If that doesn't work, after keeping a patient for about a week in his compound, the healer will probably refer him to a government hospital. (A fortune-teller may have originally influenced the family's decision to try the healer first.)

The wood dove is the Tibetans' Virtuous Bird, not to be killed. Nor should the cuckoo, which is called God's Bird because it brings the summer. A different species, called the Cuckoo's Wife, arrives even a little sooner; it was pointed out to me by one of my Tenzings, fluttering like an ouzel around the Pearl Shoals waterfalls in Jiuzhaigou National Park. A certain rare antelope, the takin, is the Virtuous Animal (though its preciousness to Tibetans doesn't prevent the Chinese from shooting it), while up at timberline grows the Tree of the Gods, furnishing firewood to herders, who at that altitude will gratefully wave a spiral of smoke scented with yak butter and barley flour as a thank-you gesture to them.

Gods have generally undergone an earlier human phase, and some hubristic miscue may tumble them down into human form again, or lower, into an animal incarnation, or even one of the eighteen circles of Hell. Some spirit mountains have historically been frightening just for the wraiths and apparitions inhabiting them, who might jostle whomever they considered an intruder off a cliff. But others were deliberately left untrodden as sanctuaries for the animals living there, where wolves, leopards, bears, pandas, dholes, or eagles could den or nest undisturbed. And still other mountains have been perceived as protectors of the villages located beneath—from flood or drought, lightning, hail, earthquake, or fire—and the grazing and hay-cutting rights to their slopes inherited only by certain clans. Even before Tibetans knew about germs, they usually boiled the water they drank, as if for tea, rather than swallowing it "live" or cold from a stream. But children are not sheltered unduly from household or dooryard dirt, lest they turn sickly later on; and because their mothers work up on the sloping shingled roofs a lot, both summer and winter—whether drying foodstuffs in the sun, or freezing meat, or sweeping off the night's snowfall—many kids roll over the edge at least once or twice and break a limb, which is regarded as toughening them. To my North American eyes, my Tibetan friends had features resembling Eskimos', but I heard Han Chinese mistake them for Mongolians.

In the old days, freelance Bon or Buddhist holy men went off to meditate in the mouth of a cave under a notable peak for a dozen years or so, and then returned to marry and father children like anybody else, yet were available for soothsaying or simple consultation, drawing on perspectives they'd accumulated. The cave might have been visible for quite a distance because of the circle of birds perching or whirling around the entrance hole, perhaps fed by the anchorite, but lending clairvoyance to him. Bon beliefs, preceding Buddhism in the Himalayas and still not wholly absorbed, are more animist and shaman-centered—surviving in spotty but potent form in isolated villages, along with the burly, "four-eyed" breed of watchdog Tibetans kept to ward off bandits, leopards, wolves: so called because of its black tuft of fur over each regular eye. Families kept a cat, as well, to guard the barley stores, and a horse for prompter errands than the yaks they rode might perform.

When I asked whether yetis still roam the spirit mountains, my friends demurred, but described the females' breasts as being so long you could run downhill to escape them because they'd trip on their teats and fall. Uphill they threw the things over their shoulders and might catch up with you. One man had not been killed when grabbed. Instead, he'd been imprisoned inside a cave for the purpose of impregnating his captor, with a stone rolled across the front that he couldn't budge. Yet once the baby was born, so much time had elapsed, she, beginning to trust him, grew careless about the placement of the stone. He made a break for it, downhill toward the river, because yetis can't swim. And her dangling breasts, as well as the child in her arms, did indeed slow her up. So when he'd swum safely across, she yelled at him, holding their infant by the legs, ordering him to return. When he shook his head, she raised it up and ripped it in half, throwing a leg, an arm, and half of the rib cage over the water to him.

Between the rocks above timberline a wild sort of tobacco grows that herders can dry to put in their pipes, with an aroma like incense, that makes them feel young again as they clamber about after their animals. For nomads on the Tibetan Plateau, stretching north from the Min Shan toward Mongolia, the most lucrative occupation may not be yak-shepherding anymore, but herb-gathering on the steppes for the medicinal trade. In particular, they'll search every May and June for a plant whose magical properties are epitomized and enhanced by its spending half of its life as an animal. Only a sharpster, gazing low as the sunrise strikes across the grasslands, can be sure to spot the twin hornlike blades before they wilt amid thicker, taller, ordinary vegetation in the midday heat. Inconspicuous as these are, yet sorcerously crossing between kingdoms—plant to animal—during the arc of the year, the organism's leaves when powdered, or the roots and stems when soaked in whiskey for a week, often bring Tibetans relief from pain or other ills. And now they're widely wanted for holistic rejuvenation, pinches being cooked, as "caterpillar fungus," into the menus of the fanciest restaurants, such as the one that slowly rotates on top of the roof of Beijing's International Hotel. "A grass in the summer, a worm in the winter," between each pair of leaves, my Tenzings said, two eyes and a mouth gradually appear.

China launched a space satellite into orbit from its experimental facility in Sichuan Province while I was there. And meanwhile the inoffensive, harlequin-colored giant panda prowled remote selected bamboo forests for shoots to loll and chew on, a remarkable recent symbol the country has chosen to represent itself. But, Tibetan monks and nuns have been beaten to death for talking to tourists as my Tenzings were speaking to me, if it was recorded in a way that could be retrieved. They and I were antsy not to be overheard. Yet one of them was talking on a cell phone to his dad, who was driving seventy yaks to their summer pasturage hundreds of miles away. Relentless logging and roadbuilding had altered the region, and the following spring, the Sichuan earthquakes would wreak far more terrible avalanche damage than might have been the case if all those earthmovers and bulldozers hadn't been chiseling at the valleys for more than a decade. However you can still encounter five-colored pools sinuously connected by rivulets wriggling through reed beds bursting with wildflower blossoms, warblers, butterflies—enough space and salience for solitude, or a fugitive moment of empathy with a porcupine wandering across a rockslide wipeout up in the sidehill woods.

In China's cities no punctuation occurs in the daylight rush of human beings. Mopeds, pedicabs, motor scooters, bikes, and pedestrians interweave with hordes of autos, vans, buses, and dump trucks in the kind of democracy which Communism did bequeath, where citizens, although now quite unequal in wealth, have the same right to the road. Even afoot, they'll step out into traffic like comrades, not peons. The street markets are ebullient, the railroad stations seethe like India's with every condition of person—nuzzly couples courting, children dashing, families glued to one another as they thread the crowds between an avenue's overpass and the terminal's maw, where beggars of all ages and both sexes sprawl.

Without killing family ties, revolutionary atheism did nevertheless put a crimp into the charitable imperative that all organized religions stipulate, substituting work-to-eat strictures that become all the more severe in a country where spirituality has long been under siege. There are few mosque or temple or cathedral plazas within which souls in need may appeal for help beyond the scrutiny of civil authorities. The whims of secularism and a robotic military reign supreme. You see it not just among the police but in the train crews and street cleaners; and the cell phone epidemic places ordinary people from whom charity might be asked at a still further remove, since, when they are text-messaging or self-absorbedly conversing with distant relatives, they are not where they appear to be. India is as crowded, and yet marbled with age-old moral contexts, Jain or Hindu, Gandhian or Gurkha.

In underpasses beneath Beijing's avenues I met blind lutenists and Tibetan silversmiths—buskers and peddlers beyond the supervision of surface constables. My guide now was a Sanskrit scholar who, even without crossing the Himalayas to worship with the Dalai Lama in Dharamsala, could have been loyal to him, since no one knew what he was reading. Nonetheless, he'd braved the snows, lived on forged papers, evaded the Kalashnikov patrols. On the other hand, he'd never been in the capital before or flown on an airplane (as we did from Chengdu; I showed him how to stop his ears from hurting), ridden a subway or hailed a cab. He was skeptical of the economic-powerhouse model when no backstop of ethics was also provided. His Tibetan secondary school had been closed by the government for its forbidden curriculum and the studies he completed as a fugitive in India would have sent him to prison if they had been known. Seeing me off at Beijing Airport was scary for him because when my bags were searched, if his Tibetan face had aroused sufficient suspicion for my notebooks to be looked at, he could have been seized and starved for years in jail. But all that happened was that the customs inspector yelled at me because, without Tenzing to help at the last, I was slow to follow his instructions, issued in Chinese.

Over the Pacific on the twelve-hour flight, I missed these Tenzings, now back in their precipitous valleys, milking yaks and boiling barley, or possibly employed in minor jobs where credentials aren't called for. China's strictures on freedom exact a great cost. And the panda's camouflaged face, whose black-and-white pattern is familiar worldwide, looks tear-stained, much as the cheetah's does in Africa. Tear-blotched cheetahs and pandas—whose habitats, which created their furry camouflage, have been skinned. The highway on which I drove north from Chengdu, landslide-damaged during the earthquakes of 2008, has been repaired. But China's pell-mell secularization has not, foretelling perpetual cultural avalanches far worse than the physical ones.

SEX AND THE RIVER STYX

When I was young I used to wonder about old scamps and leches, oglers, skirt-chasers, both because it might be my own fate and I didn't want their competition. Older men of some distinction appeared to retain a certain attractiveness to much younger women that their counterparts did not for a typical young man. This seemed mysterious to me, but I didn't mind in theory, of course, being male myself and midlife ahead of me. I understood that a sheen of success implied earning power in a potential breadwinner, as smooth skin and a trim torso signaled vigor, or that a romance with a real poet could be more meaty than with an aspirant. I understood, too, that since men kept their capacity to inseminate much longer than women did to conceive, there was an anthropological logic to the difference—that anyway these disjunctions between the sexes keep the world on an even keel. Without, first, young women's discipline in choosing partners, and then the fading appeal of women past menopause, and thus the gravitas of pregnancy, it could deteriorate into a welter of fornication. Even after the invention of condoms, that hadn't happened.

But how about these prosperous old crocks with their dozen books published or tenured accomplishments? How "dirty-minded" were they—and when did vim run out, how much sooner than lust? I wondered, anticipating my own arc past the procreative years. Did you need to be a genius like Picasso to remain virile practically into the grave? In theory and charity, desire and fantasy should decline simultaneously with potency. But I knew that mutation, not charity, is how nature operates, and so it encourages pushing the edge. The *New Yorker* cartoons of Daddy Big Bucks doddering around with a blonde leeched onto either arm were less funny if Daddy could still get it up, not be fobbed off with a wet kiss. Otherwise the blondes were working girls and Daddy, bathrobe and all, a veritable rooster.

I was reluctant to believe in clichés, such as the idea that codgers sat in the darkness at French films or in burlesque houses masturbating under the flaps of their raincoats at the sight of bare-ass girls younger than their daughters would be. Yet there they were, circa 1950, the old guys, along with me and other virginal Harvard undergraduates, plus some sailors from the Boston Navy Yard, in the crowd at the Old Howard theater's skin show in Scollay Square of a Saturday night. It was traditional for students and seamen to be snickering at the naked pulchritude of the cast of strippers like Blaze Starr accompanied by a drum, a trumpet, a trombone, and a sax or another suggestive wood-wind, and laughing at the "broad" jokes of the vaudeville comedians in baggy pants and oversized jackets in "loud" patterns who spelled them off. The drum and trombone mimicked how each lady swung her tits and bum and socked it to us, after the trumpet had commanded her to begin and the clarinet or sax had giggled as she slipped out of her negligee and spangled bra before the down-and-dirty part.

Now, dirt can be like the paint under Picasso's fingernails. It can represent living. But I didn't look at the old men to see if their smiles were cruel and cynical and fantasy-ridden, or wistful and memory-laden. Veterans of shotgun marriages, divorce debacles, they weren't here to be educated, like me, a freshman who had never seen a woman nude before and was embarrassed to meet anybody's eyes, just looked at the stage. We were all in a state of undress, really, beached in the plush, tatty seats of the Old Howard, unable to muster a weekend date. Even the Navy boys, with no access to Wellesley girls, like, suppos-edly, me, must have failed to pick up a high-school dropout to neck with over in the "combat zone" of randy bars and penny arcades on Washington Street. But we weren't spent, and probably concocting a script for onanism, instead of hoping somehow to "score" somewhere after the show.

I had no clue as to when men stop manufacturing semen (I've been amazed, at seventy, to find it hasn't happened yet). But who wouldn't prefer to spoon and cop a feel, with maybe a heart-to-heart thrown in, than gawk at somebody's knockers waggled at you contemptuously from the height of a stage? Well, maybe those whorehouse and "ball-and-chain" vets who had discovered over the years that marriage was also coitus interruptus, in an emotional sense. At the brothel the next customer rapped on the door just as you were possibly unbuttoning to open your soul, but if you'd tied the knot and thought you were a stud and had all night every night to prove yourself, "the wife" might regard you as impotent in more significant ways, and money could be a spoiler too, though over a longer term than in a cathouse. Such a gent might hold his hat over his lap and beat his meat, I suppose.

For a lonely college boy the headliners were awesome, Hera-like, but it was important that the show have a second-string performer who looked like the pretty girl next door: attainable, in other words. A brunette—not flame-haired—she walked out in a natural manner and in a regular blouse and skirt, peeling them off demurely, as if astonished at herself, a winsome, untrained girl you could perhaps talk to if you ever got the chance. This was thirty years before the bizarre shows of the 1980s, with contortionist partners and other intrusive stunts, like a dictatorial Dada play or rancid S&M freak show. Sex is for copulation or, failing that, for pleasuring someone or, failing that, recapitulating some unexpungeable natal drama, like nursing or being sponged, spanked, or whatever. I certainly went back to my dorm— hiking the several miles instead of riding the MTA—and masturbated, telling myself it was to avoid "blue balls," that semi-legendary ache of frustration "like the bends" that you always employed to beg girls to let you come at least in your pants, if they'd let you feel them up. I assumed the old men, in their single-occupancy hotel rooms, did too (if they hadn't jumped the gun), being still soiled by the life force that propels us. I had been writing a college paper about Boston's skid row, in the South End beyond the "combat zone," so I knew about these hotels, as well as drunk-tank derailments, but not the subtler forms of homelessness attendant upon the estrangement of children, or emphysema, varicose veins, incontinence, or kinkier dysfunctions. Virginal lads like the drama of infatuation or self-sacrifice or destitution but not the unseemliness of down-at-heels pensioners heckling a limelight strumpet. Enough already: what is sperm for? I would have thought. The notion that grown men, married in the suburbs, might jack off would have astounded me.

In my parents' well-heeled town in Connecticut there were some terrible marital stories. Mr. Robinson's wife hated him so much that she was rumored to have withheld his heart-attack medicine when he most needed it, and buried him before his friends from the office could organize a funeral. Mr. Caskey, pushing fifty, had taken up with his secretary, whereupon his wife hung herself. Later, ostracized, distraught, he ran head-on into a tree. Mr. Milligan, laid up with arthritis, and whose wife stayed away a lot, was said to have drawn his pistol on the maid and forced her to disrobe. The police picked her up, wandering on the road, but, scoffing at her claim, put her on a train for Harlem.

I could go on, but I didn't connect these men with the solitaries in seedy suits who sat halfway back in the half-empty Old Howard. Nor my college mentor, Archibald MacLeish, a three-Pulitzer poet, Librarian of Congress, and Roosevelt Brain Truster, who startled me one afternoon, walking the Cambridge streets just as the bobby-soxers were being let out of school. Before catching himself, he said, "If I

ever get 'sent up' it will probably be for molesting something like that."
He was sixty, I was twenty, and they were about fourteen. Nor my
own father, a Wall Street lawyer who read salacious potboilers, though
a pillar of rectitude who stopped communicating with friends who
stooped to getting divorced.

But what was salacious? Would Lewis Carroll have gone in for the
Story of O? I soon knew a few young women who enjoyed trysts with
very much older men. One would date Saudi Arabian princes who
came to New York on oil business or to their U.N. mission, and get a
jeweled wristwatch or gold coin in the morning. (She took the latter to
the American Numismatic Society because the prince had scratched
MOM onto it and she wondered whether that might have increased its
value.) Another friend, born to Park Avenue, set her sights on screwing the best Kennedy, and did possess the looks and access to have
pulled it off, except that her father was powerful enough in even presi-
dential politics to nix the project. She avenged herself by sleeping with
his most elderly pal—partly out of curiosity, she said, to see whether
the tycoon could still get a hard-on—like an experiment, as she used
to do also with me, testing my changes in breathing as she allowed me
different splendid things. (When she bought a painting, she'd screw
the artist under it, on the floor, after the gallery closed, then bring him
home and feed him steak if he was already rich, and spaghetti if he
was poor.) But this guy was so old he dropped the bottle of champagne
he'd bought to celebrate the evening on the sidewalk outside the store;
then went back in immediately to spend another three hundred bucks,
and, self-made millionaire that he was, managed to penetrate her for
good measure, and for both of their purposes trump her dad.

Being a "breast man," I romanticized the strippers (never strum-
pets to me), elevating them to the status of professional athletes who
earned a livelihood by exerting their bodies for the crowd's titilla-
tion. This left out the obloquy attached to what they were doing, the

shamefaced, secretive scuffle with which we customers left after a show. Blaze Starr wasn't Venus Williams; indeed, no Venus Williams could have existed then. A "sweater girl" like Ruth Roman might do pretty well in Hollywood, but most strippers wound up as waitresses, not in a marquee job in the insurance business, such as fame would bring a batting champ. In retrospect, I think Greek bellydancing may be more down-to-earth than our infantilizing of *Playboy* breasts: the navel being after all Delphi, omphalos of the world, and a simulacrum of the place that grown men head for.

And me—did I become a porno-flick fan, a peep-show habitué? Actually, my clumsiness gradually evaporated in the next decade, through a marriage and divorce (though most divorces are not caused by clumsiness; quite the contrary, perhaps), so that I could find companionship without fretting about when to take the woman's hand or sneak an arm around her shoulders. For a while later on, I even fell in with a down-at-heels showgirl, as if, like two exhausted antagonists of trench warfare, we had each had enough of this mickey-mouse war between the sexes, climbed out of our emplacements, and embraced in what had been no-man's-land. Her breasts were almost too sore to be touched, after a quarter-century of putting food on the table, since she had been a freshfaced Playmate, and now she had to go to a dental college to get her periodontal work done, plus act as janitor in her building to win a cut in rent. So sometimes when my head lay between her legs, she would make as if to crush it in a scissors squeeze in a fantasy of revenge. Yet I was not Hugh Hefner, and she was not a narcissistic misanthrope like some of her sisterhood. We were friends, joking about what breeders people are, easy to manipulate practically till their attenuated end. If men seek to pant and women a safe harbor, the impetus can go askew, and asking how dirty old men are—retired from a clockwork job and sitting in the dark—is to wonder what life did to them.

———

If the purpose of sex is so transparent, why isn't the pleasure simpler, like handling firewood, warmth and cooking being as necessary as procreation? Obviously the woman must test a man to see how gentle yet brutal he is—gentle at home but a protector and breadwinner, not a pushover—and compete with other women who have ample hips by swaying hers, a bit honky-tonk, while seeming reassuringly respectable too. That complicates it, as does our having been so totally in the power of a member of the opposite sex during babyhood. When we grow up to replicate a good deal of the power of the parent of our own gender, it dissipates some of the mystery he or she had held. But there is still the omniscient other one, that big mommy or daddy we didn't grow into, who, although garbed in other personalities, must be confronted. My first wife—a dear friend—and I had a blindman's-bluff sex life. I was mainly the clueless one, but she liked to be bounced on my knee the way her father had done before he left the family as she turned thirteen. And once a boyfriend of hers had shot himself while pleading on the phone for her to take him back. My second wife died before my mother, sadly enough—at sixty-one, versus ninety-five—and except for politics, we'd argued less than my mother and I, which naturally is what enabled us to stay married for twenty-five years. My mother took disputation with men to be a form of flirting: attention-getting in the flapper mode. She had witnessed the boom of the twenties, the bust of the thirties, the service ethic of the forties, the solipsism of the fifties, the rebel chic of the sixties, the disoriented seventies, the greedy eighties, and seemed rather content to drift toward dissolution in the nineties, secure in her Episcopalian faith.

Both she and Marion liked men more than women, at least as company, and—valuing the sanctity of marriage—especially homosexuals as pals. But Marion seemed more interested in homosexuals, for their often protean learning and nihilistic wit, than "straights." At the *fin de siècle*, they seemed gay and acrobatic conversationalists with a gallows humor, and she liked people who were "bent" if they aroused her considerable sympathy or had a funny shtick. Marion was more literary and empathetic than my mother, who dallied most, instead, with men of the cloth (professionally unavailable and wary, themselves, about appearances), and so when our sex life tailed off because neither of us could make love as well with people we loved as in the fever of pursuit, she hung out principally with them, while I veered off more in order to seek pursuit.

But this is about old age, not marriage, and Marion died, alas, before she even reached old age. Born in the Edwardian epoch, in the same year as Charles Lindbergh, Ogden Nash, and Richard Rodgers, Mother didn't die till 1998, when I began collecting Social Security checks. By that time we'd had peaceable relations for a long while, and, from the distance of Vermont, I had been supervising her care. She'd ceased regarding arguments as flirtation after my father's death, three decades before—when the umbrella of his protection was removed— and I had also lightened up. Her series of small strokes didn't impair her much until her eighties, however. I would visit every three months, and she would visit us in the course of enjoying a life of quiet rounds. She'd bought a house on Martha's Vineyard for $40,000 in 1965 for her widowhood, after she realized that my father was dying of cancer (angering him when he fathomed her purpose; he hadn't resigned himself at that early point to the irrevocability of his diagnosis) and she would be leaving the suburbs.

About twenty years passed before abruptly, quite belatedly, I realized that she needed real help in managing her affairs. It's a discovery carrying responsibilities and portents that children wish to avoid; and I had certainly done so. A bookkeeper was needed, and a woman to live with her, prepare some meals, help her move about, and put in her glaucoma drops. A "juvenile delinquent" could do it, her doctor said, including his own daughter, whom we hired. But we'd generally use some college-age girl who was not in college; and when I visited to relieve her and talk to various other people who needed seeing, I'd enjoy sleeping in the girl's bed in the guest room, especially if she hadn't thought to change the sheets before she left (in my fifties, already a dirty old man, quaffing her twenty-year-old's scent), while Mother and I would go through family scrapbooks for the weekend and watch TV. Later, as her enfeeblement increased, she needed help on the stairs and rarely summoned herself to speak, so we hired older women who came to sit with her in eight-hour shifts, in case she climbed out of bed to wander the house. She evaded one person and broke her hip. From another, who had a cold, she caught pneumonia. And another, an artist who slept with her boyfriend on the rug under the nineteenth-century portrait of Great-uncle Hickok in order to *"épater le bourgeois,"* went out and lived on the beach with some hippies for a couple of weeks, still pretending to inhabit the house.

But these were the bad eggs. I grew to be friends with the conscientious ones (fortunately my father had left enough money to see her through), who slept in a lounge chair beside her bed. Karen waitressed at a steak place before her midnight-to-morning stint with us, and then went out scalloping in all weather with her husband through midday, while worrying about a nephew she'd raised. Nancy ran a daycare center at her house, after her shift with my mother, and had four school-aged kids of her own. Claire, who was older, had a husband, himself a stroke victim, who required substantial care. And two others suffered marital disasters while caring for my mother. One tried to stab her husband, after catching him in an affair, and had to be hospitalized herself, though she was otherwise the liveliest of the women to talk with, and wrote poetry to boot. And the one I thought was the most intuitive or inspired of the caregivers—and who had a kind of haggard, haunting, oblivious beauty—might come to work black-

and-blue. Then when she ejected her husband, she was so pressed for money that she tried to fake an unemployment insurance claim and was put on probation. She had no idea, I expect, that she was beautiful, being engrossed in the troubles of her children and perpetually at work at menial, all-hours jobs, washing and spoon-feeding old people in nursing homes, witnessing their debilitation and pain, their desolate, fearful exits from life, and then getting beaten and bruised when she went home. My mother, seventy years after graduating from Vassar in 1925, was temperamentally and physically incapable of complaining of neglect, as she rafted through her flapper dreams and memories, and scarcely aware, I think, of the rare occasions when there was a screwup. We moved her downstairs into a hospital bed when the steps became an obstacle, and later into the utility room off the kitchen. Because it tends to be ladies in distress who take these endgame jobs, the first who stayed a long time came directly from leaving her husband, although by then she was my own age. She'd had ten children—sometimes needing to hitchhike to the hospital with contraction pains because her husband was too drunk to drive her—and tragic troubles with several of them. Accidents, a suicide. Much as Ellen, the haggardly intuitive, gifted caregiver who had also been abused by her husband, finally resorted to embezzlement in desperation to try to ease her financial dilemmas, Arlene, whose emergencies were now more in the past, plunged into religion as a poultice. She became obsessed with miracles, and traveled when she could to shrines in Italy and France, as peremptory as a traffic cop about the priorities of the saints, and so possessed by miracle-working that after a few years we had to let her go.

Yet, we don't speak of "dirty old women." They don't covet pretty men at their bedside, or cross the River Styx joking of blondes, having a different concept of dignity. An old coot may want to seem cocky right to the end, still in play, and not only because his wallet may be thicker than a younger man's. He's worldly, he's wise, has tricks up his sleeve. A white-haired friend of mine went into the hospital for cancer surgery that was going to end forever his capacity for sexual intercourse, and joking with the buxom nurse who was preparing him (and knew him from previous visits), he suddenly realized and wistfully told her that in all his half-century of activity, he'd never slept with a blonde. Middle-aged, touched, she motioned for him to get up on the gurney. "We still have a couple of minutes. Just so you can say you have, let's get it done."

As our life spans are artificially elongated, the "monkey gland" jokes are going to proliferate, but that some men keep an eye peeled for a final chance to implant themselves clear to the last seems a stance more anthropological than pathetic to me. And I seem to be among them. On the island, I used to eat at an old-fashioned, round-stooled, dockside diner where the waitresses, like my mother's caretakers, were stalled by a thicket of problems. A husband arrested for dealing drugs meant the lady's tips went straight to his lawyer and she couldn't leave town before the trial. She maintained the veneer of prosperity she had acquired in Cancún and such spots, however, by bleaching her hair and remaining a cheery stabilizer for the carpenters, fishermen, plumbers, and other early birds facing her over their coffee. Her counter-partner, a blowsy, sleepless, sympathetic woman with a tendency to weep, who was lonely enough to eat here even when off-shift, worked otherwise in an animal hospital, which provoked a lot of friendly cracks. Men notice women's vulnerabilities with a falcon's eye—it's surely instinctual—yet not just for predatory purposes: also protectively.

Meanwhile, big spender that I was, I'd given $10,000 of my mother's money to a former girlfriend of mine, from three decades before, now sixtyish and in some difficulty. And driving south one time from my home in Vermont, I'd picked up a young hitchhiker right at our cloverleaf on the interstate, who confided after a few miles that she had just shot her husband. Flustered, having grabbed his gun from the drawer to escape a punch, and instinctively aiming low, she had only injured his leg, she said. She was fleeing not so much the police as his family, who would be coming after her. They were famous burglars and fences by reputation in our corner of the county (one of her husband's uncles had even robbed my house, I suspected, though my best proof was the way that he had smiled at me afterward in town), so I silently agreed with her that if their young man had suffered a flesh wound they were likely to seek an informal revenge. She stole a glance to see if she had cooked her goose by confiding in me. But white-haired guys with glasses don't stop to pick up a slightly unkempt young woman with black hair and a blue windbreaker over a fluff-dried blouse, standing by the blacktop at the edge of the woods with no suitcase, and rubbing one bare leg as if she had just emerged from the brambles, in order to turn her in. Her hand was raised to catch a ride, but her posture was hunchy and noncommittal, as if she wished to remain inconspicuous.

A damsel in distress was a powerful image to my generation, so I'd swerved over immediately. The snow had melted temporarily, but she was lightly dressed for the weather and looked to be four or five years out of high school, at that point when the bloom goes off some of the choices a person might have made, up in the sticks. Wary, fatalistically, she had slid in beside me, accepting the luck of the draw as if she wouldn't have trusted her judgment anyway. Denise was her name.

"Do you mind classical music?" I asked. As a college professor, I was used to quizzing young women about their plans and prospects without feeling nosy. Her faded makeup made her look pale, but I didn't detect any bruises and she was fingering a wedding ring. She fastened her seat belt when I asked her to and slipped out of wet sneakers that she said were squishy, but scrunched down low whenever a car passed us from behind. I'd cleared my throat coolly, though the engine coughed when my foot left the pedal, at the news of why she wouldn't want anybody tailgating us.

"No, no, I left the gun. I didn't want nothing of his," she offered as a nervous non sequitur, in case I was worried.

"Maybe we'll get you out from under the storm front. It's not supposed to rain below White River Junction," I said as we approached the Lyndonville exit, because she seemed apprehensive that I would swing off. Both of us omitted any reference to how far we were going. "Have you got money for your trip?"

When she nodded, I ventured a joke about a story in our weekly newspaper that there had been seventeen unsolved murders in our county in seventeen years.

"That's what frightens you," she said.

"You were afraid?"

Her thin face was more strained but more calculating than a younger girl's would have been, and her wrists and hands resembled a middling stage of life. In our county it's almost a tradition that every few months some married woman or "live-in" will leave her house at an unseemly hour—at least if she has no children at home—after getting socked once too often, and wave down the first car that passes, to escape harm's way. Then they may work in the village at the laundromat, folding clothes, pillowed in the comfort of clean linens, soaps, toddlers, and mothers, sleeping upstairs where they're safe, until perhaps they try Florida for the winter, bedmaking in a motel or bagging in a supermarket, with a new boyfriend, who manages a cemetery's lawn maintenance, while living more scuzzily than they expected. There is a parallel kind of country code that the accused batterer or rapist who gets out on bail will go to work in the woods on a lumbering crew with other "rejects" (as you'll hear them joke at night in the Crystal Saloon) until his case is resolved, in a tacit quarantine—staying out of sight again when he is out on parole—though you may notice a dog looking out of the passenger side of his vehicle that says to the world, *there's two of us*. (And a gun in the glove compartment would make that three.) In marginal climates, people cling to the weather's rough edges for additional equanimity. The tiresome snowdrifts, storms icing the windshield, and then mud season, furnish a keel that may balance them. And they'll put on some ornery-looking fat for extra ballast and insulation, pigging out when a mood of depression threatens. The individuals who strut down Main Street tend to be those on welfare, however. For them a strut is medicinal. And the cattle dealer has the smirky, sidelong air of a slave merchant trucking suffering coffles to the slaughterhouse.

Denise looked so wan that I told her she could lie in the back seat out of sight, if she was tired or scared. She said she had met her husband on Cape Cod, where he was working at a construction job, and been "wined and dined" by him until she quit the computer course she was enrolled in; thank goodness they'd had no kids. Her own family, down near New Bedford, was as close-knit clannish, and messed up as his—"just not crooks"—and would take it personally if the Vermonters came all the way down there searching for her.

"Same old, same old," she said, when I asked whether she might have found a job that interested her in our neck of the woods. Nervier, stringier than the box-shaped honorary lunks you'd see knocking back beers in the Crystal Saloon, and not gaunt or pudgy like some of the welfare moms ("I don't want to go there," they'll say, if you chat with them at the lunch counter, falling back on the argot of their group-therapy sessions when the topic skids toward dicey experiences), she indicated with her hand that she wanted to stick with me, when I offered to drop her off at the White River Junction bus station. I said I had watched girls who had tried Arizona or Florida, after marrying some North Country palooka, but then crept back with their self-esteem lamed and moved in with their parents again, saying that "the pace" had been too fast. She sniffed at that silliness.

"Was it a ricochet that bloodied him?" I asked—dirty old Polonius—to open an alibi for her.

She would have none of it. "I hate guns."

"But there'll always be guys with guns around. The trick is for you to avoid them. You should look on the Internet for where unemployment is lowest."

She nodded, and for a loony moment I thought we might even make a pair: her youth with my wisdom. For a long-in-tooth male, the next best thing to sleeping with a much younger woman is to protect her from the machinations of men of her own age. Although Denise would no doubt have dumped an old fart like me in Las Vegas or Key West or Seattle at the end of our road trip, I actually felt a hard-on, enjoying a deep-seated, predatory sense of repletion for this interval that she sheltered with me. With her rubber-banded ponytail, blue cotton socks, unironed blouse, and blinking air of sleeplessness and tremulous bravado, she was just about ready for a new linkup, and probably too far along to run home to her mom and dad and stick there anyway. The homely truth was that she needed to be driven to a cozy mid-priced motel somewhere off the beaten track, with a Jacuzzi and a pool, for a week of rest and recreation. Then after the dirty old man had thoroughly pumped the tension out of her (being a good ten years older than Lolita, she would not be weeping at night, as Lolita did), he could give her a couple of hundred bucks to outfit herself with a nice change of clothes—the jeans, tank tops, pullovers, and other basic wash-and-wear stuff that, with a hairbrush, shoes, toiletries, and a few nights of healthy dinners and beauty sleep, will prepare a twenty-something-year-old to go practically anywhere and start over, if she has the spirit for it.

But because this is a real-life tale, there was no succinct denouement. I had common sense enough not to drop everything and begin living out of ATM machines. A bit regretfully, I slowed to exit at my turnoff, hoping that she wouldn't wind up with some eightball on a motorcycle. Indeed, she seemed to feel the same. "I wish you'd wait till I get my next ride," she murmured. She had a hint of scoliosis in the posture of her back, I noticed, while watching from the ramp as she waved reticently at two or three fast cars. But a black pickup soon braked to a quick stop.

"Do you need a lift, darlin'?" I heard the stranger say, with an accent from a thousand miles away. And her bold, scrambling timidity in entering his truck—with her blouse collar turned up, her scoliosis, her sneakers—touched me extremely.

In a Third World city such as Bombay or Nairobi, where people live on a dollar or two a day but Islam's disciplines do not also apply, I've sometimes given money to a young woman who approached me, desperately needing it for her children or a visit to the doctor, and asked nothing of her in return except maybe a day or two of companionable conversation with a lonely traveler. The impulse was not demeaning or sadistic, in other words, but protective (and it would be she who had the hungry, coughing children, not the men or older women who were also asking for money). And yet my penis might secretly swell at the manliness of providing her with half a dozen weeks or so of future security. Was that dirty-minded?

Well, you may ask, tell us more before we judge. At home in the United States, as a college professor, do you sometimes fantasize about your female students? No, I don't, ever. I may feel attracted in the classroom to certain individuals, but I don't daydream alone later on about them, or at night when my consciousness is turned off. Two or three decades ago, when professors at many institutions were routinely allowed to sleep with undergraduates and I was middle-aged, I didn't do that either (though I did with a few graduate students, believing at the time that there was enough of a difference in self-direction in the older women). We live in a sort of wind tunnel, each of us a test pilot for the blowback of social change. In the 1980s, during the same years that faculty-student romances were outlawed, a considerable loosening occurred in permissible homosexual public conduct, however, as well as in the parameters of acceptable white-collar corporate behavior. And divorce—exceptionable at mid-century—had become commonplace.

Human nature is as many-footed as a centipede and doesn't alter with rapidity, but interpretations of course do: egalitarianism, hedonism, uprightness, Darwinism, wealth and sex as taint or virtue. My mother had a yardstick for marriage in the era when divorce was unthinkable, which still seems pretty apt: "Would you let her use your toothbrush?" Marriage is for the morning after, between the poles of friendship and infatuation, where burps and farts won't derail it. Many men, in the passion of lovemaking, might go down on a woman whose toothbrush they wouldn't use two hours later. But a woman I know, pushing fifty and wicked-tongued, has a blanket method of expressing it when someone puts the moves on her. "He wants me to have his babies," she'll say, with her disheveled flair and bartered swagger. The seventeen unsolved murders in our county mostly relate to a spousal or sexual crescendo, because felons teeter further from the norm than the rest of us do, but in an arc that we are familiar with. Even a web-surfer in a swivel chair who pendulums between chat rooms may tap his feet as restlessly as a hunter-gatherer with authentic walking to be done.

As our obesity and insomnia increase, the social workers hereabouts have begun handing out snowshoes each winter to families that need more exercise, as well as the usual sacks of macaroni and surplus bricks of cheese. Claustrophobia is more of a problem than hunger for those on (to employ an ancient term) "relief." But in a rural community everybody knows the halt and lame, the biblical unfortunates "ye will always have with you," as Matthew says, who used to be warehoused in vivid destitution at the proverbial Poor Farm, whereas now the Visiting

Nurse drops in on them in subsidized housing. Turtling down, they tend to grow faceless, if they don't adopt that righteous, medicinal strut in heading for the post office for their food stamps—while some of the rest of us travel, pharmaceuticals in hand (lest it become real travel), to places labeled the Acropolis, and so on, or to an equatorial climate where wages are a fiftieth of ours, hopping about by Boeing with a photo ID, borrowing camaraderie from the stranger in the aisle seat, or a waitress for an hour.

A friend of mine explored his fascination with waitresses, or "rented wives," as a dirty old man, by compiling a whole book of interviews with them. All around southern California, he ordered the pot roast and asked the lady about herself, a respectful listener, pining over her in a manageable manner. I haven't gone that far, but once or twice, when beached in some catfish town like Venice, Louisiana, I've offered a roadhouse chum a ride north, if she looked put upon enough that she might want to jump in my car. It must have sounded crazy to her: nor did I know what we'd do once we reached Manhattan, being at that time a married man—in deference to which I hadn't attempted a spree with her during my week on assignment in Venice.

The chapfallen guy lingering at the counter as if the soup had been home-cooked, who has memorized the schedules of the different "girls" so as to time his meal to coincide with and win a smile from his favorites, is a staple of transient America. He knows the names of their kids and mums, and needs them, these public wives, for survival beyond the Social Security check. Men's energies so often skid askew that the waitresses eye the unattached joe who strolls in for the difficulties he may pose, like intrusive flattery, a bullying gaze, as he stuffs his mouth revoltingly. But I've met waitresses who were lonelier than me. Once, about dusk, I was the only customer in a small-town eatery, when the waitress, with bleached hair, on the far edge of middle age, took out a little store cake that she said the owner had left for her when he went home, and trifled at it with a fork. Then, although I was a stranger, she cut me a sliver too, shyly confiding that it was her birthday, licking her fingers when some icing came off. So we nibbled together from paper plates with the counter between us, as if on French pastry (she'd been born in Quebec), and talked of our children's birthdays and her new grandchild, and such. When she offered me a second slice, I asked if she shouldn't take it all home to share with her husband, but she told me he might not regard her birthday as an occasion to celebrate. We mused over our chocolate frosting, and I went to a cylindrical rack of inexpensive watches displayed near the wall and made it rotate, pointing to each of the ladies' models as they swung around. When she nodded at one, I paid for it. She unlocked the glass case and put it on, keeping the receipt, without our exchanging a word about the uncommon intimacy of the exchange. But we both felt good, and huddled over coffee and my supper of chicken salad on opposite sides of the counter until closing time. And it meant I had a friend on other lonely evenings when the tables were turned, later on.

I love teaching as a sidewise form of parenthood; and a couple of years after my mother died I became a grandfather belatedly (having been belated about having children as well). When the phone call came, I got on the nearest Amtrak train, in Albany, New York, and glided south along the Hudson River through resplendent scenery that had inspired so many nineteenth-century landscape painters and is not too badly dimmed even now. Being in a ferment anyhow, I was alive to the Catskills' voluptuous grandeur—the curling, widening, pewter-colored water, with flittering ducks or a standing bittern, a pair of swans occasionally, or a gray-blue heron in the marshy sloughs, with amber or obsidian water, a bristly island of splendid willows, and all backed up by the wild-looking contours of mountains loping off toward a serrate horizon, or plunging straight into the river in lion-colored palisades.

It's as lovely a stretch of railroad as any I know of in the United States, and primal enough to befit this rare journey to lay eyes on brand-new Oren: whose name means "cedar" in Hebrew.

I simply wanted to feast them in the meantime, yet felt hassled by my daily tic of poring over the newspaper. Because this wasn't related to what was happening in the actual news, my eyes would stray discordantly from the eely, silvery river to some mayoral news conference or culture bookie's prognostication about who was in and out. A skirmish went on in my head between gazing at a birchy copse and the personable oaks, a cruising osprey over a water meadow, or egos crowing over the minutiae on the op-ed page. I'd be pining intensely out the window at the handsome headlands of the river, and a tributary in a glen, a butternut tree in a forest, and watching the weather brewing, with serenity and excitement twinned—as if on the point of fathoming primordial memories within myself—when, like the White Rabbit consulting his watch, I would twitch back to my newspaper habit, absurdly checking off sections that I'd finished with, like Metro or Style and Trends, as if I were killing time in a greasy spoon. The shining river unspooling behind me barely held its own.

Then we were in the rail yards of Manhattan, pulling into Penn Station. Exuberantly I extricated myself from underground and walked across town to New York University Medical Center to get a glimpse of—a gander at—*take in* my grandson. Lying in my daughter's arms (she purring with triumph), he was a great deal closer to the Hudson, I immediately realized, than to a newspaper, being a reddish, wriggly, and gloriously amphibious creature, as miraculous as a mythical salamander, and now air-breathing. He was still slope-headed, for his outward passage, and, newtlike, squirming toward shelter and warmth. But unlike a newt, his upper lip appeared to be his most developed muscle, attuned to suction, as he rather quickly mammalized and vigorously began priming the pump. Thus was he protean, this newborn citizen of the island at the mouth of the Hudson—like the leap of a fish I had seen that morning, or the beating of a trio of geese downriver—until he would collapse once again in a momentary nap, or gaze bedazzled off toward the pewter-colored and obsidian world out the window.

We tend to get things wrong, such as not discovering Herman Melville until decades after his death, or not peering out the window much while traveling down the Northeast's signature river toward the birth of a baby as if right out of that great germinal, artesian, selfsame river. *So, get serious*, I instructed myself. *You're a grandpa and pretty soon headed back toward that immemorial water.* When my daughter shooed me away so Oren could sleep, I went uptown to the FAO Schwarz store to muse in their river of toys. It's a wonderful spot, and despite the cash registers discreetly placed, the imagery of wild things—both animals and "animorphs"—remained tumultuous and profound, as though I were dowsing, walking around. Amazonian and Congo beasts were heaped unmanageably together with Inuit symbols, Bushman dream-time facsimiles, and Sesame Street. The gorilla with a sturgeon, and a graveyard mask with an android togged out in a spaceman's suit. Oren had no tics yet. He could grow into the Last Mohican or a Cro-Magnon Man if we let him, or walk on the moon. Like a marmot emerging out of hibernation or a tadpole with its legs sprouting, he was the soul of atavism and animalia. He was everything at once: no options closed.

An ecstasy's synapses are amoral. They fire off from friction, in a convulsion, whether it is sex for hire or an affair of the heart. Like the crab bite of a cancer, they are a process, not judgmental, but unlike ancient illnesses, they threaten to become a kind of hall of mirrors, what with the invention of Viagra and vibrators, Internet pornography, and the more interactive wrinkles that will likely follow. Because nubile women need a long-term partner, not a one-night stand or a creaky pasha, in order to raise children, we frown on liaisons where the age differential looks wacky—yet fill the media with young women as eye candy in the equivalent of underclothes, and often grotesquely posed to tweezer the libido.

So what do we do, us geezers with brains still sparking? Silence is dignity? Sex is strenuous, so live in your memories? "Keep your thoughts to yourselves"? Well, we do, of course, as everyone over eleven mostly does, but my memories are so tangled with the gristle of life that if I try to replay scenes of lovemaking with one of the women I have genuinely loved, it swiftly ramifies into the complexities of the entire relationship—the sadness, the disconnects. The sex in the package cannot be extricated from the stymieing cowardice or passivity, the misperceptions that diluted our passion. Poignance overwhelms my sensual memories. Why, I wonder, wasn't sex the best during my marriages, but rather on the sly? Or rotating that around: when and where it was the best, why didn't we simply get married? I bridle at this, not really wanting to know the reasons. I've never visited a psychiatrist and plan on dying unshriven by that priesthood, but do recognize some of my selfishness, obtuseness, and "fear and trembling" nevertheless. My life seems like a snail shell whorled with recalcitrances that slowed me to a crawl, whichever pairing I think back to. And my friend's progression as well, because there is an equal solipsism to the female: created to outlive that needlessly pugnacious lunk who impregnated her, and find another by jutting a round hip and showing a nipple or a belly button.

Old men have to shave more carefully than young ones, lest they look not rugged but bummish. And they'll stoop and stumble anyway, so they need to choose clothes to draw the eye away from a wattling neck, irregular gait, not just any old sweatshirt that can be stripped off for the beach. Everybody wants to flee from a dying man, but for the preceding dozen years or more he may exude a certain twilight, or candlelit, appeal: that stability, humor, perspective, with so little of the macho bluster of a younger guy, and no worrisome consequences from a mild flirtation. He can be confided in without the danger that he will start calling, stalking, peeping, or driving past.

I'm a person who dreams of strangers more than about people I know, and although I seldom have real nightmares—the mind, when reasonably healthy, seems to keep a safety catch on the dreams one has, like a gun that doesn't fire or the monitor that prevents grown-ups from wetting their beds—these tend to be hedged about with red tape, anxiety, lost passports, or a slight vertigo. They're not the "sweet dreams" my mother claimed to have enjoyed. Nonetheless, I look forward to them. Although more dicey than my daytime life, they're also more interesting. And if (every week or so) I start to kiss a stranger, the dream will mellow into a willing friendship and delight. Before a resolution is achieved I'll wake up, which is frustrating, but not more so than the natural blunting of most of the denouements of life itself. And the odd part is that these night dreams—where my unconscious is given its head and I can't directly censor its anagram-matic recapitulation of forgotten memories—are cleaner of kinks than my daydreams are. The sex is simpler, in other words, more wholesome and affectionate and like the evolutionary mating position. I might be embarrassed to recite my daydreams, but seldom the night dreams I recall. This paradox might be explained by the old saw that "you're always thirty" in your (night) dreams, whereas perhaps you are resent-fully dragging your heels, always aware of your age, and not going gently "into that good night," during the day. I remember my friend John Berryman was the opposite of me in this regard, and dreaded falling asleep because he sometimes dreamt of killing his children. Being asleep, he could not turn off or dodge the visions, and finally killed himself. Old age unstrings you. Better the hoary Milton Berle joke. "How many times a month do you make love with your wife,

Mr. Berle?" the straight man or the pneumatic babe beside him on the vaudeville stage would ask, when he was gray. "Oh, almost every night!" he answered pertly. "Last night, almost. And the night before that, almost. . . . And the night before that, almost . . ."

A seventy-year-old is quite harmless, if he isn't reduced to gumming his food. Dotage itself is inappropriate behavior, so whether he spills his peas or harbors outré fancies, he is hardly a clear and present danger, like some creepy, snoopy fifty-year-old. Instead, what does it say about life that we even wonder—is there no plateau of equanimity? Maybe there shouldn't be. We eat, pay bills, maneuver through the social pleasantries of an average set of acquaintanceships, and try to maintain the cock of whatever hat we have chosen to wear through the terrain of an entire life. Fifty years ago I wrote a book about prizefighters and saw how they were able to preserve a mask of aplomb through withering punishment. Endurance was panache—right to the brink of being knocked out. And I remember Paul Sann, a fabled old-time, cynical, swashbuckling New York tabloid editor, whose girlfriend, a leggy, undernourished model maybe thirty years younger than him, was my wife's friend. Marion also liked Paul, as everyone did, but they used to commiserate angrily that aging newshounds in green eyeshades were allowed to have druggy brunettes for arm candy, to display in clubs and restaurants and at the fights, who made their living by the shape of their cheekbones, or selling their gams in stocking ads—and the old guy only able to perform cunnilingus on her at night, and too old or too cheap to marry her.

Nylons and nightlife: the Walter Winchell game. I once saw Sam Spiegel, the Hollywood mogul, stroll across the tarmac to an Air France plane in Nice, with three nearly identical blondes carrying his briefcases and suitcases. This was in the early 1960s, and the sun on the runway illuminated their hair, which was bobbed to shoulder length and styled to the same tint—all in their thirties (he was fifty-eight at the time), and of the same height, wearing the same smile, and trim in the same secretarial suit jackets, with the breeze swinging their gray skirts. Although their limo had bypassed the terminal, they boarded our flight late to occupy first class. And short, strutting Sam, all putzy energy, made his threesome walk briskly to keep up with him, but bestowed an auxiliary confidence on them that, with the luxury of the shooting locale, may have compensated them for looking like a harem.

I've never known men of my own age who were rich enough to take on trophy wives, but have run into them at New York parties or talked to them when they were stalled in traffic on the highway to East Hampton and using a cell phone, with the Vegas-voiced spouse kibbitzing in the background. Also, I've seen distinguished writers like Robert Lowell, in their late, shaky years, waving over a succession of young groupies to sit on the great man's lap and be fondled by him for a few minutes at a soiree. Kenneth Burke, Conrad Aiken, William Faulkner, and other gurus used to stroke the hair of other people's wives at dinner parties without objection, as a privilege of the famous elderly, whose grizzled, mystical look and cranky, persistent virility were assumed to be a signal of unquenchable vitality—like Saul Bellow's fourth child, born when the author was eighty-four and still publishing scintillating fiction. Such genes should be perpetuated, whereas we say to the ordinary snickery-minded lech, why would the world want yours ever again?

And most old crocks agree. We don't attempt to conceive children we don't have enough years left to father. If you want to do good, there are plenty of needy kids around. Just ask that red-eyed waitress who brought your meatloaf; then double the largest tip she says that she has ever received—and go home with her to meet her mother, who babysits when her shift doesn't match the children's schoolday. Help the boy search for the arrows from his archery set that he lost in the grass; help persuade the girl that the doctor is right and her eyes are too young and still growing to put contact lenses in; and give them both some books. Their mother is sleeping with a knife under her pillow after kicking her husband out, because his logger friends are barreling past her isolated house, hollering in the wee hours. The catcalls frighten her—plus several survivalists have been camping in the woods nearby, which makes it worse. The grandmother assiduously counts the silver she brings home each night in tips, as if that might somehow enable their small family to escape.

So do you now, as a visitor in the parlor, feel like a dirty old man in search of "jollies with a dolly"? Old Adam, in fact, isn't that bad. Even in his nether regions he knows that kindness is the priority, and has stopped calibrating cup-size and the straightness of the woman's nose, for a surge of altruism. Life is an earful, after all, and while the twoness of a lady's breasts and buns invite the twoness of one's hands, our ears exercise a different role. They hear anguish, they hear danger, and seem more linked to our intuitions. Our eyes appraise and calculate, and can trigger pity or anger, in feeding upon body language. They hunger or they envy or they lust, as ears—less snobbish and less squeamish—scarcely do. Our ears are gentler, and almost patient, attuned to a breeze's music more than to athletics, though as quick as repartee when called upon. They hear emotions, and may well with empathy or curdle from suspicion. They deal with intimations, indirection, more than our eyes do, and consequently are being submerged by the racket of a civilization that is motorized. Like the whiffs of scent our noses no longer catch, much of our former sound palette is being lost. Instead we hear mechanized or scripted, broadcast, instrumental sound, and people squawking their voice boxes.

Civilization is so much a matter of scheduling, not the seven-decade-long rhapsody one might expect from the premises of organized religion, that our smiles become a social device. You'll get nowhere without a smile, we hear, and a milestone of preadolescence is when you recognize that your parents are really not as happy as you may have presumed. Not just not as omniscient, secure, or in control, but less happy? *So, I'm pretty much going to have to go it alone?* Yes, pretty much: you realized that they couldn't serve as paradigms or be a lot of future help, as children will ordinarily have assumed. And they are authentically tired. "Tired" had just sounded like a family excuse for saying no, but now you grasped that they were indeed exhausted, their faces sometimes masks of resignation. And it appeared to be a deeper disillusionment than merely bellyaching about money, bad teeth, or the boss. Although school for you was necessarily tense, adults ran their own affairs, didn't they, so shouldn't life be smooth sailing for them, once they knew the ropes? What was the trouble? Wasn't God's world made for them?

We gradually learn that, on the contrary, the world we negotiate nowadays is mostly man-made, and curiosity is going to be our approximation of reverence; or that, at any rate, like generosity, it complements it. It is praise of God distilled to common sense but implying the marveling that religion used to tap and without which many of us would be simply bores. Marveling is a form of joy, and what might be called the "mating flight" that young people do on their honeymoons, or probably before, tests this, as well as each partner's vim and sensitivity. Girls with new diplomas used to look perhaps for a flamboyant protector, steady but funny, a good-looker but not a cheater, inventive but predictable, strong and smart but considerate and self-deprecating. It was a tall order, but nobody wants to feel that they are trudging, 24/7, toward oblivion. Meanwhile, just make it happen, nature is saying, although sex—a redoubled preoccupation in our addled society—occurs relatively rarely, compared with other pleasures and necessities.

Orgasm and ennui—frenzy and languor. And the ennui is more puzzling than the ecstasy is, because what is the purpose? More than "resting up," it often involves a sort of turning-away and shutting-off, as if to clear the decks for the pursuit of another love partner, another go-around. That doesn't happen, but silence, the languorous switch-off (traditionally a time to douche and smoke), advertises the possibility. And yet coition is so peremptory and unambiguous, after the to-and-fro that preceded it—the flattery and flowers, the tentativeness and gulling—that such a seesaw of emotion, from ritual to screwing, almost demands a spell of indifference. If such perfervid tenderness, like the simulated brutality of hard intercourse, has been out of proportion to what the two participants actually feel, the pendulum brings it back to normalcy.

Like oil and vinegar, courtship and coition are a beguiling combination. And neither is complete without the other. The public bodies displayed on TV don't do it, any more than the paperback covers on twenty-five-cent copies of *God's Little Acre* or *Tobacco Road* in the bus-station book racks of my youth. They were intended to draw the quarters out of your pocket, as the salt on pretzels keeps you coming back. But salt—the shorthand version of hackneyed stuff—befits old guys again, after vinaigrette is unobtainable. Old skirt-chasers come a cropper in classic plays and operas as well as in life: old moneybags who try to steal the bloom off young girls' cheeks. And if they aren't rich, they're violating the social compact by which middle-aged folk pay taxes to bankroll a decent dotage for the elderly on condition that they quit looking accipitrally at schoolgirls if they're men, or smearing on ruby lip gloss, chalk-white cheek powder, and black mascara if they're not. (In general, as with many problems lately, it would help if people of both sexes would stop trying to live so unnaturally long and gave the world more breathing room.)

Curiosity, like a gopher, can pop up unexpectedly from myriad redoubts, but more than before, even the polymath or Renaissance man must choose what he has time for. We're so belly deep in a buffet of news cycles and celebrity gossip, sociological theories and scientific breakthroughs, that we could easily gourmandize ourselves into informational butterballs if we didn't throttle our intake to a considerable extent. We want to know everything about what might selfishly concern us, like cholesterol, attention deficit disorder, or West Nile virus, but not genocide or AIDS on the Nile. And because insight is a type of sight, not proof, we have seen so many breakthroughs merely eclipse previous breakthroughs that we stilt-walk a bit among them all, knowing that received wisdom will continue to shift. Eggs will be good for you or not; cancer metastasizes because of unhappiness or not; cell phones and fluoride are harmless or not. Certainties are so squishy now, we'll fall back on what we sometimes say about the arts—"I know what I like"—although the idea itself tends to truncate experience.

There is inevitably a spiritual dimension to speculation, and faith is speculative too, but fluctuates partly because our interpretations are subject to the influences of body chemistry. A headache can spoil a church service or museum visit, not to mention the effects of depression. As a people, the more we learn about the human genome, global-positioning coordinates, dark energy and matter, the ancestress of man in Chad, and the origins of the universe, the more antacids, tranquilizers, and sleeping pills we seem to consume. We are disoriented—our learning curve doesn't free us up—and sex has been a dragging anchor, instead of holding fast, as one might have expected it to do. It slides into androgyny, or orgy, or again monogamy, not in the course of centuries, as before, but in close sequence, like other New Age pulsations that wilt and flourish as revulsion follows excess, and then overreaction again. I expect a century of crises that will surpass the last century's because they will be environmental; and the priapic absurdities that interactive games in cyberspace may bring in the way of perpetual lubricity (what will men and women do, crank the chair-side dial to Ecstasy?) will be a sideshow.

Old men with dirt under their fingernails may be of some help. Old dogs who've paid their dues and been "around the block," who can look at their grandchildren and see a little ahead. I remember a senior anthropologist in Boston whose house was a couple of blocks from a five-alarm fire that broke out, interrupting his work. When he heard the sirens and bells he stepped outside, looked at the smoke and the ladders going up, wet a finger and lifted it, and then went back inside to rap on the keys of his typewriter again. He had been around the world and assessed a lot of fires, bar fights, auto crashes, divorce wrangles, tribal cultures, guerrilla wars, and had that dash of Churchillian dignity a wicked old, randy old sea dog has. Such a one is a good judge of character and can hold his brandy, outtalking, outliving his juniors, and not sink in a storm that panics the pups. He knows that the woman we really love is usually a "Jeannie with the light brown hair" and not some bottle-blonde, and is deft at avoiding spurious quarrels, nimble at sidestepping angst, recognizing how much of life's unpleasantness is avoidable, really, or if it isn't, knows the moves.

Most people construct a personality for themselves, and if they don't start kiting checks or kissing showgirls' toenails by the age of forty, they probably won't later on. It is an edifice born of mimicry, admonition, trial and error, and maybe movie-watching. We want to be debonair yet diligent, congenial but a little austere. Society instructs us to live responsibly, with moderation, but also and subliminally, *Don't be a fool, live to the hilt, you only have once!* So we may finally bemoan our timidity in not having traveled more or had more children or risked a big change in midcareer. Here for scores of years, and that was all we signed up for? "Cocky" is the word for that old scamp who still manages a swing to his shaky walk—does he still have the balls to go with it? But did he stay in the game and push further than us? The loves that we perhaps passed up as secondary a quarter-century ago don't seem so now, as we sit on the porch. When we tell people what we were interested in, it may not seem enough. God formed man "from the dust of the ground and breathed into his nostrils the breath of life," says Genesis, so naturally he stays a bit dirty to the end. Do you think that I, at seventy, never want to enter a woman again? Sex remains an unfinished business, which keeps our antennae up. Our eyes, indeed, with their focus upon curvaceousness, may feel as if they have withdrawn partway into our heads after an attractive woman has passed by—the way a frog's do when he swallows a fly. But our ears keep right on listening for information and premonitions, soaking them into our emotions. Intuition has other purposes besides being a sexual appendage or enabler. Soldiers on a killing field may pause in hacking up civilians to spare a certain individual, but more mysteriously than on the basis of whether she has breasts. Sound waves or sixth-sense vibrations may penetrate the bestiality to invoke a spike of remorse, or arouse the rare dissident who will refuse "unlawful orders." A child's voice that isn't just a scream; a man's words spoken with uncommon clarity. Like predators (I remember bayonet training in the 1950s army), we are tempted to try to kill whatever runs away from us or weakly feeds our sadism, and rape is also an historic soldiers' sport.

But most old men haven't the stomach for even verbal cruelty. They omit being violent, and in general will wear a special squint when forced to watch bad stuff, as you'll notice at an accident scene or an untimely funeral. Their temperamental flashpoints wane, and "do no harm" is a grandparent's mantra. Not that they try to reform the world (if they ever had a zest for that); but they do bear witness. And that's not an inconsiderable recipe for life—to do no harm and to bear witness. The second is often harder than the first.

Do they have a glint of divinity in them? At this strange millennium we tend not to think so, having denatured our sense of religion—taken the bite of authenticity and joy and somberness and charity out of Christianity, for instance. Nor do we much like the idea of going from "dust to dust" anymore either, having denatured nature as well. We prefer cremations, burial vaults, and the like: tidier forms of termination. "Deceased," we write on mail, to notify the government, the lawyers. The world has become too packed to believe that each person in the crowds may have a spark of God in him. And as our life expectancy is assured or extended, our apprehensions about death are diluted, as if the unknowables had been dispersed. We are still a bit afraid of disease, discomfort, or debilitation, but if death is simply a void (with the new, ecumenical agnosticism), and not the entry point to an afterlife, then it is going to appear a great deal less complex or fearsome. If it is regarded as a biochemical process, not a kind of reckoning, then, although the grief of the survivors won't be appeased, people become rather relaxed about the prospect. It's not a passage, a crossing-over toward a radiant (or fiery) confrontation. Things are merely at an end. The tick-tock stops. The blood pools and blackens. Dirty old men.

EDWARD HOAGLAND has written more than twenty books, both fiction and nonfiction, including *Cat Man*, *Walking the Dead Diamond River*, *African Calliope*, and *The Tugman's Passage*. He worked in the Ringling Bros. and Barnum & Bailey Circus while attending Harvard in the early 1950s and later traveled around the world writing for *Harper's*, *Esquire*, *The Nation*, *National Geographic*, and other magazines. He received two Guggenheim Fellowships, Brandeis and National Endowment for the Arts awards and two awards from the American Academy of Arts and Letters, and was elected to the Academy in 1982. Hoagland edited the thirty-volume Penguin Nature Classics Series, and has taught at The New School, Rutgers, Sarah Lawrence, CUNY, the University of Iowa, UC Davis, Columbia University, Beloit College, Brown University, and Bennington College. He is a native New Yorker.

Howard Frank Mosher is the author of *Walking to Gatlinburg*, numerous other novels, and a travel memoir. His awards include Guggenheim and National Endowment for the Arts fellowships, the American Academy of Arts and Letters Literature Award, and the American Civil Liberties Award for Excellence in the Arts. Three of his novels—*Disappearances*, *A Stranger in the Kingdom*, and *Where the Rivers Flow North*—have been made into acclaimed feature films. Mosher has lived in Vermont's fabled Northeast Kingdom since 1964.